This is a very human and touchi[...] to adjust to a new land and at t[...] Without parents to guide him, the boy is forced to learn a new language, practice new customs, and absorb different attitudes to life. As he grows up, he encounters kindness and selfishness, decency and mindlessness, compassion and heartlessness—the entire gamut of human nature. The book is both gripping and fascinating, and is a must-read for anyone who wants to gain a new understanding of what it was like to be a Jewish war refugee in the USA during World War II.

> Rabbi Emanuel Feldman
> Rabbi Emeritus, Cong. Beth Jacob, Atlanta, GA
> Former Editor, Tradition Magazine
> > Author of seven books: *The 28th of Iyar*, based on his experiences during the Six Day War; *Jewish Law as Theology; The Biblical Echo; Reflections on Bible; Jews and Judaism; On Judaism; Tales Out of Shul; The Shul Without a Clock;* and *Biblical Questions: Spiritual Journeys.*

Benjamin Hirsch has done it again. Again he has carved out a block of history, known to many of us through textbooks and archival photos, and he has made it alive, peopled by real and breathing citizens, characters, loved ones. He is an artist and draughtsman not only of the architecture he has created in his professional life, but of history and the human spirit. Like his buildings, his books will stand to shelter and illuminate the lives of those who follow.

> Melissa Fay Greene
> Author of *Praying For Sheetrock, The Temple Bombing* and
> *There Is No Me Without You.*

Distinguished Atlanta architect Benjamin Hirsch has written a fascinating and historically significant account of his escape from Nazi Europe and resettlement in 1941 Atlanta. Nine years old in a strange land, Hirsch recalls his days in public schools, living arrangements with strangers, and adventures in the streets of war-time Atlanta. Concluding with enrollment at Georgia Tech and joining the army, *Home Is Where You Find It* will delight readers interested in history, biography, and human interest.

> James Taylor
> Librarian
> Atlanta-Fulton County Library
> Host of "Writers in Focus" on cable-access television

Home
Is Where You Find It

To Isabelle and Albert friends since longer than I'd like to remember.

Home
Is Where You Find It

Benjamin Hirsch

Author of: HEARING A DIFFERENT DRUMMER
A Holocaust Survivor's Search For Identity

iUniverse, Inc.
New York Lincoln Shanghai

Home Is Where You Find It

Copyright © 2006 by Benjamin Hirsch

All rights reserved. No part of this book may be used or reproduced by any means, graphic, electronic, or mechanical, including photocopying, recording, taping or by any information storage retrieval system without the written permission of the publisher except in the case of brief quotations embodied in critical articles and reviews.

iUniverse books may be ordered through booksellers or by contacting:

iUniverse
2021 Pine Lake Road, Suite 100
Lincoln, NE 68512
www.iuniverse.com
1-800-Authors (1-800-288-4677)

ISBN-13: 978-0-595-39002-1 (pbk)
ISBN-13: 978-0-595-83393-1 (ebk)
ISBN-10: 0-595-39002-1 (pbk)
ISBN-10: 0-595-83393-4 (ebk)

Printed in the United States of America

This book is dedicated to the memory of my siblings, Sarah Hirsch Shartar, Flora Hirsch Spiegel and Jack Hirsch, who survived the Holocaust and came with me to the United States, but who are no longer with us. Each of them made their mark in this land of our refuge and will be remembered, no only, by their loved ones but all who came in contact with them;

and in honor of my surviving sibling, Rev. Anselm Asher Hirsch, may he live in good health for many years to come;

and to the members of DSI, Devoted Sons of Israel, with whom I shared experiences growing up in Atlanta in the 1940s and early 1950s, but are no longer in life;

and to the memory of the jolly giant, Doyle "Whitey" Kugler, who put an end to my having to defend myself on a daily basis and whose young life was brought to a tragic end in a crash of his U.S. Air Force fighter jet in the early 1960s.

Benjamin Hirsch
Atlanta, Georgia

Contents

INTRODUCTION xi

I   COMING TO AMERICA—August and September 1941 1

II   FIRST HOME IN ATLANTA, September 1941–January 1943 12

III   ESCAPE FROM EUROPE/THE FRENCH CONNECTION
      December 1938–August 1941 32

IV   SECOND FOSTER HOME, January 1943–June 1944 54

V   THE SUMMER OF '44 67

VI   FRANKFURT MEMORIES, September 1932–December 1938 76

VII MRS. GONCHER—JUNIOR HIGH,
      September 1944–August 1947 89

VIII NEW LABELS, NEW BEGINNINGS,
      September 1947–August 1948 122

IX   FINALLY, AN END TO FISTICUFFS,
      September 1948–August 1949 144

X   LIGHT ON THE HORIZON—SENIOR YEAR,
      September 1949–June 1950 169

XI   A YEAR IN TRANSITION, June 1950–December 1951 186

XII GEORGIA TECH, A NEW OUTLOOK,
      January 1952–October 1953 202

EPILOGUE 227

ACKNOWLEDGMENTS 237

INTRODUCTION

From the time that I had landed on the shores of America at the age of nine, until I was in my sixty-ninth year, there were questions about how my four older siblings and I were able to escape Europe and come to the United States in mid-1941. These were questions that, in spite of my research efforts, I had been unable to answer with any degree of certainty. The United States of America had not been a country known for having an open immigration policy during the 1930s and 40s, a period of grave danger for all European Jews. Yet somehow, two small groups of European Jewish children, one of 100 and the other of forty-four, from the OSE Jewish children's homes in southern France were able to escape Europe on a Portuguese liner and arrive at New York Harbor. The first group arrived on June 21 and the second on September 1, 1941. Who organized, who orchestrated and who financed these escapes? How were selections made of which children were to be included in each escape and who made the selections? Who made it possible for almost 150 Jewish children to enter the USA at a time when immigration for European Jews was prohibited? What organizations from other countries were involved?

In 1976, my oldest sister Flora Spiegel, of blessed memory, sent a copy of a then recently published book, *Out Of The Fire* written by Ernst Papanek with Edward Linn, to each of her four living siblings with the inscription, "Lest you forget whence you came." Dr. Papanek was the director of the *Oeuvre de Secours aux Enfants*, better known as OSE homes, from its inception in 1938 until he fled to New York where he arrived on September 12, 1940. He had fled occupied France to avoid imminent arrest as an enemy of the Reich and, as stated in his memoirs, his plan was to set up the escape mechanism and immigration for some 1,600 OSE children. In the book, he chronicles how OSE was transformed into a viable organization of children's homes for mostly Jewish children left without parents as a result of the Nazi onslaught. He writes of the generosity of those who financed the procurement of châteaux and villas to house the facilities and support the operation of the children's homes. Included are stories of some of the children and of the adults who turned the châteaux and villas into caring homes. He further writes of the world organizations involved in the escape of some of the children, and of the disappointment to the would-be rescue organizations when the German army had taken over Vichy before all, or at least a large percentage of, the children could be rescued.

I gained much from this book and continue to discover more information every time I read it. I was even able to make contact with Ernst Koppstein who was quoted in the book as having left Château du Masgelier at the same time I did. We did not remember each other from France, since he had been at least four years older than I, but we met and related through our shared experience. At the time we got together, he was a doctor in Baltimore, Maryland. The book was informative in that it included names of many organizations that had a hand in trying to save the OSE children. The story, however, did not detail the relationships these organizations had to each other, how their involvement came to be or if there was any coordinating entity in all of these efforts to save the lives of endangered children. There were still too many holes in the story to definitively answer my questions.

Then, after twenty-five years, out of the blue, two things happened in 2001 to shed more light on the story. Iris Posner, a social science researcher and co-founder of One Thousand Children, Inc. (OTC), contacted me to apprise me that I was, in fact, one of the "1,000 children," ages one through sixteen, who had fled Europe without parents and arrived in the USA between 1934 and 1945. She and Lenore Moskowitz, also a researcher, had formed OTC and wanted help in tracking down the one thousand children, who, by then, were adults. They sought to research and document the journey and fate of these one thousand children, (although, in actuality, it has been established that the number is closer to twelve-hundred children), and to discover how they were allowed entry into the United States by the State Department in spite of adverse immigration policies and the apparent isolationist mood of the American public. Suffice it say, this non-adherence to established immigration policy saved these children from being among the million-and-a-half Jewish children murdered by the Nazis in World War II. Iris also wanted to chronicle America's role in saving these children which, while not matching Great Britain's hospitality to twenty thousand *Kindertransport* children, was more than most had anticipated.

In July, I received an e-mail, probably sent to everyone on Iris' list, from a woman named Michelle who had been searching for her true identity for over twelve years. Michelle had been in one of the OSE homes in Montmorency and her picture was on the back of *Out Of The Fire*'s book jacket. She came on a ship to the USA as a four or five year old and was taken by train directly to Louisiana. The woman, most likely a case worker, who brought her to either New Orleans or Shreveport handed her over to a Cajun Catholic couple whom Michelle claims destroyed all of her documents and brought her up using their dead daughter's birth certificate. Therefore, her official name became Mary Victoria. She remembers her real mother's and her grandmother's first names and she remembers Dr. Papanek from Montmorency.

I was touched by her search for her identity and was one of the many who responded to her plea and offered to help. It turned out that she had been gathering data for quite a few years and had about exhausted all avenues known to her when she heard about OTC. Among the data she had acquired since 1984 was a photograph taken from a ship arriving in New York. The camera lens was pointed toward the Statue of Liberty, and the photo showed the backs of children standing at the ship's railing waving and a woman carrying a young girl. Michelle also has a photo that was taken of her shortly after her arrival in Louisiana. The girl being held on the ship's deck was facing the photographer and not only bears a striking resemblance to Michelle's photo taken upon her arrival in Louisiana, but the dresses worn in both photos are identical. I remarked that the source of the boat picture could lead to the identity of the little girl on the ship, which almost assuredly was Michelle.

It turns out the photo was reproduced from a book that had been sent to her by the curator of the Marshall Field archives. It is entitled *Transplanted Children, A History*, by Kathryn Close, and was prepared for The United States Committee for the Care of European Children, Inc. While the book is a hard cover, there was no publisher noted and was copyrighted by the U. S. Committee in 1953. It is a historical review of the U.S. Committee, formed in 1940 and disbanded in 1953. Unfortunately, the book gives no provenance to the photographs, an omission that put us back to square one as far as Michelle's identity was concerned. It has a wealth of information, however, for anyone researching America's role in saving children fleeing the Nazis, including British children fleeing the *Blitzkrieg*, Germany's bombing of Great Britain in 1940. The U.S. Committee had officers and a board of directors. Its president was Marshall Field and the honorary president was the first lady, Eleanor Roosevelt. Both remained in their respective offices for the entire twelve years of the Committee's existence. It appears from the book that the U.S. Committee, which operated for twelve years, was the coordinating committee under whose auspices other world organizations worked to save European refugee children. These organizations included the American Jewish Joint Distribution Committee, the American Friends Service Committee, the Unitarian Service Committee, *Secours Suisse*, European-Jewish Children's Aid, the National Non-Sectarian Committee and the French child welfare organization, OSE. Most of these agencies had been functioning separately before May 1940, and in fact, the book notes that the European-Jewish Children's Aid had brought 443 refugee children to America by 1940. So, of the thousand plus

Jewish children that were saved from 1934 through 1942, only 309 came to the U.S. under the Committee sponsorship. My four siblings and I were among those 309 and our "affidavits in lieu of passport" had been prepared by the American Friends Service Committee.

The following excerpts from Kathryn Close's book, *Transplanted Children, A History*, give some perspective as to the peril facing the Jewish children of Europe and the roles of the agencies that were concerned about their plight.

> As far back as 1934 Jewish groups in the United States, deeply concerned over what was happening to the Jews under Hitler, had been exerting efforts to bring whom they could to safety. They had conceived the idea of a program for the migration of unaccompanied children when they learned that many Jewish parents in Germany, appalled at the grim future held out to their children in their native land, sought to send them out of the country; and that the growing brutality of the Hitler regime was depriving many children of their parents. To carry it out they set up the German-Jewish Children's Aid, for which the State Department first set the corporate affidavit agreement pattern. As the terror spread over Europe this agency appropriately changed its name to the European-Jewish Children's Aid. By the beginning of 1940, it had brought 443 refugee children to America.
>
> Aside from these efforts, however, attempts to offer haven in America to the endangered children of Europe had failed, the main obstacle being the quota restrictions in our immigration laws. In 1939 the National Non-Sectarian Committee led efforts to get Congressional legislation which would have enabled the United States to equal Great Britain's hospitality to 20,000 Jewish refugee children, but to no avail. Then the storm had broken, cutting off one by one the avenues of escape.

It should be noted that the U.S. Committee's first goal was to bring British children to safe haven in America for the "duration." After the fall of France in 1940, Britain feared an invasion by Hitler's forces was imminent since the Germans launched daily bombing raids, this *blitzkrieg*, posed sufficient danger to Britain's children and prompted many parents to sign up for a temporary haven for their children. Continuing from *Transplanted Children*:

Members of the Committee met almost daily with officials of the U.S. Children's Bureau, the State Department and the Attorney General's office in an effort to find an opening for groups of children in <u>immigration laws [that had been] written to prevent the exploitation of foreign child labor</u> [emphasis mine]. They found it in mid-July when the Attorney General's office issued a ruling that preserved the individual character of immigration but made it possible for the Committee to import numbers of unaccompanied children, including those unknown to anyone in this country as well as those specifically requested.

The magic tool was a device called the "corporate affidavit" which allowed a non-profit organization to guarantee the support of a specific number of children and within forty-eight hours to receive as many "blank visas." These it could send abroad to be filled in with the names of children awaiting exit. Six days after the ruling the State Department issued 1,000 visas on the Committee's corporate affidavit.

[In America, requests from Jewish households] trying to offer haven to the children of relatives and friends in both occupied and unoccupied Europe, began to pile up. The Committee turned over requests for children from occupied countries to the European-Jewish Children's Aid which still had contacts with Jewish groups in those countries. Requests for children from unoccupied France it kept on file until migration procedures could be arranged with American groups there and ways found of cutting through the Infinite entanglements of shipping arrangements, transit visas, exit permits and quota numbers. <u>In the meantime the State Department declared continental children ineligible for visitors' visas, [that had been] used by the non-Jewish British children</u> [emphasis mine].

In spite of that setback, about two hundred "continental" children managed to get through to America in that grim half of 1940. Some came to private sponsors on individual arrangements, others through the arrangements made by the European-Jewish Children's Aid. Of those,

twenty-five represented a kind of "trial balloon" to test the feasibility of a Committee sponsored continental evacuation program. They were brought from occupied France through Spain and Portugal, where they embarked for America, through the joint effort of the U.S. Committee and the Unitarian Service Committee.

This was the escape route used by the group of children which included my two brothers and, three months later, by the group that included my two sisters and me.

Action stepped up a bit in 1941 and 1942, though never to the point of untapping a real flow of children from the continent. The Committee made formal arrangements with the American Friends Service Committee for selecting children for emigration from France and with the European-Jewish Children's Aid for providing temporary shelter and allocation to local communities for the Jewish children who reached the shores. As the non-French Jewish children in France were those in the most desperate circumstances, they represented the majority of the 309 continental children brought to the United States under the Committee sponsorship by August 1942.

As time went on, the desperate plight of the Jewish children in unoccupied France became clearer. Dark rumors of Nazi plans to force the Vichy government to deport all Jews to a mythical Jewish reservation in Poland took on grim substance in August 1942, when word came of the departure of the first trainloads of non-French Jews from Gurs, [purportedly the largest concentration camp in France.] Then came frantic cables from numerous overseas agencies asking for refuge for 5000 non-French Jewish children doomed to deportation and probable death by the Vichy agreement with the Nazis.

After a few weeks of negotiation that eventually included the President himself, (F.D.R.), the State Department announced that 5000 refugee children could be admitted from France by a special emergency arrangement...Arrangements were nearly complete when word came that the Vichy government would give exit permits to only 500 children. On the morning of November 7, 1942 [the U.S. Committee] sent the remaining twenty-eight doctors, nurses and child care experts off on a Portuguese ship to fetch the children. One hour after the ship steamed out of Baltimore came the announcement of the Nazi occupation of Vichy, France. The last door to escape for any of the 5000 children had been sealed shut.

To summarize what I had gleaned from *Transplanted Children*, after years of cajoling and politicking on behalf of thousands of Jewish children in soon-to-be Nazi occupied Europe, and only after President Roosevelt himself got involved in the negotiations, the State Department finally allowed five thousand refugee children to be admitted into the United States providing, of course, that their support would be vouched for by private sources. Then the quisling Vichy government reneged and would commit to visas for only 500 Jewish refugee children. When the Nazis occupied Vichy, France on November 7, 1942, all of the posturing and negotiating turned out to be for naught.

However, 309 orphaned children, mostly from the OSE homes in southern France, did enter the United States between May 1940 and August 1942. Each one has many stories to tell, stories about their journeys, escapes and unique experiences growing up in America as orphaned Jewish foreigners at a time when anti-Semitism was at a peak, even in America. While my story is just one of those, I feel compelled to tell it.

My story is comprised of layers of memories from that time, over fifty years ago, and is bolstered by my files from the Children's Service Bureau of the Hebrew Orphans Home in Atlanta, Georgia. These files had first been offered to me in 1988, after the Bureau's board of trustees voted to no longer provide the children's and family services it had offered for decades and instead to focus only on distributing funds for free educational loans. JF&CS, Jewish Family & Career Services, which had been simultaneously providing similar services to the Atlanta Jewish Community, would take up the slack.

The Bureau became JELF, the Jewish Educational Loan Fund, and no longer had any need for its old files. Accordingly, Fritzi Lainoff, a caseworker for the Bureau who continued to work for JELF, had been instructed to offer the personal files to any clients who were still living in Atlanta. The trustees, concerned about confidentiality, met to decide if the sensitive files should be made available to clients, and they decided against it. According to Fritzi, their decision to make the files available only to researchers had been predicated on the fact that they contained periodic caseworker evaluations of the clients which may have been unfavorable. A few years later, when JELF no longer had space to keep the files, Fritzi was finally able to give me partial files about my siblings and me. The remainder of the files had been donated to the archives of the William Breman Jewish Heritage Museum. At the same time, I had been working on the design of the *Absence Of Humanity, The Holocaust Years*, a signature exhibition for The Breman Museum. Sandy Berman, the museum archivist with whom I had been working closely, offered to make my family's files, as complete as she had them, available to me for the first time.

My memory was also jogged by reviewing old issues of *The Vanguard* and *The Senator*, newspapers from Hoke Smith Junior High and Senior High School, respectively, along with other items of memorabilia that I had saved along the way.

It should be noted that I am fully aware that memory is a very personal process of recollection of events. Therefore, for the most part, events recounted herein have been told from the perspective of my memory and could easily be remembered differently by others who had been party to the same events.

Lastly, it should be noted that this book is a prequel to *Hearing A Different Drummer, A Holocaust Survivor's Search for Identity,* my first book. Much of the amplification of my family's experiences in Europe, as well as the details of our escape, its planning and the organizations involved, has been included after considerable research in response to many comments and requests from readers of my first book. In doing so, some stories that appeared in my first book appear in this book as well, though somewhat modified. To leave them out would have made this book incomplete.

Map of Europe showing Ben's odyssey from Frankfurt am Main, Germany, through Strasbourg, France, to Paris, Montmorency, to Château du Masgelier in Creuse, to Marseilles, to Broût-Vernet, back to Marseilles, through the Pyrenees Mountains, to Madrid, Spain, to Lisbon, Portugal, where he boarded the *S.S. Mouzinho* for the journey to the United States of America.

I

COMING TO AMERICA—
August and September 1941

It was over sixty years ago, but I remember it as if it were yesterday. It was September 1, 1941. Our ship, the *S.S. Muzinho*, had crossed the Atlantic Ocean from Lisbon, Portugal in about two weeks and now we all had to stay on board another day because it was Labor Day in the United States of America. All, that is, except for the two stowaways who were escorted off by the U.S. Coast Guard. They were black as the ace of spades, although they were Caucasians, because they had been hiding in the coal compartment until they were discovered and put into custody by members of the crew. They were escapees from a Lisbon prison who hid in the ship to escape the Portuguese authorities. Rumor had it that they had killed a member of the crew, who inadvertently discovered them, and had cannibalized him. I fought my way through the crowd of curiosity seekers to get a glimpse of them as they were being escorted off. The rumors about them, since their capture, had made them legendary to the gullible youngsters aboard. Getting a glimpse of them was one of the highlights of the trip for me.

My sisters Blimel and Gustl, who changed their names to Flora and Sarah upon arrival in the United States, and I were among the small group of Jewish children from OSE homes traveling without parents and escaping from Nazi controlled Europe. There were many Jewish adults and individual families on board who were also escaping Europe, but to our group of forty-four children, this was the culmination of an escape out of Europe that had started in early August in Marseilles, France, through the efforts of organizations of which we had no knowledge. While the others aboard had booked their own passage on the *Mouzinho*, our group of children was a part of the second and last escape convoy of children selected from the OSE *(Oeuvre de Secours aux Enfants)* children's homes.

Our escape, we now know, was organized through the cooperative efforts of several organizations including, but not limited to, HIAS, German-Jewish Children's Aid, Inc, American Joint Distribution Committee and American Friends Service Committee (Quakers.) The escape route had taken us from Marseilles where we were among those gathered from the various OSE homes throughout southern France. We took a train across the Pyrenees Mountains, through Spain to Madrid where we stayed overnight in a convent, then on to Lisbon where we stayed for ten days to two weeks and were hosted by the Lisbon Jewish community while awaiting the departure of the *S.S. Mouzinho* to the United States of America. The United States, according to what I had been made to believe, was a place where the streets were paved with gold and President Franklin Delano Roosevelt surveyed them daily while riding on his white stallion.

With a sense of wonderment, I watched the stowaways as they were being escorted off the ship. I knew they were dangerous criminals, but the fact that they had made such a daring escape out of prison and that it had almost succeeded made them seem bigger than life to me. Of course, this was the impression of an almost nine-year-old child, among this group of forty-four children and in the final stages of his own clandestine escape. Granted our escape was from the Nazi regime that threatened to take the lives of all Jews in Europe and ultimately succeeded in killing six million of us, while their escape was from a Portuguese prison for criminals. Still, I related to them, and even felt a distant kinship to them, although I had no idea of the severity of their crimes.

As memorable as the stowaways were to me, my two sisters, who apparently had their own priorities, paid no attention to this event and years later when I brought it up, they did not even remember the incident at all. Flo was almost sixteen and Sarah had turned twelve in April. They had their own group of friends whom they impressed with the fact that they were responsible for their skinny little nine-year-old brother who weighed a mere fifty-two pounds soaking wet. The remarkable thing was that I had gained eight pounds since being weighed in Marseilles not quite three months earlier when I was scheduled to leave with the first convoy. When the first group, which included my two brothers, left, I had been forced to stay behind due to stomach cramps that were diagnosed as appendicitis. The fact of the matter was that when I first arrived in Marseilles and noticed the lines for hot soup and hot bread, I was so excited that I went from one line to the other several times. Hot food had been a rarity for me in Château du Masgelier and I decided to take advantage of this opportunity. My stomach cramps were the result of my over-eating and as soon as I had recovered, I was sent to Château des Morrelles in Broût-Vernet outside of Vichy where my sisters Flora and Sarah had been residing for several weeks.

We stayed in Château des Morrelles, one of the kosher OSE facilities, which was more like a villa than a château, until about the beginning of August, 1941. After news came that the first convoy had arrived safely in New York, preparations for the second convoy were under way. The three of us were selected to participate even though, based on the agreement made between the Vichy government and the Nazi occupiers of northern France, Flo who was already fifteen and one half years old, would not have ordinarily been a candidate. According to that agreement, she would have had to be turned over to the Nazis when she turned sixteen. Ostensibly, she was put on the list to take care of me, the younger brother whom they felt was too small to take care of himself. I don't remember if we traveled to Marseilles by bus or truck, but when we arrived there and met with the other fifty-some-odd participants for the second escape convoy; I made it a point to go through the hot food lines only once.

People are fond of saying that God works in strange ways. You have to believe in this when you consider that an eight-year-old kid could save two lives, as a result of his over-eating in hot food lines. Helen, the person who took my place on the first convoy, would have turned sixteen before the second convoy was ready to leave France, and her chances of surviving would have been slim-to-none. Among her contributions to this world, she and Rabbi Ebstein, her husband, were the founders of HIDEC, a highly respected institution of Jewish learning for the hearing impaired in New York City. Had I not stayed behind because of the stomach cramps, gone to Broût-Vernet and left with my sisters on the second convoy, it would have been highly questionable whether my oldest sister Flora would have been allowed to participate in that escape. Among Flo's many achievements, she was the mayor of Corona, California in the 1980s.

The *S. S. Mouzinho* was a sizable and sturdy ship. Even though the Atlantic was a bit choppy, the Portuguese liner smoothly cut through the waves without making the sea rough for its passengers. As we passed the Azore Islands, the voyage started getting rougher. Gale-like winds had started to blow and the massive ship started to feel less sturdy. We were warned not to walk around the decks alone when the sea was choppy, whether it was day or night. I had been ignoring that warning on a nightly basis. I so hated being cooped up in the lower deck where all of us slept on tiered hammocks. The large room was stuffy and claustrophobic, the air was stale, and I found it virtually impossible to fall asleep at night. The second night out to sea, I decided to do something about the sleeping conditions. I waited for my sisters to fall asleep then I sneaked out to the bow of the ship and fell asleep on one of the lounge chairs that would have been off-limits to me during the day. The fresh sea breeze provided the proverbial breath of fresh air. At dawn I sneaked back into our compartment and nobody was the wiser. I had learned to improvise in the children's homes when conditions were not acceptable.

On the night that this caper blew up in my face, I was lying with my eyes open on a lounge chair, keeping an eye on the storm that seemed to be brewing. As the gale-like winds started getting fiercer, I realized that I better get myself back below deck into the safety of our crowded compartment. I quickly gathered myself together and started walking along the narrow promenade with cabins on one side and the ocean, beyond the steel railing, on the other. The wind was exceptionally fierce. I had to bend my body forward as I walked to keep from moving backwards. All of a sudden, the strip of carpeting on the narrow promenade deck broke loose and started moving up and down with the wind in a serpentine fashion. The carpet, propelled by the force of the wind, lifted me into the air and, as if I had been a piece of newspaper, hurled me over the rail.

Had I not been able to grab on to a post and hold on for dear life, I would have been blown overboard. Luckily, one of the stewards heard me screaming and ran to my rescue. After he helped me down, he proceeded to scold me for being up on the promenade at night, and for being out of my quarters in such dangerously windy weather. I pleaded with him not to report me to the Captain, or to my sisters, who seemed to cherish the responsibility of watching over me on the journey. We made a deal that I would stay below in our compartment every night until we reached calmer seas. In return, he would not report the incident to anyone, especially my sisters. He half jokingly suggested that I take up eating as a hobby so that I might gain some weight and cease to be a human kite. Every time we ran into the steward after that incident, Flo and Sarah wondered where and how he and I had developed what appeared to be such a special relationship.

After being without parents or siblings for over two-and-a-half years in France, one would think that I would have been ecstatic to finally be with my two older sisters. The problem was that each of my sisters decided that she should be my surrogate mother. I soon found out that the only thing worse than not having a mother around was having two mothers around, each trying to assert her authority. The most humiliating of many mothering incidents on the ship was when they both ganged up on me to bathe me. Granted, I was a bit grungy, not having bathed in several days. After being overpowered by my sisters who appeared to have my best interest at heart, I finally acquiesced to allow them to clean me off. I never could have dreamt that they would bathe me in front of their friends who, of course, were all girls. Needless to say, that was the last time that my sisters had anything to say or do about my bathing. I was understandably relieved when I found out, upon our arrival in Atlanta, Georgia, that I would be placed in a foster home with my two older brothers.

On Tuesday, September 2, we finally set foot on American soil. We disembarked at Staten Island, New York and were greeted by a group of energetic young social workers. I seem to remember one French speaking young man who was assigned to me. He asked me if there were anything in particular that I might want, even something that I had never had before. Without much thought, I asked for bubble gum. I had heard of it but never had any. He laughed and told me I was a "cheap date" as he proceeded to grant my wish.

I was disappointed when it became apparent that President Roosevelt was not there to greet us on his white horse. I had been so anxious to see this great hero, especially at that time when the world seemed so in need of heroes to look up to and leaders to believe in. On the other hand, I had not really expected the streets to be paved with gold, figuring that this rumor had been an exaggeration. However, when I found out that this giant of a man, the President of the United States of America, was in a wheelchair, crippled by a disease called polio and would never ride a horse again, I was taken aback. After confronting my shock and disappointment, I felt very sad for him. As far as my great expectations were concerned, I had been accustomed to disappointments and certainly was not going to allow my spirit of excitement for this new country to be dampened.

We were taken to a dormitory-type facility where we stayed for almost a week while our foster homes were being prepared for our arrival. The fact that our two brothers had preceded us apparently predetermined in which city we would be settled. Anselm and Jakob, who changed their names to Asher and Jack upon arrival in the United States, had arrived on the *Mouzinho* on June 23, 1941 with the first convoy among 100 Jewish children from the OSE homes traveling without parents. From there, most of the children were sent to Chicago for distribution. Asher arrived in Chicago on June 27, while Jack had to stay behind in Ellis Island to be treated for impetigo on his legs.

When Jack arrived in Chicago five days later, attempts were already being made to place them with relatives. Asher had an address book in his possession that our mom had apparently given him. It listed two close relatives in the United States. Uncle Eli Auerbach, our mother's brother, lived in California and he was the closest relative. When contacted by German-Jewish Children's Aid, Inc., Uncle Eli declined to take in his two nephews, subsidized or not. He wrote that he was not nearly as religious as our parents were and knew that he could not bring up the boys in the religious atmosphere that they or their parents would want. He also stated that he had just recently arrived in the United States after escaping a concentration camp in Germany and had to focus on getting his life together. He sent a pair of *Tefilin* (phylacteries) for Asher's Bar

Mitzvah, which had taken place the previous May in France, and suggested that our cousin Selig was a more fitting foster parent for Asher and Jack.

Rabbi Selig Auerbach lived in Rome, Georgia, and he, our mother's first cousin, was the next closest relative. While he gave it a great deal of thought, he also declined to take in the boys. He was the rabbi of Rodeph Shalom Congregation, a synagogue composed of about twenty-five families in Rome, Georgia. His salary was only $100 per month and he was paying off a $300 loan to the congregation that they had granted him to bring his mother-in-law out of Europe. He and his wife and baby were living in a small apartment where his mother-in-law was expected to join them soon. The other consideration was that Rome had too small a Jewish community for bringing up two very religious Jewish boys. He, therefore, requested that the boys be sent to Atlanta where they could be placed in Orthodox foster homes. This would allow him, he added, to visit the boys on a regular basis so he could be a mentor and offer moral support. His request was taken to heart and the Children's Service Bureau, formerly the Hebrew Orphans Home, an organization supported by the Atlanta Jewish community, was contacted and asked to find a foster home for Asher, age thirteen and Jack, age ten.

Mrs. Armand Wyle, director of the Bureau, notified cousin Selig of the positive response of the Board of Trustees of the Children's Service Bureau to his request, and in short time Asher and Jack were placed in a strictly kosher Jewish foster home in Atlanta. By the time the second convoy with my sisters and me was well on its way and sailing the Atlantic Ocean, a telegram was sent to the Hebrew Orphans Home/Children's Service Bureau stating that three more Hirsch children were en route to the United States. The message requested that they find foster homes for these three siblings as well, so that the five Hirsch children could reside in the same city.

The Children's Service Bureau graciously accepted the challenge. When I arrived in Atlanta I was placed at the home of Sam and Sarah Bregman at 266 Atlanta Ave. SE, the same foster home where my brothers Asher and Jack had been staying since August 6. Flo and Sarah were placed with Mr. and Mrs Abe Wolbe at 853 Mentelle Dr. NE, on the north side of Atlanta. Our cousin, Rabbi Selig Auerbach visited us a few times before he moved with his family to Cincinnati, Ohio.

The *S.S. Mouzinho*, the liner that brought the Hirsch children to America.

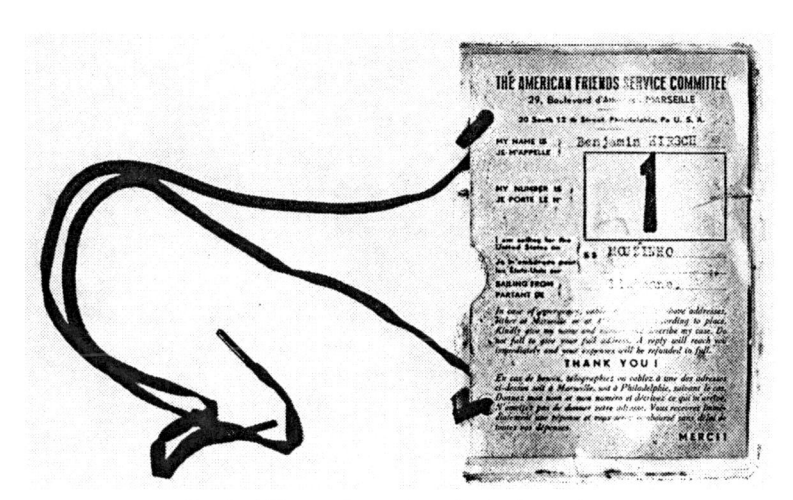

Ben's I.D. card on the trip to America.

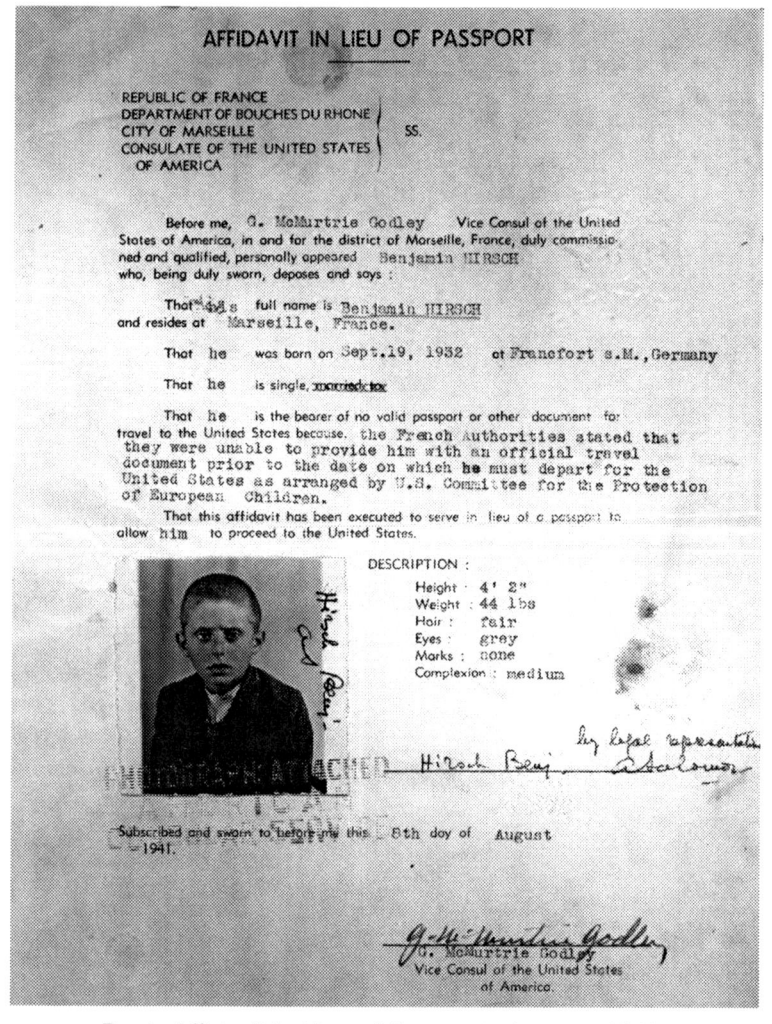

Ben's Affidavit in Lieu of Passport, August, 1941.

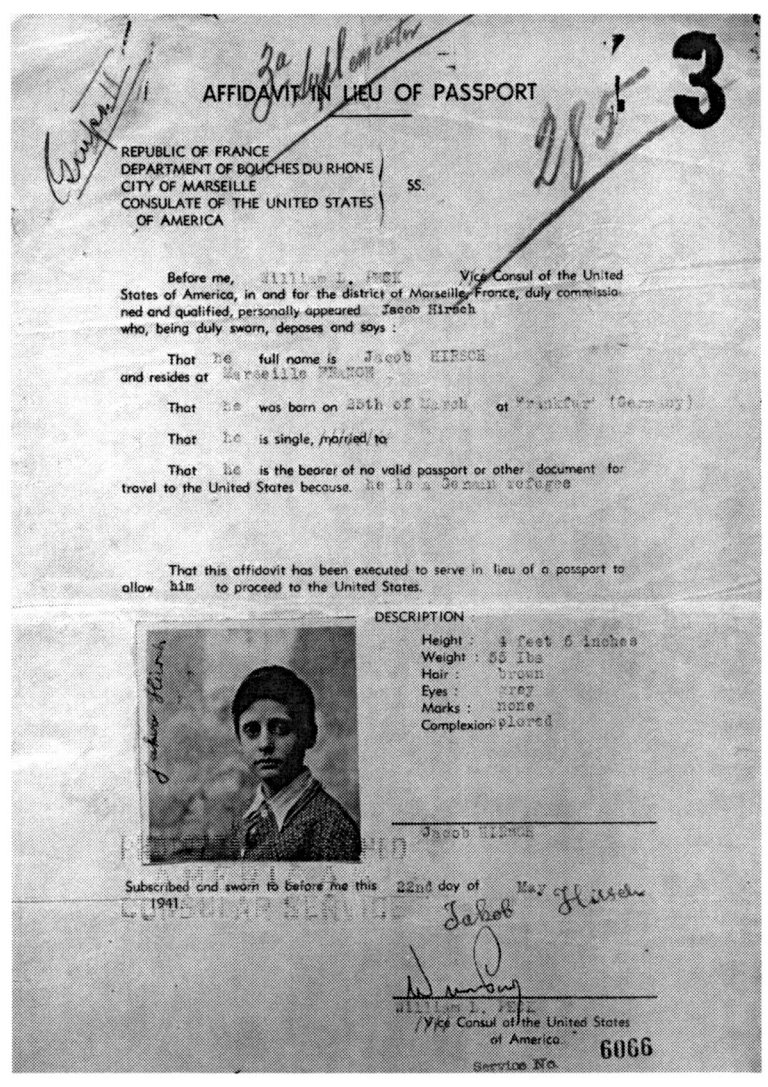

Jack's Affidavit in Lieu of Passport, June 1941.

Sarah (2nd from left) on the deck of the *Mouzinho* with friends from the group of escaping children, August 1941.

Some of the 100 refugee children on the deck of the *Mouzinho* upon their arrival in New York Harbor, June 23, 1941.

II

FIRST HOME IN ATLANTA, September 1941–January 1943

The five of us had been without parental supervision for almost three years and for the greater majority of that time, I had been without the companionship or influence of my older siblings. It wasn't surprising, therefore, in reading various evaluations and reports that Sarah, Jack, and I were, to put it mildly, disciplinary problems. The amazing thing was that all five of us had maintained a great amount of the religious training we had received from our parents while still in Frankfurt am Main. Asher, of course, had the highest degree of practice and learning. He was so steadfast in trying to maintain the degree of religiosity that he had promised our father that he was often thought to be overbearing and judgmental of others. He felt strongly that the burden of guiding his siblings in keeping the faith was his responsibility alone. This dynamic was part of the baggage we brought with us to the various foster homes that were gracious enough to take us in, at least initially.

It amazes me to think that at nine years of age, after being without parents or siblings for 2½ years, I was still "a very pious boy." According to the caseworkers' reports, I was "a boy who prayed each morning and would never take his beret off his head (not even at night)." These reports described me as "a slight boy, rather short for his age-much quieter than Jacques," and as "phlegmatic," which must be a term taught in social worker schools, since it was used by so many different social workers in describing me. To this day, it embarrasses me to admit that I still occasionally wet my bed at my first foster home and would not be able to cure myself of doing so for at least another year.

Before Asher and Jack came to Atlanta, there had been concern about finding a foster home religious enough for them, but the only requirement that Asher had insisted upon was that the home be strictly kosher. The Bregman home fit the bill. Sam and Sarah Bregman were not strangers to being foster parents for the Children's Service Bureau. By the time Asher and Jack arrived in Atlanta, they had picked up a little of the language in Chicago and New York and were able to speak a little English. Eager to master the local language, Asher immediately requested that Mrs. Bregman speak to them in no other language.

My brothers came to the Bregmans' with hardly any clothes. Jack had only the socks he was wearing, some underwear or shirts, and his shoes didn't fit. The Bureau requested that Mrs. Bregman immediately purchase the necessary items of clothing for both boys for which she would be reimbursed. A week later, Mrs. Bregman called for permission to buy the boys an additional pair of *tzitzis*, the four-cornered undergarment with fringes at each corner which religious Jewish males are biblically enjoined to wear. Asher and Jack each had only one pair and, Mrs. Bregman had reported, "they refused to take them off even to be washed." I, on the other hand, had been without *tzitzis* since a camp incident in France. I had been sent to a summer camp setting ostensibly to fatten me up. Upon arrival, I was greeted by two counselors who immediately took the *tzitzis* off my body and tore them to shreds as I stood by with a bewildered look on my face.

The Bregmans had three children. Larry was the oldest and least friendly. He always appeared very serious. Maybe that was because he was a student at Emory University in pre-med. It seemed as if he considered himself the leader of the household. Petty was sixteen and in high school. He was a very amiable and outgoing young man with an active social life. Then there was twelve-year-old Pauline, affectionately called "Pookie." The Bregmans also had a maid, Martha, who had been with the family for years. Mr. Bregman spent long hours in their grocery store on Martin Street and Mrs. Bregman went there often to help him out. Whenever his parents weren't around, Larry felt that he was needed to keep the foster children and his younger siblings in line. My brother Asher, on the other hand, although he was closer to Petty's age, also had a strong feeling of responsibility for the behavior of his siblings. In Asher's case, he was exhorted by our parents in the few letters that we had received from them to see to it that Jack and I behaved in such a way as not to bring embarrassment or disgrace to our family name. As would be expected, there was some friction between Larry and Asher.

The first *Shabbat* that I was in Atlanta, we went to Friday night services at the 'Big *Shul*,' as Ahavath Achim Synagogue was commonly known. A. A., as it was also known, was the largest of the three Orthodox synagogues in Atlanta at the time. The synagogue was at least two miles from our home on Atlanta Avenue but I don't seem to remember any concerns over walking to and from the synagogue on the Sabbath. Asher and Jack were already acquainted with many of the worshipers including Rabbi Harry Epstein and Cantor Schwartzman for whom Asher had already been singing in the choir.

After services, we started walking home with a small group of men that were walking in our direction. My main language was still French though I had picked up few words of English in the few days I had been in the States. Even though I had been introduced to all of the men and wanted to participate in the conversation, I realized that I had to learn the language first. I therefore listened intently to the conversations, focusing on the English words being spoken. I later found out that what I had been listening to was the broken English spoken by people who had immigrated from Europe, most of them fewer than ten to twenty years earlier. In spite of that, I was still able to make out a word or two from what I had learned by then.

I was so intent on listening to the conversation going on around me that I didn't pay attention to the path in front of me. The rain had stopped just before we left *shul* and the sidewalks of uneven hexagonal concrete pavers had plenty of traction to keep us from slipping. The asphalt streets, however, were quite slippery. I believe we were crossing Richardson Street when I slipped and started sliding into an equally slippery cast iron curb inlet. My brothers, reacting very quickly, each grabbed one of my arms, as my four foot-two inch, fifty-two pound frame slid almost totally inside the drainage structure. I had not thought of myself as having been that small before that experience. I quickly became very conscious of the need for me to start working on gaining some weight. Asher and Jack regaled in telling the Bregmans how they saved their little brother from being washed down the sewer system. Of course, I was chastised for getting my newly acquired *Shabbos* suit filthy.

Jack and I were both enrolled in James L. Key Elementary School. Jack had already been in the U.S. for over two months by the time the school year started and was proficient enough in English to be placed the grade level indicated by his testing. He was placed in Five-High although he was only ten and one half years old. Apparently, the education we had gotten in France was at a higher level, especially in math. I, on the other hand, with my fluent French and almost non-existent English, was put in Three-Low with Mrs. Green as my teacher. Asher was placed in Nine-Low at Hoke Smith Junior High, Flo entered the tenth grade at Commercial High School, and Sarah was placed in the sixth grade at Clark Howell School, taking courses ranging from Five-High in English to Six-High in Math.

Mrs. Green tried valiantly to communicate with her refugee student and I in turn tried equally hard to keep up with the class, or so I thought. Reports have it that I was "incorrigible, wild and disobedient." In my selective memory, I remember cherishing the colorful stickers that she would put on papers with good grades. To my recollection, there was no such system in France of rewarding students for doing their work well and on time. I even remembered, for many years, a poem that she had the class memorize likening children chewing gum to cows chewing their cud. The verses to that poem were among the things that disappeared from my memory when I had open-heart surgery in 1988. Math had not been a problem, but subject matter requiring comprehensive understanding of the language took me a little longer than the rest of the class. After school, Miss Stern tutored both Jack and me in English. Jack had been making great progress while Miss Stern complained that I had deliberately closed my mind. I think she failed to realize that since Jack had arrived three months before me, his progress made me look like an underachiever. By the end of October, I was placed in Four-Low, because the teacher, Miss Gillman, could speak French and believed she could do more with me. At the same time, it was decided that I should take lessons apart from Jack because he persisted on talking French to me when I should have been learning English.

When I first came to James L. Key, I was kind of an attraction, or better put, an oddity. One particular student, Jimmy Bloodworth, whose mother and father were devout Baptists, had asked me to come to his house after school at his parents' request so they could talk to me about what was going on with the war in Europe. They displayed a great deal of interest in my experiences under the Nazis and those of my family. They seemed to be aware that Jews had been singled out as enemies of the Third Reich, but were lacking details that they hoped that I could fill in. While there was very little I could share of the current situation in Europe or about my family in particular, they thanked me for speaking to them and expressed genuine concern for my parent's welfare and for that of the Jews of Europe. I didn't know what to make of that encounter. I was heartened that a non-Jewish stranger would show genuine concern for the travails of my family and my people, but still, I felt uncomfortable. It was like I was being viewed through a microscope and I wasn't sure of what they were trying to learn. Most of the other students were just curious about the fact that I spoke a foreign language, or that I had traveled through nine countries before coming to Atlanta. The fact that I was half the weight of the average student in my class, wore a skullcap called a *yarmulke* almost all the time and would come to school in a tee shirt on snowy days probably piqued their curiosity as well.

Two of the most popular sixth grade girls, one of them Jewish, decided that I was their pet. They 'oohed' and 'aahed' at my every minor accomplishment, whether it was acing a math test or learning a new word; they made me feel as if I had climbed Mount Everest. Needless to say, I fell in love with both of them and was crushed when I found out that one of them had a steady boy friend.

On October 18, 1941, Asher received a letter from Mom. Actually it was addressed to all of us, but only he and Flo could read and translate the

German. The letter started with Mom expressing her joy that, finally, the five of us were together in one city and safe. Then she wrote that our dear Papi, our father, had again taken very ill. This was understood to mean that he was incarcerated again in a concentration camp, something she couldn't write because all of the outgoing mail was censored. She then added "the doctor comforted me that even he can emigrate if he soon gets better." This meant that if he could get out of the camp soon and if the papers for Cuba would arrive, they would be able to emigrate.

Flora had received a cablegram from Mom and we had received letters from Dr. Möller, a distant cousin from Germany now living in New York City, saying that Hermann Hirsch, our father, urgently needed a Cuban visa. At first we were told that the Cuban visa would cost eleven hundred dollars. This put tremendous pressure on Flo and Asher to try to raise this unbelievable sum. Asher had been in touch with a Mrs. Rothschild in New York, a friend of the family for years, and she informed him that Dr. Möller had raised a sum of money but it was not sufficient for the entire transportation cost which by then was up to fourteen hundred dollars. Even though the time had come and gone to obtain the Cuban visa, Flo saved her pennies for years to buy visas for our parents and siblings to come to America. As it turned out, those who were able to raise the required amount for Cuban visas in late 1941 got no visas for the money submitted. A small consolation indeed for the anguish Flora and Asher went through.

My first major confrontation in school came when the other third grade teacher, who happened to be Jewish, asked me to report to her while everyone else was at recess. I dutifully went to her classroom, not knowing what she had in mind. She proceeded to inform me that I was not only causing her embarrassment by wearing a *yarmulke* in a public school, but that I was embarrassing every other Jewish teacher and all the Jewish students in the school. I listened intently to her arguments for me to cease-and-desist from coming to school with a *yarmulke*. As I had been brought up to do, I was trying to respect the opinion of a teacher, but I could not understand how my decision to wear the traditional head covering that I had been taught to wear by my parents could cause anyone else so much angst. She was not very convincing and, while I made a point of being respectful, I excused myself and said I would have to think about what she said, knowing full well that I had no intention of going along with her idea.

The next day at recess, a large boy who happened to be in her third grade class, started hanging around close to me. He may have been the largest boy in the school but he was in the third grade and I was in the fourth, so I had no fear of him. As it turns out, he had been held back several times due to failing grades. Had he never been held back and received social promotions, as non-achieving students do in public schools today, he would have been in the sixth grade. I found out later that he was the school bully. Not paying any attention to him, I found an empty swing and sat in it swinging as high as I could go. As I was getting up some speed and altitude, he stood behind me, to the side of the swing's path. As the swing passed by him, he grabbed the *yarmulke* from my head and started running. Precious time passed before I could slow the swing down enough to get off and chase him. Too agitated to be patient, I jumped off the swing before it came to a stop and started chasing after him, not knowing if he had been playing a joke or if he had actually meant to make me feel as violated as I did. Whatever his motive, I was fuming. I caught up with him, tackled him by his ankles and started pounding on him as if my life depended on it. I don't how long I was hitting him before he handed me the skullcap and asked me to stop. I don't remember him hitting me back but I'm sure he did. I was so enraged and focused on making him pay for what he had done to me that I probably could not feel his blows. A large crowd had gathered and two teachers came to break up the fighting that was over before they got there.

My only reason for fighting with him was to get back my *yarmulke* and to protect my turf, my right to be the arbiter of what I would wear. Had I been more aware of who he was and where he stood in the school "tough guy" hierarchy, I'm not sure what I would have done. Be that as it may, now that my mission was accomplished, I was a marked man, all fifty plus pounds of me. Not long after that, pressure started coming from all sides. Everyone, except Asher, counseled me to stop wearing my *yarmulke* at school. Even the principal, Mrs. Cates, for whom I had the utmost respect and I knew cared for me, told me that "Americans didn't do that." It wasn't long after she spoke to me that I made the decision to no longer wear my *yarmulke* to school except when I was eating lunch in the cafeteria or in the school yard.. I can't remember when it was that I stopped wearing it there as well.

Asher had his share of problems with wearing his *yarmulke* at school too. Aside from being picked on by bigger boys, I guess for daring to be different, Asher got a sermon from our cousin, Rabbi Selig Auerbach telling him that wearing a *yarmulke* in public was not appropriate in Atlanta where no one else wore one on the street. He advised Asher that if he must cover his head for religious reasons, he should wear some kind of cap that didn't draw so much attention to him. Rabbi Auerbach followed that up with a letter to the Bureau (Children's Service Bureau of the Hebrew Orphans' Home) stating that he, who was also religious but had been living in America longer than Asher, knew how much better it was to follow American customs. In his discussion with Asher, Cousin Selig pointed out that main-stream orthodox Jews in Frankfurt had the custom of not wearing *yarmulkes* outside of the home or synagogue unless they were eating or saying a blessing. Asher knew this to be correct, however, this made little or no impression on him and he continued wearing his *yarmulke* at all times.

Not everyone in Atlanta was exerting pressure on us to become acclimated to Jewish life in Atlanta by changing or giving up certain religious practices. The Heflers lived on Washington Street across from Rabbi Geffen and they took a great interest in all of us, especially Asher. They were New Yorkers who had come to Atlanta for business reasons and were quite Orthodox. They invited us over often and tried to encourage us to maintain the religious practices of our parents as we had done for the most part before we had come to this country. Max Lieberson, a European immigrant who had maintained his religiosity along with of his financial success, was also very interested in Asher. He and Mr. Hefler paid for private *Talmud* lessons for Asher with one of the older and more pious teachers at Ahavath Achim.

Asher went to morning services at the "Little *Shul*," Congregation Shearith Israel, just two blocks south of A.A., virtually every day and tried to get Jack and me to come along. Jack had been with his older brother throughout Europe and knew how to get out of doing things Asher wanted him to do. I, on the other hand, was more prone to go along with my oldest brother's wishes, and found myself going with Asher more often than not my first couple of years in Atlanta. Besides becoming familiar with the morning prayers there were other perks to going to morning *minyan* with my brother. Being the youngest person among the mostly adult worshipers gave me almost celebrity status. Jack and Nathan Maziar were brothers who attended the morning services regularly. They were both successful businessmen and were younger than most of the regulars. They decided to make it worthwhile for youngsters such as Jack and me to attend. Almost every day that I came to services, I was rewarded with anywhere from fifteen cents to a quarter. In a time when I was getting twenty-five cents a week for spending allowance, that was a huge incentive to get up early enough each day to accompany Asher to *shul*.

Joe "Paratrooper" Aranoff had a strong interest in what was going on in Europe and he took a special interest in our family. Every time he saw me he would ask if we had heard any news from our parents. Then he would talk about joining the army and parachuting into Nazi held Europe to kick butt.

Maybe that's how he got the nickname "Paratrooper." He took a particular liking to me and started calling me "Frenchy," the moniker that stuck with me through grammar school. I didn't object to that nickname, I actually enjoyed it. I figured that any reference to the French part of my background might divert attention from the reality that I was actually born in Germany.

On certain days of the week, the Ahavath Achim school bus would pick up the boys who were going to the A. A. Hebrew School. The driver (As I recall, his name was Leo) was one of the first black men I ever came to know. I was picking up English rather quickly, but some of the nuances, such as words with two or more meanings, escaped me. For example, Herbert Mendel, who was a year or two older and much taller, taught me a song that he said I should sing out loud and out of the bus window whenever a pretty girl passed by. The lyrics I had been told to sing were, "She has freckles on her——but she's pretty," with emphasis on the "butt". I dutifully sang the song every time a pretty girl passed us, unaware of the double entendre, while Herb and friends laughed uproariously at my expense.

My Hebrew teacher was Mr. Leon Steinberg, a short jovial man with a little mustache and a pot belly that made it easier for students to stay ahead of him when he chased them around the classroom, ruler in upraised hand. He was a very likable man, but he had a short fuse when it came to mischief and chicanery. By the time we had put in a full day's schedule at public school, it was difficult to keep us focused on Judaic studies when all we wanted to do was play. On the afternoons that we didn't have Hebrew school, especially after Mr. Bregman became ill and Mrs. Bregman had to spend more time at the store, I occasionally walked over to the Bregmans' grocery store on Martin Street and ran errands. On the days their housekeeper, Martha, wasn't working, we would all go to the store and Mrs. Bregman would have supper there for us.

On November 3, 1941, Flora received a letter from our father that had been written on October 3 from the police jail in Frankfurt am Main. She translated the letter for us.

> My dearest children: I was so glad when Mama wrote me that she understands from our cousin, Selig Auerbach that you, dear Flora, Sarah and Benjamin, are in Atlanta, so I want to tell you, my best welcome wishes. It is really nice that you, dear Benjamin, can live now with Asher and Jack. Give this letter to the girls, too, whose address mother forgot to write me. Now that you are already there after three years, you must try all possible means that we can come

over there perhaps by way of Cuba. Now you see on the top of this letter that I cannot practice my job now, but I hope that when you will read this letter I shall be already at home again. Try all you can and write to all your relatives and people you know how things are, and perhaps they can help to bring money together to let us come over to America. You know that your Daddy knows how to work, and that he'll work hard until the whole sum is paid back.

You, dear Flora, will have your sixteenth birthday, and I hope that you know what you are to your brothers and sisters, and to your parents who are far away. I was already here when Benjamin had his birthday, and that's why I couldn't write him, but I send him my best wishes in this letter. I will be glad if we could celebrate the next birthdays of our family which will be in March in the country of liberty, and all together. And so I hope that the next year will bring us only good things and good luck. Please pray for us, and we'll pray for you. Perhaps God will hear our prayers. For today I'll finish with my best wishes, I am,

—Your Father, who thinks always of you, and who hopes for you.

On November, 20 a letter from Mom was received addressed to Viola Wyle of the Bureau and Mrs. Bregman, which was dated September 10, 1941, in which she alluded to our father being arrested again and spoke of their hopes for the long awaited emigration papers to come soon. She added a note about Werner and Roselene:

> The two babies, of three and four years pray every evening. "Dear God, make my father well, and let us come to America soon to our brothers and sisters."

In the letter, Mom made a point of thanking the addressees for taking such good care of her children and expressed her regrets that it had been necessary for her to let them out of her hands so soon. She closed with a parable:

> "Man thinks and God leads, but I hope that it is all for the best."

Then she asked that we, the children, write. I don't remember having Mom's letters shown or read to me. Either I forgot, or I could assume that my older siblings had been protecting me, but I'm not sure from what. When I finally saw the letters, decades later, they broke my heart.

I heard about tryouts for a choral group at James L. Key. The choral group's main performance would be for a Christmas program, which I was told was an annual event. I had always loved to sing and did not feel that the program would pose any conflict for me. So, I went to the tryouts a little excited and full of anticipation that I would be able to show off my singing voice which I had been told was quite good. The first song they had everyone sing together was "*A Horse That Knows the Way Back Home*," which everyone seemed to know except me, but I found it easy enough to sing along. Next came the individual tryouts. I was asked to sing "*Onward Christian Soldiers*," and I found myself unable to sing the words. For some reason, I couldn't mouth the words without thinking that the Nazi soldiers, who were murdering Jews in Europe, were Christians. It is even possible that I had been taught about the Crusades, and their slaughter of Jewish communities in Germany, in my early Jewish education. Be that as it may, I excused myself and sadly accepted the reality that I would not be singing with the school choral group.

In December, the war that I had escaped from in Europe was suddenly extended to the United States. Thankfully not on American soil, but American young men were enlisting and being drafted into the armed services, many that I knew, to train for engaging the enemies of freedom in battle, albeit on foreign soil. The stated goal was to defeat the enemy before they could bring the fighting to our shores. I felt sufficiently a part of my country of refuge to think in terms of "our soil," but it was not long before I found out that my status in my new country had changed from "refugee" to "enemy alien."

December 7, 1941, we were told by the president of the United States was, "a day of infamy." We heard that the Japanese navy and air force had attacked Pearl Harbor and America was plunged that quickly into the Pacific theater of World War II. I had wondered if and when America's involvement would extend to the European sector of the world conflict. As it turned out, it was only a matter of days, December 10 to be exact, that President Franklin Delano Roosevelt declared war on Germany and its allies, joining Great Britain who had already been fighting Hitler's war machine for two years, all the while, pleading with the United States to join the battle.

Prior to America's entering the fight against the Axis, few if any students at James L. Key knew or cared very much about what was going on in Europe. To them, I was just a kid from a foreign land who was learning to fit in. With the exception of the fight over my *yarmulke* and a few minor incidents, I had no reason to feel threatened. I had disliked being pitied by some of the older students and faculty for coming to this country as a parentless refugee, but in retrospect, it was preferable to being singled out because I happened to be born in the country that was now at war with ours. While most of my schoolmates and their parents understood that I had been a victim of Nazi Germany's tyranny, there was no shortage of those who were eager to brand me as an enemy alien and who relished engaging me in fisticuffs. It was at that point that other students started picking fights with me on a fairly regular basis, ostensibly-at least initially, because I was an "enemy alien." This aspect of my growing up in Atlanta did not fully stop until 1948.

From all indications, my schoolwork, as well as my behavior in school, improved dramatically once I was placed in the fourth grade. I was feeling more comfortable with the language and with my schoolmates, although fisticuffs had still been the major unsolicited activity of my week. If I could keep it down to two fights a week, I could have been a candidate for a peace prize.

There was one classroom incident that illustrates how easy it was for me to get a reputation for misbehavior even when I was not necessarily misbehaving. The teacher decided, one day, that it would be enlightening for the class to explore the parental roots of each student. She asked each of us who had at least one parent that was not born in Atlanta, to state where his or her parent(s) had been born. One student's mother was a New Yorker; another student's father was a Charlestonian, and so forth. Finally my turn came and I truthfully said that my father was a Frankfurter and my mother was a Hamburger. Without missing a beat, Dicky Bradshaw yelled out, "What does that make you, a meat ball?" The whole class burst out laughing and I was sent to the principal. I told Mrs. Cates the whole story and I explained that my father was in fact born in Frankfurt, Germany and my mother was born in Hamburg, Germany. Mrs. Cates came to my defense and explained the facts that led to my response. The teacher, however, remained convinced that I was a troublemaker and that I had been waiting for the opportunity to spring this little tidbit of information in the most comical way possible. Dicky, incidentally, had not been called down for his outburst. Somehow that didn't surprise me.

My teachers were aware of my flair for art and they encouraged the Bureau to have me take art classes to develop my talent. My caseworker tried to get me to sign up for classes at the High Museum of Art which I was eager to do until he said the classes would be on Saturday. I explained that as much as I would have liked to go to art school, I could not violate the Sabbath.

Since I wasn't going to start art school over the summer, my case worker gave me the option of going to summer camp for a two week session. My first reaction was negative. My only experience with summer camp had been three years earlier in France, and that was an experience I did not want to relive. I was assured that this camp was run by the Jewish Educational Alliance and not only was it kosher, but the camp was respectful of observant Jewish practices. So in July, I was sent to Camp Daniel Morgan in Rutledge, Georgia for the first session. I was sad that the doctor would not allow Jack to go as well because of his heart murmur, but I soon made a lot of friends such as the Edelson boys from LaGrange, Georgia whom I still see on occasion today.

My introduction to the great American pastime, baseball, was a learning experience. Baseball was the camp's major athletic activity next to swimming, and try as I might, I never could understand why it was such a popular sport. I was always put in the outfield and couldn't get excited about standing around waiting for a ball to be hit in my direction. I suppose if I would have been pitching or catching or even playing the infield, it would have been more enjoyable for me, but those positions went to the experienced players and I just couldn't wait to gain that experience. So, I played in order to be one of the boys and looked forward to the swimming after the game. I did enjoyed keeping score, however, and that's where I found my niche in America's favorite pastime. All in all, in spite of my earlier misgivings, summer camp was a good experience. It allowed me to put the horror of the camp experience in France behind me for the time being. I couldn't wait to get home and share my experience with my brothers. The summer was not over yet and I, who had been used to swimming everyday, was in withdrawal.

Paul Muldawer and I were the same age. He also attended James L. Key, and lived three or four blocks away from the Bregmans. We occasionally hung around together and he offered to take me with him once or twice a week to swim at the Jewish Progressive Club where his family had membership. I learned that there were two more Jewish private clubs, the Mayfair Club and the Standard Club, and that the social standing of Jewish families in Atlanta was based on which club membership they held. Originally, I was told, the Standard Club had been the club for German Jews most of whose families settled in Atlanta before the turn of the twentieth century. The Mayfair Club had been for Jews from the Polish immigration of the early twentieth century, and the Progressive Club was for Jews from the later Russian immigration. I was very happy to be allowed as a guest at the Progressive Club with its beautiful swimming pools. It was a good summer, but even before summer was over, I was ready for school to start again.

It wasn't long before the novelty of having his little brother around wore thin for Jack. Like any little brother, I wanted to hang around with my older brother and like older brothers, Jack didn't want me following him around. Sundays we would go to the movies. The first few weeks we would go to the Empire Theater on Georgia Avenue, which was in the direction of the *shul*. Later Jack decided he liked the Kirkwood Theater better and, since I did not know how to get there, he would hide until I was gone so he could go to the movies without me tagging along. One of the Maloof boys from across the street clued me in on what Jack was doing and to assuage my hurt feelings, the Maloofs let me browse through their vast comic book collection. I never knew that so many comic books existed. The Maloof family, being Middle Eastern Christians, was also a part of a minority group and told me that they felt an affinity to the Jewish community. They made me feel wanted and I looked forward to being invited to their house when Jack snuck off to the movies with his friends or by himself.

I don't know how the idea of selling magazine subscriptions door to door came about but, when the opportunity presented itself, I gave it a try. As I recall, it was promoted by the school as a patriotic extra-curricular activity for students who wanted to make some spending money. *Liberty Magazine* was probably a new publication toward the beginning of World War II and it recruited elementary school students to go door to door selling subscriptions. The commissions were very low, but there were prizes for sales incentives including college scholarships if you sold an unfathomable number of subscriptions. I worked hard at this for a while, but with minuscule returns for my efforts, I soon became disillusioned with the endeavor. Yet, it was my introduction the art of selling which, as I later found out, is crucial to being a success in almost any endeavor. The biggest lesson I learned from that brief experience was that I would never want to depend on selling anything door to door for a livelihood.

In the few letters that our father wrote, he exhorted Asher to remain steadfast in his orthodox religious practices and he put the onus on Asher to see to it that Jack and I followed suit. I had no problem going along with the traditions that I had remembered from Germany and trusted Asher to guide me on those things with which I was not familiar. Jack, on the other hand, had been living with Asher throughout our stay in France and had had his fill of being told what he could and could not do as far as religious practices were concerned. I can still remember the Friday night that Jack purposely turned on the bedroom light and defiantly looked at his older brother and said, "See! Nothing happened." I was aghast. I couldn't believe that Jack had the inclination or nerve, for that matter, to do such a drastic thing. I thought, had our father been there, he would have beaten Jack until he was black and blue. But Dad was not there and it turned out to be a turning point in Jack's life. For Asher, it was a major setback to his aspirations of having Jack and me follow the level of religious observance of our parents.

That incident aside, Jack continued to keep Jewish observances while living with Asher at the Bregmans'. I remember the time that all of the children under the auspices of the Children's Service Bureau were invited to go to a movie together at the Fox Theater. The sticking point was that the movie outing was on Saturday. Realizing that this was something that Jack and I really wanted to be able to participate in, Asher arranged for the tickets to be waiting for us at the box office so we could walk to the theater and avoid violating *Shabbos*. All the other children were meeting at the Jewish Educational Alliance on Capitol Avenue in the early afternoon and going by bus from there to the Fox. Jack and I started walking from the synagogue shortly after *Shabbos* morning services. As we approached Whitehall Street on Mitchell Street, the bus carrying the other kids passed us. The driver honked and the kids, our peers, waved at us. By the time we reached the theater, everyone else had just gone in except for one adult who was waiting for us to make sure that we got our tickets and that we would join the other children. Asher didn't go, taking offense that anyone would schedule an outing for Jewish kids on *Shabbos,* but we rather enjoyed going the extra mile, literally, to avoid desecrating the Sabbath while still participating in a community event.

Though we were still getting letters from Mom on rare occasions, we had little information about what was happening in their lives other than that our father had been arrested again and sent to Sachsenhausen, a concentration camp in Oranienberg just outside of Berlin, and that they desperately wanted to immigrate to Cuba, as soon as he would be released

Our last letter from Mom and Dad addressed to *Anselm and Bob* (Asher and Jack), as usual, was dated August 24, 1942. All the letters from Mom and Dad were written in German, which may be part of the reason that I never saw them when they came. The fact that the letters were no longer coming did not register with me, since I don't remember ever having the letters read or translated to me. I kept up with the war and the sprinkling of information on the concentration camps in the newsreels that were played in every theater between feature films. I fantasized about growing big and strong and joining the army to go back to Europe and to get my revenge on the Germans.

In the newsreels, we heard that Hitler turned on his ally, the Soviet Union, and ordered his Generals to conduct an "unmerciful" and "unrelenting" war against the USSR in March of 1941. There was nothing in the newsreels, however, about the establishment of the Warsaw Ghetto, in October, 1940 and its being sealed off from the rest of the city a month later. It was a 3.5 square mile area that would house upwards of 450,000 Jews with virtually no food, medical supplies or other basic necessities of life. Nor was the American public told of Heinrich Himmler's plans to expand the Auschwitz complex to make room for more Jewish slaves and prisoners doomed to be murdered and incinerated. Maybe it was for the best that my siblings and I knew no details of the horror that was the life of our family and all of European Jewry.

I have since learned that our father had never returned from that camp near Berlin. In fact, he was evacuated from Sachsenhaussen in October 1942, when S.S. Chief Heinrich Himmler ordered it to become *Judenrein*, free of Jews, because of its proximity to the "holy city of Berlin." My father along with virtually all of Sachsenhaussen's Jewish prisoners was sent to Auschwitz. Approximately thirty Jews who were bookkeepers or accountants were left behind to finalize the records. In 1995, the curator of the Sachsenhaussen Museum looked through the list of those who stayed behind and verified that Dad was not among them. As recorded in the Gedenkbuch, published by the postwar German government, my father was killed in Auschwitz on November 5, 1942.

Our mother, along with Werner and Roselene, was deported from Frankfurt am Main on September 24, 1942. They ultimately ended up in Auschwitz where, in the fall of 1943, they were seen by my uncle, Philip Auerbach. Uncle Philip, who survived as a chemist in Auschwitz, told my brother Asher that he had been shown a list from an incoming transport which included the name of Mathilda Hirsch née Auerbach. He maneuvered as close as he could to the staging area and he saw his sister with her two youngest children waiting in line to enter the delousing showers, which were in fact gas chambers. My mother had no means of communicating with us that last year of her life and I still have no verifiable information as to where the three of them were between their deportation from Frankfurt and their arrival in Auschwitz about a year later.

Apparently Jack and I were quite precocious. While I don't remember many specific things, it seems that we were always getting into trouble whether together or as individuals. We were both very curious kids, always trying to find out why things were the way they were. Jack was more aggressive, however, in seeking answers to questions that puzzled him. The one incident that I remember was when Jack wanted to find out just when the light went out in the refrigerator after the door was closed. Like a true scientist, he went straight to the source. He opened and closed the door to the refrigerator trying to catch that split second when the light went out. The fridge broke before Jack could reach a scientific conclusion and, for Mrs. Bregman, this was the last straw. At least that's what I remember her saying and shortly thereafter we were told that we would be moving from the Bregman house. The fact of the matter was that Mr. Bregman still hadn't fully recovered from an illness and required a great deal of attention and help from Mrs. Bregman, who was spending full days at their grocery store. That, along with the burden of trying to keep two wild things in line, plus taking care of her own children, was wearing her down. One of the social workers told me, in jest, that they had decided that for the good of Atlanta, Jack and I would not be allowed to live on the same side of town.

Late in December 1942, the Bregmans officially requested to have the three Hirsch boys placed elsewhere, and Mrs Wyle promised to find another foster home for us as soon as possible. On January 22, 1943, Asher and I moved to 172 Atlanta Avenue, the home of Mr. And Mrs. Philip Hershberg where Flora was already living. At about the same time, according to The Holocaust Chronicles:

> At Les Accates, near Marseilles, France, twenty-nine Jewish children were seized by the Nazis at the La Rose Orphanage. Their guardian, Alice Salomon, insisted on remaining with the children and was gassed with them at the Sobibor death camp two months later.

Among the many noteworthy positions taken by world leaders in January 1943:

> Pope Pius XII, in response to the request of the Polish president, Wadyslaw Raczkiewicz, that he publicly denounce German atrocities against the Jews, announced that the Vatican can help oppressed peoples only via "our prayers."

Also, in Casablanca, Morocco at the meeting at which Winston Churchill and Franklin Delano Roosevelt discussed the future Allied invasion of Western Europe,

> Roosevelt proposed to French North African official General Nogues and later to Free French Forces General Giraud that the French government in North Africa should discriminate against local

> Jews just as Hitler did in the 1930s. FDR specifically stated that "the number of Jews engaged in the practice of the professions…should be definitely limited to the percentage that the Jewish population in North Africa bears to the whole of the North African population." He added that limiting the number of Jews in the professions "would further eliminate the specific and <u>understandable complaints which the Germans bore toward the Jews in Germany…</u>" [emphasis mine]

Leaving a foster home comes with strains of separation not unlike breaking an engagement or splitting up a partnership. For this ten-year-old boy, it was difficult to sort out how I was supposed to feel about the Bregmans. I barely kept in touch with the Bregman family while I was growing up. In our adult years, Jack made a point of keeping close ties them and, thank God, he pulled me along. Pauline was like a sister to Jack and me before he passed away. When Larry, who had been my children's pediatrician, passed away his wife and daughters asked me to say *Kaddish*, a traditional recitation praising God in memory of the deceased, for the year of mourning. Petty was unfortunately too ill to do this for his brother's soul. I felt honored and privileged to be entrusted with that awesome responsibility.

Letter from Ben's mother to Mr. and Mrs. Abe Wolbe, Flo's and Sarah's first foster parents, thanking them for taking good care of her children, dated September 9, 1941.

Letter from Ben's mother to her five children in Atlanta, written on the back of the letter to the Wolbes, giving news of the two younger children and instructing us to be well behaved and to show gratitude to our foster parents.

James L. Key Elementary School class, c.1942. Front row: Benjamin Hirsch (3rd from left), Dick Bradshaw (5th from left), Paul Maldawer (far right); middle row: Peggy Milam (6th from left), Mary Thomas (7th from left); rear row: Stanford Firestone (far right).

III

ESCAPE FROM EUROPE/THE FRENCH CONNECTION
December 1938–August 1941

I had been in Château du Masgelier, located in Creuse, a region in middle France, for well over a year when I was told that I was on a list of children who would be going to Marseilles by bus in mid-May. We were going to be part of a group of about fifty children who were to attempt an escape from Nazi Europe to the United States. The exciting part was that I would rendezvous with my brothers Asher and Jack, whom I hadn't seen since they visited me on my birthday in September 1940. Somehow all three of us were put on this same list.

I was sort of getting used to Masgelier. I had been there longer than any other place I had stayed in France. It was one of the homes run by OSE, *(Oeuvre de Secours aux Enfants)* the organization for the security of Jewish children whose parents were either imprisoned or killed by the Nazis. I had come there from Villa Helvetia, in Montmorency, a suburb of Paris, which was the OSE children's home where Nathan and Helen Samuels had placed me in 1939 after they realized that, with the impending occupation of the French capital by Nazi Germany, Paris would no longer be safe for Jews. They visited me often and made sure that I was taken care of and then they made plans to go into hiding outside of Paris. Ultimately, they ended up working in some of the OSE homes. The Samuels family was not related to me but they took me into their home when I arrived in Paris from Frankfurt am Main, Germany on December 6, 1938.

I came by *Kindertransport* train, along with my four older sisters and brothers. That was almost a month after *Kristallnacht*, November 9 and 10, 1938, when our father, Dr. Hermann Hirsch had been arrested and sent to Buchenwald. After that horrendous experience, our mother, Mathilda Auerbach Hirsch, made the bold decision to send her children that were old enough to travel, out of harm's way. My twenty-one months old brother, Werner, and my nine month old sister, Roselene, were deemed by my mother to be too young to travel without a parent and remained in Frankfurt with her.

The train stopped in Strassburg, apparently a scheduled stop, where we were met by our mother's cousin, Jacob Cohn. Bo, as Asher referred to him, took the five of us to the house of Martha Margot Klein, a distant cousin of our father, who served us lunch and got us back to the station where we boarded the train for Paris along with our cousin, Bo. I don't remember seeing of hearing of Cousin Martha again.

Upon our arrival in Paris, several people were waiting at the train station to greet us and take us to our respective places. I had no idea that the five of us were going to be split up; but then again, I apparently had no clue as to why we were in Paris in the first place. Our cousin, Marcus Cohn, Bo's older brother, was there to pick up Asher and Jack and take them to his mother's house. Sara Cohn was our mother's aunt. Marcus was the director of École Maimonides, an Orthodox Jewish boarding school. It was a yeshiva day school with the curriculum of *Lemudai Kodesh*, religious studies, in the morning and secular studies in the afternoon. Asher and Jack lived with Aunt Sara for four weeks then, after the *Chanukah* vacation, they moved to École Maimonides, where they lived and attended school for the next semester. By then the OSE home for boys from religious families, Villa La Chesnaie, opened up in Eaubonne and they moved there.

Uncle Gusti was there to meet my sisters Flora and Sarah. August Hirsch was my father's older brother. He was the seventh of nine children and my father was the eighth. Mom, as she had done with Asher and Jack at the Cohns, had arranged for my sisters to stay with Uncle Gusti and Aunt Helen, who had no children. Mom had also arranged for me to stay with Uncle Yaki's family. Yaki, Jacob Hirsch, was Uncle Gusti's older brother; he was the sixth of nine Hirsch siblings. Apparently something happened after our *Kindertransport* train had left Frankfurt that made Uncle Yaki and his family decided that they could not take me in to stay with them in their house. He went to the synagogue on Rue de Julien LeCroyx for morning services on the day of our arrival. There he made a public appeal for someone who could provide a home for a six-year-old boy from a fine Orthodox Jewish family in Frankfurt, Germany who was arriving in Paris later that day.

Mr. Nathan Samuels was one of those present at that *minyan* (minimum of ten men required for a prayer service), and he offered to take me in. As it turned out, Uncle Yaki, Aunt Mila with their son, Pierre, and daughter, Jacqueline (Margot), lived in the same apartment complex at19 Boulevard d'Indochine. I had not known that my uncle was supposed to pick me up at the train station, and I would not have recognized him if he had, so it had not bothered me that a nice man, who was a total stranger, picked me up and took me home with him. What did bother me was that I was being separated from my siblings. While each of them had another sibling with them, I, the youngest, had been suddenly left without parents or siblings in a strange city. It was no wonder that in less than two weeks, by the time I had my first day of public school, I had forgotten how to speak German. It was clear that I was the new boy in town and my new classmates asked me where I was from. They seemed to have some doubts when I responded that I was from Frankfurt am Main, Germany and they challenged me to speak German. When I was unable to meet the challenge, they were convinced that I had been lying to them and beat me up.

I enjoyed living with the Samuels family. They had a two-year-old daughter, Fanny, who was very cute, and also very possessive with her toys. Like most two year olds, she had a hard time sharing. In spite of that, we learned to get along in no time. On one occasion, she indicated the desire for me to reach in the fish bowl and get a goldfish for her. Wanting to oblige, I stuck my hand into the bowl, which had been out of her reach, and pulled out a wiggling goldfish. At first, I snickered when she opened her mouth widely. After a slight hesitation, I shrugged my shoulders and dropped the goldfish in her mouth, like a mother bird feeding worms to her young. From that incident a legend was born. Over thirty years later, in 1973, I found the Samuels family in Paris, just six months before they would be moving to Jerusalem. I was in the Samuels' apartment, when Fanny, who had been living in the same building on a higher floor, walked in the front door. She looked at me and shouted, "You exist—I thought you were a legend." Then she chuckled as she continued, "You used to feed me goldfish!"

Helen Samuels reminded me recently that Aunt Mila often asked her to have me come by their apartment for a visit. Aunt Mila's apartment was very to close to the Samuels', but I never wanted to go. Mrs. Samuels guessed that was because Aunt Mila's home was furnished and decorated like a show place and I was afraid that, even if I had been allowed to play, I might have broken something expensive. I must have visited the apartment at least once, to have been aware of the touch-me-not nature of the pristine decor. That may have been the reason she and Uncle Yaki felt they couldn't take in a rambunctious six year old to live with them, in addition to their own children, Pierre, who was fourteen, and Jacqueline Margot, who was eleven.

As much as I enjoyed living with the Samuels, from time to time, I would get lonely for my family. Asher and Jack came to visit me occasionally and when it was time for them to leave, invariably, I started crying. I still remember how Mr. Samuels would take me on the elevator and ride it up and down, as many times as it would take, to get my mind away from my brothers' departure. The building had seven floors, as did all the buildings in the apartment complex. I remember this because Mr. Samuels had explained that Paris had an ordinance limiting buildings to seven stories in height. Both Nathan and Helen Samuels made me feel like I was a part of the family. I wondered if I would ever have the opportunity to express my appreciation to the Samuels for their hospitality.

One day, I noticed an open can of black paint, with a paintbrush lying on it sitting on the toilet room floor. In Europe, most apartments had a separate small room for the toilet fixture. The lavatory and/or bathtub would be in a separate room. After giving it some thought, I surmised that it must have been Mr. Samuels's intention to paint the bathroom black. Why else would the open can of paint and brush be there? Grabbing the opportunity to do a kind deed, I started painting the walls.

After I painted the walls as high as I could reach, I climbed on top of the toilet seat and continued. I was standing on the toilet seat, painting as high as I could reach, when Mr. Samuels let out a gasp as he saw what I was doing. Apparently, painting the toilet room black was not on his agenda after all. That incident preceded my move to Montmorency by less than two weeks and I had always assumed that I had been sent away because of that ill-advised deed. When I first saw the Samuels again, in 1973, and we shared anecdotes, it appeared that neither of them had any recollection at that entire incident.

Villa Helvetia in Montmorency had been my first OSE home. The director of Helvetia was Margot Kahn, who later married our cousin Jacob Cohen, in 1945. Jacob had also been working with OSE through the war years. Helvetia was evacuated in 1940, shortly before the German troops reached Paris. From there I was among the few Helvetia children who were sent to Château du Masgelier in Creuse, out of the jurisdiction of the German occupation. The other children had been disbursed among the various OSE homes in the "Free France" area.

I don't have too many memories of my stay at Helvetia. I do remember that when I first arrived there, I felt distance from the other children who all seemed to know each other and stuck together in cliques, leaving out the new kid. I was just six years old and I was in need of friends. My solution to that problem was to announce that the following day was my birthday. The adults and children alike hastened to put together a party for me and, though sugar was rationed, all of my new peers had cake and ice cream. I became popular overnight and no one ever realized that it was not my birthday.

I remember bringing my prized possessions with me; the green velvet Bavarian suit and gray tweed jacket than Mom had packed for me, as well as the two drawings I had made while living with the Samuels and wanted to save. One was a detailed sketch of the Arc de Triomphe and the other was of the Eiffel Tower. I had prized these items so much that I took them with me everywhere I traveled in France. I often wonder what happened to them.

I was encouraged to do a lot of drawing at Helvetia and that kept my mind off things that might have made me sad. I wish I could remember the name of the beautiful little girl who taught me to tie my shoe laces there. She was my first love. I remember drawing pictures for her and trying to do various athletic stunts to impress her. There was another suitor who also drew well and was more athletic than I was, it was a friendly but serious competition and she made us both feel like we were the one. When Helvetia was evacuated and she was not among the children at Château du Masgelier, she was the one I missed the most.

Flo and Sarah were still living with Uncle Gusti in Paris and came to visit me a couple of times, as did the Samuels, as long as they were still in the area. Asher and Jack had already moved to the OSE home for children from religious families in Eaubonne. I have never gotten a satisfactory answer as to why I was not sent to that home.

Asher became a Bar Mitzvah in Eaubonne on May 25, 1940 and Jack was the only other family member present for the occasion. Uncle Gusti and Uncle Yaki were supposed to be there, but war-time travel restrictions made it impossible for either of them to come. Uncle Philipp, who had gone to France when he and his family escaped Belgium, was also unable to make it. I was probably still in Montmorency, restricted to the premises during preparations for the evacuation of Villa Helvetia. On June 3, nine days after Asher's Bar Mitzvah, Villa La Chesnaie was evacuated and only eleven days later, on June 14, 1940, German troops marched into Paris and started the occupation. Asher and Jack were sent to Château des Morelles in Broût-Vernet, also an OSE home for religious children, outside of Vichy, the capital of Marshall Petain's "Free France."

Somewhere between the beginning of my stay in Villa Helvetia and the end of my stay at Château du Masgelier, I had been sent to a camp-like place that turned out to be a very hostile environment for me. To this day, I still cannot remember when I went there, how I got there, where it was and how I, mercifully, got out of there. I could only assume that I was sent to this place to put some meat on my bones. (Giving the benefit of the doubt to whoever was responsible for having sent me to this place,) I had been very skinny and definitely could have benefited from gaining some weight. Be that as it may, this turned out to be an experience from Hell that left me with nightmarish memories for many years.

My first adverse memory was an incident which occurred upon arrival at the facility which seemed to be a summer camp. I remember it because of the manner in which the people in this camp welcomed me. After looking over the way I had been dressed and the items of clothing I had taken with me, they proceeded to take off my *tzitzis*, the four-cornered undergarment with fringes that I had been brought up to wear under my shirt. Then they went through my suitcase and found the extra pair of *tzitzis* that I had packed and tore them both up in front of me. I was too intimidated to ask why in the world they would do such a thing. It certainly wasn't to make me feel at home. I had been under the impression that these people were Jewish and that the place was a Jewish establishment. Why then, I wondered, would they revel in destroying items of Jewish ritual. I was totally confused and apprehensive about what may lie ahead.

If this were a camp, it was already in session. I was escorted to the lunchroom which was just emptying as I arrived. My escorts sat me down by myself at a small table for two against the exterior wall. Within minutes, they served me a plate with only a thick slice of ham on it. I looked at the meat in dismay. I was hungry but I knew that I couldn't eat meat that wasn't kosher. Two young adults stood over me, exhorting me to eat the food that had been served if I knew what was good for me. I suspected by that time that they had little concern for Jewish dietary laws, but I tried to make them aware of my situation anyway. I explained that as an observant Jew, according to *Torah* law, I was not allowed to eat ham. Not surprisingly, my words fell on deaf ears. Once it became apparent that I would not eat the ham, someone took the plate away and told me to go to my bunk and unpack.

At dinnertime, the dining room was full of people but I was made to sit by myself at the same small table with the same plate and the same piece of meat on it. By this time, we had reached a standstill. They knew that I was not going to eat the non-kosher meat and I knew that there was no point in trying to explain why I would not. The irony of the situation, I think in retrospect, was that they were supposed to be fattening me up, and instead they were starving me. When the evening meal concluded for everyone else, someone took my untouched plate without offering any alternative food and I was told to go to bed. I was exhausted but hunger pangs were keeping me awake. I must have fallen asleep at some point because before I knew it, it was morning.

The dining hall was full again for breakfast. I noticed that some people were eating eggs with rolls and others had cereal. Again, I was told to sit at the same table by myself. They served me the same plate with the same piece of ham one more time. By this time, the piece of meat had started to show its age, and I wondered if any of the other people in the dining hall noticed what I had been going through. Hungry as I was, I still refused to eat the ham much to the disappointment of the counselors watching over me. One of counselors grabbed my arm and dragged me outside toward a large animal pen enclosed by a wire fence.

Inside the pen was a huge sow. One of the adults went into the pen with a butcher knife in his hand. Two people held the sow still; one at each end, while the man with the knife knelt down and thrust the knife upward into its belly. Someone placed a metal bucket under the bleeding pig to catch the blood. While this was going on, I was being held at the side of the pen and forced to watch the proceedings. When the bucket was filled with blood, one of the people picked it up and heaved the contents in my direction.

The blood barely missed me only because I had been allowed to jump out of the way. As my feet landed on the ground, I was so nauseated that I grabbed on to the wire fence and leaned over to throw up. There was nothing inside of me to regurgitate. It seemed like the dry heaving would go on forever. I have no memory of what happened after that. I have no idea how much longer I stayed at this place, if I finally succumbed and ate the ham, or what transpired that finally had me taken away from that place. Maybe I don't want to remember

I recently visited the *Centre de Documentation Juive Contemporaine* (Jewish Documentation Center) in Paris, trying to find some information that would identify the camp, as well as who ran it. While I had no success, I was shown a book on the activities of the OSE children's homes after the Nazis took over all of France. This book had references to some of the institutions taking younger Jewish children and training them not to act Jewish or look Jewish in any way lest they be arrested and/or killed. This had taken place in 1943 and by all accounts the methods used to train these children to save themselves were very harsh. Maybe in 1940, the people in my summer camp from Hell were three years ahead of their time, or maybe that was not their agenda at all. The questions still persist, but at least a fathomable answer is on the table.

Masgelier was a different experience. The château was in a rural setting and was probably four hundred years old. There were plumbing fixtures although there had been no sewer system in the area. All of the waste was dumped into a large subterranean pit which had to be opened up for repair all too frequently. As a result, the sanitary conditions were less than optimal. The walls of the dining hall were so full of flies that one could not tell the color of the paint on the walls. To satisfy our juvenile competitive spirits, we would cup our hands on one of the walls and in a sweeping move attempt to catch as many flies as we could. The one who caught the most flies would be the winner. I held the dubious honor of catching twenty flies in one sweep of the hand. To the best of my knowledge, that record still holds.

When we arrived at Masgelier, we were told to avoid interacting with the local people. Even though we had to walk more than a mile to the public school, we were cautioned to avoid conversation with kids from town who were our schoolmates because no one could be sure whom we could trust. All of us had been issued *sabots*, wooden shoes, which was the indigenous footwear at our rural school. *Sabots* did not come with instructions, not that wearing wooden shoes required any special skill in normal weather. Maneuvering in *sabots* during wintertime in the snow presented a challenge for those of us who had not been brought up in the rural areas of France, Belgium, or Holland.

A group of us were walking back to the château from school. Snow had fallen while we had been in class and at least twenty inches had accumulated on the ground. As we were walking back to the château, two of us were lagging behind because snow was caking on the bottom of our *sabots* and we didn't know how to handle that. Putting our heads together, we figured that if we continued to walk, the snow would eventually fall off. We kept waddling along while the rest of the group was already out of sight. After a while, walking started getting precarious. The snow caked to the soles of our *sabots* was getting deeper and tapered to a point. It was as if we were walking on stilts with nothing to hold on to. We each grabbed hold of the nearest tree to keep from falling flat on our faces in the snow. We were both crying when one of the local people came along and knocked the snow stilts off of our *sabots* and told us to stop periodically to do that in order to avoid the type of snow accumulation we had just experienced. We thanked him profusely. He was one of the people we were supposed to be afraid of, yet he knew we were from the OSE home and did not hesitate to help us.

Strangely enough, I recently found out that there had been another OSE home on the other side of Cruese. Château de Chabannes was very different from Château du Masgelier, in that the people in charge there believed in interacting with the community around them. They encouraged the children to interact with the local citizenry and successfully involved the local political leaders in their protection from the Nazis. The documentary film, *Children of Chabannes* that I had the privilege of seeing at an OSE reunion in 2000 highlighted a very supportive local community that was greatly affected by the refugee children in their midst. The townspeople went out of their way to foil the gendarmes and

German soldiers in their attempts to arrest the children. I marveled at what a difference a few kilometers made.

Air raids were among the many hazards of wartime. Whenever the air raid siren would sound, we knew to rush to the shelter. At Masgelier, the shelter was in the dungeon of the very old castle. Our first air raid came and went without catastrophe. It was an exciting experience to rush down the narrow stone steps to what probably was a place where enemies had been imprisoned hundreds of years before. As air raids persisted, the shelter soon lost its glamour. It was cold and dank and a very crowded place to have to sit for, sometimes for as long as two hours until the all clear siren blew. Out of boredom, on a dare, I once drank a bottle of blue-black ink. I was reprimanded, but they figured that having a blue-black tongue for a week was punishment enough. The air raids were invariably at night and, after several months, I had my fill of getting out of bed to run to the dank shelter. Every time we had an air raid I ended up with a bronchial cough.

I had made up my mind before the next one that I was going to stay in bed and take my chances. What I failed to consider was that we had a buddy system in which each child was responsible for seeing that his buddy made it to the shelter. I shared a bunk bed with my buddy and, when the siren sounded, I told him I was not going to the shelter. I had just gotten over the cough from the last raid and was not in the mood to start another one. He pleaded with me, saying that since he was responsible for me, as I was for him, he could not go without me. I cursed the buddy system and rushed down to the dungeon with him. Two hours later we emerged from the depths and found that our portion of the large dormitory room in which many kids slept had been damaged by debris from a blast thirty yards or so away. Surveying the damage, I didn't think it would have killed me, but it definitely could have wounded me. I thanked my friend and promised him that I would not try to avoid the shelter again.

The food at Masgelier was not that bad. The problem was that the older kids got to the food first while it was still hot while the smaller kids, the category that I was destined to be in, got their portion last. For some foods, that could have been acceptable. But for hot cereal, like oatmeal or farina, it was far from acceptable. Any of these breakfast foods, when they were served cold, would be so lumpy that trying to swallow it would make me gag. To this day, I will not eat oatmeal or farina; just the thought of it makes me gag.

I used to love making drawings of the château, especially the curved steps leading to the castle. I wished I had watercolors or oil paints so I could capture the beauty of the colorful snakes that crawled in and out of the open joints of the stonework at the steps. I eventually learned, and none too soon, that the more colorful a snake, the more dangerous its venom. My brothers Asher and Jack, who were living quite a distance away at Château des Morelles in Broût-Vernet, somehow were able to visit me for my eighth birthday, the real one this time. They even brought me a chocolate bar for a present, forgetting that I didn't like chocolate. I was aware of how rare chocolate bars were and I pretended to be ecstatic with the gift. After they left, I doled out small pieces of the chocolate bar to all the boys and girls my age and became a hero for a day.

The directive to go to Marseilles to rendezvous with Asher and Jack and be among 100 OSE children on an escape convoy came as a complete surprise. I had not even been aware that any plans to escape Europe were in the offing and I wondered why my brothers and I were on this special list. I was not unhappy to be leaving Masgelier. I had made some friends that I would miss, but I was not going to miss the château, picturesque as it was. The isolation and the rural setting, with its sewer issues, were not conducive to fond memories. All in all, however, the time I spent at Château du Masgelier was a positive, if not a life saving, experience. The stench of the open sewerage pits, their accompanying plague of flies and the sight of a dead diseased cow decaying in the field, will not be forgotten. But, I did learn the meaning of survival of the fittest at meal times.

I fondly remember the feeling of camaraderie when we went on field trips as a group, all marching together along the unpaved roads, as well as the group farming projects. Among the vegetables we planted, I'm reminded most of the sugar turnips. I remember the thrill of picking a ripe turnip that we had planted months before, and sinking my teeth into it. Today that would be considered unsanitary and dangerous to ones health, but we had other dangers to concern ourselves with and so we enjoyed the moment. The saddest thing for me is that I totally lost contact with the friends I had made in the year or so we were in Masgelier together. I don't even remember their names.

We traveled by bus southward to Marseilles. I didn't know any of the other children on the bus—all of whom were older than I was—and my guess was that they didn't know me either. That was borne out almost fifty years later when I met Ernst Koppstein who had been on that bus that left Masgelier on May 17, 1941. He didn't remember me and I didn't remember him, but we still had a reunion of sorts. Our busload had an exciting arrival at Marseilles. Siblings and friends were reuniting. Other than seeing my brothers, what excited me most was seeing the hot food lines. Being among the smallest children at Château du Masgelier meant that we were the last to get at the food platters and, by the time the food got to me, it was always cold. So, the thought of hot food made me feel warm all over. I immediately got in the line for hot bread and as soon as I received my portion, I took it with me and ate it in the hot soup line. When I finished the soup, which was deliciously hot, I went back into the bread line, then the soup line again and so on until I had my fill, and then some.

Gluttony does have its price. A few hours later, I was doubled over with stomach cramps. A doctor or medic examined me and diagnosed that I had appendicitis. I was told that I would have to stay behind while the group of children including my brothers, along with a handful of adults accompanying them, would travel by train to Spain and ultimately to Lisbon, Portugal where they would board a ship for the United States of America. I must have cried for being left behind and alone again, but I don't remember doing so. I may have been too focused on the pain in my stomach to care about anything else. Anyway, it wasn't long after the train left, a couple of days at the most, that I was feeling fine. I was sent to a villa called Château des Morelles in Broût-Vernet, where my sisters Sarah and Flo had been staying for a few weeks. Broût-Vernet is outside of Vichy, the capital of so-called "Free France," the portion of France that had not been occupied by German troops after France surrendered. It was officially controlled by Marshal Philippe Petain and his quisling government. (Petain was convicted of treason after World War II.)

Flo and Sarah had been staying with Uncle Gusti and Aunt Helen in Paris until shortly after the Germans occupied the city. At first, Uncle Gusti wanted to stay in Paris. He felt they could keep a low profile and make do, even under German occupation. Finally his fear of the antisemitic French collaborators turned out to be the catalyst for taking his family and leaving the city he loved. Not long after the Occupation on June 14, my uncle, aunt and two sisters sneaked out of Paris and settled at Le Mont Dore (Puy de Dome), a vacation town in the mountains about forty-six kilometers from Clermont Ferrand (the city where Michelin Tires are manufactured). Uncle Gusti had been active in the French underground and found out about the convoys of refugee children that would attempt to escape Nazi Europe. He decided, in the early part of 1941, that Flo and Sarah's chances of being selected to go on one of the escape convoys would be better if they were in an OSE home. He also felt that they would be safer in a group home that had a modicum of protection from the Petain government.

When he sent them to Château des Morelles, which was only 107 kilometers from Mont Dore, Asher and Jack had not yet left to go on the first convoy. So, for a short period of time, my four siblings were in the same OSE home. Uncle Gusti visited Morelles often until he increased his activity with the French underground. The last we heard of him, he had been leading a group of escaping Jews to the Swiss border, as he had done many times before. By the time the group reached the border crossing, it was Friday evening and the sun had already set. The Swiss guards insisted that everyone crossing the border would have to sign their names and show identification. While everyone in his group crossed safely into Switzerland, Uncle Gusti explained that he was prohibited from writing on Shabbat and therefore could not sign his name. He turned around to go back home and was never heard from again. I believe that Uncle Gusti was fully aware that he could violate any Shabbat restriction if it meant saving a life, but he used that as an excuse because he did not want to leave Aunt Helen behind.

Immediately upon my arrival at Morelles, a rivalry began between my sisters to establish which one was going to be in charge of little Bennie. If that was supposed to make me feel good, it didn't work. Actually Flo, according to the charge from our parents before we left Germany, was supposed to be looking out for me. She was fifteen and a half years old and had already become interested in boys. She only started to focus on taking charge of me and my behavior when Sarah tried to fill the void and challenge her authority.

I have fond memories of the wisteria-clad trellises around the villa. They smelled so sweet but attracted many bees. I was admiring the wisteria at the side of the villa one day, when I noticed a transaction going on not ten feet away. A boy several years older than I, named Manfred, was telling an even older boy that he would eat one of the live snails, which were plentiful around the grounds, if the other boy would give him the orange he was holding. The bet was made and Manfred proceeded to take the snail out of its shell and swallow it. I wondered if the snail could live in his stomach because it had been so slippery that he couldn't chew before it slid down his esophagus. He did not know that I had been watching until I started laughing as the snail slid down his throat.

I guess the fact that I witnessed his shenanigans embarrassed him. He grabbed his orange and then grabbed my arm and threatened to make me eat a raw snail. I broke his hold and started running in terror, with Manfred at my heels waving a live snail. I was so frightened that I ran through a wood-framed glass French door. I had been looking behind me to see how close he was when I collided with the door. The glass shattered on impact and a piece of it stuck in the right side of my neck. Manfred turned around and ran away, but he was caught and reprimanded. The staff doctor removed the piece of glass and told me that I was lucky to be alive. The glass had missed my jugular vein by a small fraction of a centimeter. My sisters decided to take turns watching over me more carefully.

Around the beginning of August, 1941, my sisters and I were told that we would be a part of the second convoy to attempt the escape from Europe. The first group, which included Asher and Jack, had successfully reached the U.S. We were to travel to Marseilles, along with a handful of others, to meet up with the rest of the convoy and begin to retrace the footsteps of the first group. At first, there was a question about Flo's eligibility to be on the convoy. In three months she was going to turn sixteen, the age at which she would have to be turned over to the Germans, and that was problematic with the French authorities who had to approve the convoy list. Eventually, the argument that she was needed to take care of her frail little brother was accepted and she was put back on the list. When we arrived in Marseilles, I was understandably restrained at the hot bread and hot soup lines. I had learned my lesson three months earlier and did not want to be left behind again.

I don't remember how many days we stayed in Marseilles before boarding the train to Spain. I think there were forty-two of us in all. We had hardly any baggage, and at each mealtime were given brown paper bags of sparse rations which were then picked back up after the time allotted for the meal. I remember this because my nature, and probably that of the other children, would have been to put some food aside for later, just in case. But that was not allowed, for reasons I could not explain. Recently I was told by historians at OSE, that hoarding food was not allowed to keep us from appearing to be the refugees we were. This was to keep from drawing attention to the escape convoy, while traveling in a country that was rife with Nazi sympathizers.

The train went through the Pyrenees Mountains then through the Spanish countryside, stopping at a few small stations on the way to Madrid. The stops were just to take on and let off passengers and we were not allowed to leave our seats. At one or more of these stops, I remember starving, emaciated children coming up to the train, begging for food. I was disappointed that we had not been allowed to stash away food for our own future needs. Now I was distraught that I had nothing to share with these children who apparently were worse off than we were, something that I had not imagined possible before that point.

As planned, we arrived in Madrid after dark. I was told later that the timing was designed to avoid detection by the vast Nazi espionage organization operating out of Madrid. Although Spain was officially neutral in World War II, it was no secret that the government under Generalissimo Franco cooperated in any way it could with the Germans. The sole purpose of these German spies was to intercept any Jews who were fleeing the areas of Europe occupied by Nazi Germany.

We were taken to a convent and were bathed, fed and allowed to sleep just long enough so that we would be able to leave before dawn. I was very impressed with the care and kind treatment we received from the nuns. They were focused on what had to be done in a short period of time, but their efficiency did not take away from the warmth, compassion and tenderness they showered on us. We were all aware of the danger of being discovered and sent back. The fact that we were children, who, under normal situations, might balk at being ordered around by authority figures, was not a factor.

We boarded the train well fed, clean and rested and it left the Madrid area early enough, again to avoid detection by the ever-present Nazi spies. By the time we reached Lisbon, Portugal, there was a feeling of exuberant relief that was contagious among the group of children. I had been living under a cloud of fear and uncertainty for the past two-and-a-half years. Actually, I had been brought up in an atmosphere that inured me to have fear of those around me since I had been old enough to take note of the hostile environment in Frankfurt am Main. I was not alone, I was sure that what I experienced was typical for most of the kids in our group. We were housed in a large villa where we awaited the return of the *S.S. Mouzhino*. This was the Portuguese liner that had taken Asher and Jack with the first convoy to New York Harbor. Once the ship arrived back in Lisbon, the crew had to make her seaworthy again for us to try the escape route once more.

We stayed in Lisbon for ten days to two weeks and, for some reason, it seemed as if the sun was always shining there. We were given more freedom of movement than we had since we left the confines of the secured OSE homes. I remember one morning I was walking along the beach by myself, something that would have been unheard of in France or Germany. I had this strange sensation of something that I had never felt before. I couldn't figure out what it was and did not know how to describe it to my sisters. Years later, as I was trying to put my thoughts together about my experiences in Europe, the answer dawned on me like a flash of lightning. I had been born, just four months before Adolph Hitler became Chancellor, in a country that was obsessed with oppressing Jews. From the time that I was able to walk, I knew that I should never walk anywhere out of the house by myself, or if I did, I knew to always look in all directions in case I had to flee from a dangerous situation. No one was to be trusted and no place was safe from danger. A stranger, or even someone you knew, could try to hurt you, maybe kill you, or turn you in to the Nazis.

That mindset of constant suspicion had been the norm for me. I knew nothing else. On the beach in Lisbon, I had no fear. I didn't feel the need to look in all directions for possible danger. What I was experiencing that day in

August 1941 was freedom, a new and welcome addition to my life. It amazes me how so many people take freedom for granted—that is, until they lose it.

We boarded the *Mouzinho* with hundreds of other Jews fleeing from Nazi occupied Europe. I have since met some of the people who had booked cabins for the voyage, many with at least part of their families. The forty-two of us were without parents but we were on our way to America, the land about which we had heard such utopian legends. Actually all that hype had not been necessary to build up our anticipation for coming to America.

It was not as if we had many choices, so we were understandably ecstatic that our country of refuge was also one that valued freedom and was willing to fight for it. We had few expectations other than to have the opportunity to make new lives for ourselves and the hope that our parents and extended families could survive and join us in America. An interesting statistic to note is that of the 144 parentless refugee children on the two *Mouzinho* convoys, no one ever went on welfare and almost all became college graduates.

Villa Helvetia, OSE children's home in Montmorency.

The Jewish refugee children living at the Villa Helvetia OSE home in Montmorency await the arrival of the SS St. Louis children. The children wait on the steps of the villa underneath a large banner that says 'welcome' in German and French.

Château du Masgelier, where Ben lived with other parentless children in 1940 and 1941. © CDJC/Fonds OSE.

Children at Château du Masgelier, 1941. Ben in front row, 2nd from right.

(above) Masgelier children with counselors, marching to an outing. © CDJC/Fonds OSE.

(below) Children of Masgelier on a truck, going for an outing. © CDJC/Fonds OSE.

L-r: Oswald Kemberg (now Arthur Kern), Jack Hirsch and Asher Hirsch at La Tourelle Home for Refugee Children in Soisy, France, 1939. *Courtesy, Arthur Kern.*

Children from Masgelier working on an agricultural project, c.1943. © CDJC/Fonds OSE.

Group portrait of Jewish children in the OSE children's home of Château des Morelles. Asher Hirsch, 4th from right, middle row. *USHMM, courtesy of Marc Horowitz.*

L-r: Sarah, Asher, Flora, and Jack Hirsch at Château des Morelles at Broût-Vernet, France, c.1941.

(above) Nathan and Helen Samuels, c.2003. Once Ben located them in 1973, he visited them on every trip to Israel.

(at left) Flo and Jack visiting Château des Morelles. Gladys (Jack's wife) in background with caretaker.

IV

SECOND FOSTER HOME, January 1943–June 1944

Whether the social worker's prediction had been a joke or not, Jack went to Mrs. Fannie Asman on Sixth Street in North Atlanta where Sarah had already been living. Actually, Sarah had asked for one of her siblings to be placed in the foster home with her, since Flora had gone to live elsewhere. Aunt Fannie, as she was fondly called by everyone, had a house full of foster children. Since Jack was closer to Sarah's age, Mrs. Asman felt that he would adjust to her home better than I would. Also, Henry Birnbrey, another boy who came from Germany without parents and had been living in her home since he came to Atlanta in 1938, said he would be glad to share his room with Jack. Asher and I were approved to stay with Mr. and Mrs. Philip Hershberg, a few blocks up Atlanta Avenue, where Flora was already staying. Yeta Hershberg knew Asher and me from the times we had visited Flo and since her youngest son, Harold, had just been taken into the armed services, she had an extra room available. For some reason, both Asher and I had taken to calling Mrs. Hershberg "mamma" even some time before we knew that we would be living in her home.

We lived next door to Lee Gilner, a beautiful girl for whom Asher carried an unrequited torch. Harry Kruger, who lived a few doors toward Capitol Avenue, played the flute and was quite a gifted musician. He was one of the oldest boys in the neighborhood and was respected as a leader among the kids. Years later, as an adult, he became assistant conductor for the Atlanta Symphony Orchestra and probably went on to greener pastures from there. Two or three houses up the block, on the corner of Greenfield Street, was where Paul Muldawer's family lived. Paul was just four days older than I and kind of took me under his wing. He had an older brother, Harry, and two very attractive older sisters, Evelyn and Marilyn. Marilyn reminded me of Rita Hayworth, so I decided to have a major crush on her. That part of Atlanta Avenue was full of Jewish families that had boys within two or three years of my age.

Across the street had been Jakie Froug and his brother. June Senilia's house was very close to Jakie's. She was one of the boys, even though she wasn't a boy and she wasn't Jewish. Her father had the most beautiful gardens I had ever seen in the back of their house. School groups used to take field trips to see the gardens. A few houses down the block, across the street from the Hershbergs' house, the Teplis family lived, with their sons Paul and Nathan. They were a good deal older than the rest of us. Paul had joined the Navy at the beginning of the war and thus received a free medical school education when his tour of duty was over. He was my general practitioner until he retired in the 1990s. Arthur Bartell lived on my side of the street down toward Connally Street. The last I heard of him, he was living in Florida and was still aspiring to become a professional singer.

On the corner of Connally and Atlanta Avenue was the Shartar family. Mrs. Shartar was Jack and Nathan Maziar's sister. Ruth, Edith, Harry, and Martin (Buddy) were quite a bit older. Bud, the youngest, was at least five years older than I. Harry was in the U.S. Army serving in Asia. When he came back he started dating my sister Sarah. They were married on May 9, 1948, on Mothers' Day, at the A. A. Educational Building on 10th Street.

On the other corner of Connally were Jerry Zimmerman and his sister Hannah and next door to them lived the Haver family, with Bernard and his sisters. On occasion, whenever Mrs. Hershberg would go out of town, I would stay with the Havers. The Havers had a grocery store and I remember how impressed I had been the first time I saw them serve Coca Colas to everyone at their table for a meal. I always looked forward to being invited to the Havers for a meal and share in that luxury. There had been no shortage of Jewish peers in the neighborhood.

The Shartars were very interested in the story of how we came to Atlanta and they would offer cookies and iced tea to Asher and me if we would stop and talk to them about what we remembered of Europe. I wasn't that comfortable talking about my childhood experiences in Europe. I felt as if people were looking to be entertained and I didn't feel that my stories or experiences were of enough interest, and certainly not of enough entertainment value, to make good conversation.

Asher and I moved in with the Hershbergs in late January 1943. About a week before, the Children's Service Bureau received a letter from Rabbi Selig Auerbach, who had moved to Cincinnati, Ohio and was with the Bureau of Jewish Education there, inquiring about his cousins. He said he had written to us but had received no reply. He suggested that he and his wife would like to have Asher spend *Pesach* (Passover) with them, but that he could not afford the train fare. To Mr. Wyle, this request was fraught with problems, none the least of which was that U. S. Government approval was required for us to travel since we were classified as aliens. That, along with lack of travel expenses and the fact that we were to be transferred to a new home, made the Bureau's decision a simple one. Asher stayed and celebrated *Pesach* with us.

Connally Street, between Ormond Street and Atlanta Avenue, was very steep, but that did not keep us from using the street, which dead-ended into Atlanta Avenue, as our playground. We played touch football there as well as softball. The games had always been very competitive and often ended in fistfights. Jerry Zimmerman owned a Flexi, which had a flat surface of wood boards with a rounded front. It had four wheels and hand operated brakes on the front two wheels. The objective was to lie, stomach down, on the Flexi and coast down any slope, building up speed along the way. If one needed to slow down or stop, he would twist the hand brakes clockwise down on to the front wheels, putting friction on them, thereby slowing up the Flexi. I used to love gliding down Connally, building up speed until the bottom of the hill and coasting to a halt just before reaching the busier Atlanta Avenue. I'll never forget the time I was racing down the hill when a cat crossed the street in front of me. My first reaction was to twist the brakes to avoid running into the cat. At the speed I was traveling, that was not a good course of action. The front wheels stopped and the Flexi flipped over. I landed on my back and slid about ten feet on the pavement, tearing my shirt and most of the skin from my back in the process. If I ever rode a Flexi again, it would have been a long time after that incident.

While I was learning to play American sports games and to ride a Flexi, Werner and Roselene were traveling somewhere in Eastern Europe with our mom under less than the best of circumstances. I have conflicting information regarding the ultimate destination of their deportation transport, the last train of the mass deportation of Jews from Frankfurt am Main on September 24, 1942. Each transport, in keeping with German efficiency, was scheduled to include one thousand deportees, except for the last one which carried only two hundred and fifty, the last remnants of Frankfurt's four hundred-year-old Jewish community, including my mother and siblings. Actually, Jews in or from mixed marriages were not deported until a later date. Both of my sources have made studies of the Frankfurt deportations and both agree that the last transport traveled first to Berlin to fill up the transport by picking up an additional seven hundred and fifty Jewish deportees, most likely from Czechoslovakia, and thus achieved maximum efficiency in Germany's genocidal quest.

According to Ilse Kahane, who was also on that transport, and Hilde Scheraga, whose mother was on it as well, the now complete transport traveled from Berlin toward the Riga Ghetto. They traveled to Estonia on a train, Ilse added, "3rd class, tightly pressed against each other," and stopped just before Riga, Latvia, where they waited at the station for six days and nights. Once in Riga, they waited on the train for many more hours before it was confirmed that the Riga Ghetto was so full that it could not absorb them. The train then traveled back into Estonia and suddenly stopped at small railroad station where the one thousand deportees, less those that died along the way, were told to disembark. It is from this point that opinions differ.

Monica Kingreen, the daughter of a Nazi and author of *Nach Der Kristallnacht* (After Crystal Night), who has made a study of the Frankfurt deportations, agrees with Bella, Hilde's mother, that at this station "Women and children and people who did not appear healthy, or those whose nose did not please the official in charge (Herr Sturmfuehrer) were loaded into buses without any of their luggage and taken away," and presumably, killed immediately. After this, of the original one thousand only two hundred and fifty were left (Ilse's recollection is that it had been more like one hundred) and put in a camp in the forest with very primitive barracks, where they stayed for about six weeks. From there they went to Reval (Tallinn, Estonia) where they were allowed to sleep in a jail that housed political prisoners while they worked as slave laborers all day for the Holtzman Company.

Charlotte Guthmann Opfermann, a survivor and Holocaust historian, is convinced that all those who survived the deportation transports from Frankfurt eventually turned up in Theresienstadt. As sure as Monica is that my family could not have ended up in Auschwitz, Charlotte is sure that their transport went to Theresienstadt from where they could have been deported to Auschwitz. Since my mother, brother, and sister were seen entering the "showers"(gas chamber) by my mother's brother, Uncle Philipp Auerbach, in the fall of 1943, I tend to side with Charlotte Opfermann's theory of ultimate destination, even though we have found no hard proof to verify it. This still leaves me with no details of my family's travails during that last year of their lives before they were deported to Auschwitz. Also, the picture of Werner and Roselene that was found in Auschwitz, among 2,400 pictures, at least places my mother there, as does the *Gedenkbuch*, the memory book published by the Federal Republic of Germany, The picture, with its forested background, could very well have been taken in the area of Theresienstadt. Under the conditions described by Ilse and Bela, this is not a likely scenario.

The principal of James L. Key, Mrs. Willie Cates, had taken a special interest in me. When she heard that I was being transferred to a new home, she called the Bureau office to express her hope that this transfer would in no way hinder the progress of her special foreign student. Mrs. Wyle took the opportunity to discuss my behavior in school, which she had heard was not good. Mrs. Cates replied that my "so-called behavior difficulties could be traced to a real intellectual curiosity." She further reported that I no longer wore a *yarmulke* in school except when I was eating in the cafeteria, and that she would not counsel me to stop doing that since I was doing it out of religious principles. What surprised me, in reading the report, is that she said nothing about the frequent fights that continued to be part of my daily existence.

About a week after I had moved to the Hershbergs' house, I went out one evening to mail a couple of letters for my sister Flo. At the sidewalk, I was greeted by a group of at least six boys whose leader was the large third grader who had taken away my *yarmulke* some months before. I don't know how they knew that I had moved or if they had been stalking the Bregman house as well, waiting for me to show up by myself. However long the wait had been, they took advantage of finally finding me alone and beat me to a pulp *en masse*. They each took turns and appeared to relish teaching me a lesson. The lesson had been that I should never do anything that would show their gang leader in a bad light. At least they didn't tear up Flo's letters. When I came back into the house, all bloody, bruised and with torn clothing, Flo didn't bother to ask for an explanation. She ran out the door with Asher to chase down the "Nazi hoodlums," but the brave warriors were already out of sight.

In February, on my regular monthly visit to the Bureau office, I brought along two or three sketches to show to Mr. Wyle. One was of the French General Giraud and one was of Gene Autry. It appeared as though American society was beginning to influence my choices of heroes. This prompted Mr. Wyle to again offer me the opportunity of going to the High Museum of Art for Saturday morning art classes. As before, I declined, reminding him that I could not do that on the Sabbath. Only this time, I added the caveat that my brother Asher would not approve.

In school, I did not limit my associations to Jewish students. Dicky Bradshaw had been one of the first to pick a fight with me, after the incident over my *yarmulke*. In fact, for the first year or so, our fisticuffs had been on a regular basis. I suppose, since virtually all of our fights ended in a stand-off, he either started respecting me for not backing down to someone considerably larger than me, or I just grew on him. In any event, we started hanging out together and became friends. Mr. Hershberg was very uncomfortable with my bringing home non-Jewish playmates. He was from Eastern Europe where apparently Jews and *Goyim*, as he called them, did not intermingle. This became a very touchy subject. I did not want to be unreceptive to my non-Jewish friends, but I had to respect that my foster parent did not want them in his house.

We managed to work around that by playing elsewhere, but Mr. Hershberg would still question me after I got home as to with whom I had been playing. I knew he was just looking out for my welfare, using his experiences as a child in Europe as a basis for his fears for me, but I was really quite comfortable with the few non-Jewish friends I had developed. Of the half dozen or so bullies who had picked fights with me on a regular basis until I started filling out in junior high school, Dicky was the only one who had made a complete turnaround. In fact there were several times that he had the occasion to take up for me and seemed to relish doing so.

Even though I was getting some meat on my bones, I was still being challenged almost daily to duke it out with anyone who was aspiring to be a tough guy or a bully. If two days went by without someone picking a fight with me it was cause for celebration. I was a good student and maintained good relations with my teachers. By the time I was in sixth grade, my teacher, Ms Brown, for whom I had done several art projects, approached me about becoming a patrol boy. She pointed out that there was a shortage of patrol boys and that, with one exception, I met all of the criteria. Patrol boys and girls directed traffic at street corners near the school and assured safe passage for students crossing streets. Being asked to be a patrol boy was a status symbol and was limited to good students without behavioral problems.

Her invitation had a caveat. If I could go for a week without getting into a fight, she would automatically make me a patrol boy. I thanked her and told her that I would do my very best but that I was not in total control of that aspect of my behavior. I reminded her that I had never started a fight since the *yarmulke* incident in the fourth grade. Also, I pointed out, that even if I would walk away from the challengers, they would continue to hit me until I responded—but, I repeated, I would try. Suffice it to say, I never became a patrol boy.

The war effort was very much a part of everyday life. Even school children were aware of the rationing of essentials, and the saving of newspapers and flattened tin cans. All the movie theaters showed newsreels before the main feature. Students were asked to do their part as part of the school curriculum. We were asked to help out during the cotton harvest season. Students who would volunteer to pick cotton were given special credit, and it was done on school days, thus making volunteering even more attractive. Like most of the kids in my class, I had never picked cotton before. I'm sure that there must be an art to picking cotton without totally destroying your hands, but I never acquired that talent. I was among those who did not take to the picking cotton adventure naturally. I don't know about anyone else, but I convinced myself that I would never want to make the effort to become an expert cotton picker and would have to find other ways to volunteer for the war effort the next season.

Everyone had been encouraged to plant and tend victory gardens. Mr. Hershberg did not want me to dig up his back yard so I put all of my effort into helping Paul Muldawer with his garden. Even though it wasn't my garden, I took great pride in seeing the vegetables grow and ripen. It brought back fond memories of the group farming we did at Château du Masgelier and of the exhilaration of picking of the first vegetables to ripen.

The first couple of years I was in Atlanta, Paul had been my best friend. We shared an interest in drawing and, like the garden, there were other activities that otherwise would have been off limits to me, that I experienced through Paul. For instance, I was not allowed to have any pets. When we were 11, Paul had been given a dog, a black Scottish terrier, as I recall. Paul did not seem to mind that I used to run home after school to play with his dog. Some months later, the dog must have gotten lost. When he didn't show after a day or two, he was considered missing. I had been very concerned for the pet's welfare and I spent all of my spare time looking for him. I must have obsessed over trying to find the little fella, to the point that I got on Paul's nerves. He told me to let it go and quit searching, that it was just a dog, and his dog at that. It may have been just another pet to Paul, but it was the closest that I had ever come to owning a pet. Even though I had no illusions as to whom the dog belonged, I had been so close to the little animal that I felt the loss deeply.

One afternoon, Paul came home from a basketball practice with a new club that was just being formed for boys our age. The name of the club was DSI, which stood for 'Devoted Sons of Israel.' He wasn't sure that I would be eligible for the club but said that he would check it out. He was excited about this new sport and thought that I would like it very much. That was my introduction to basketball, which became my favorite participatory, as well as spectator, sport. I became a charter member of DSI and worked at trying to learn this new game. My brothers had learned to play soccer in Europe, but I must have been either to young or in the wrong place at the wrong time since I never played that game.

Most of the boys in DSI had either been in school with me at James L. Key or in afternoon Hebrew school at Shearith Israel, or both. Afternoon Hebrew school was an activity that had been mandatory for many Jewish kids, at least until their Bar Mitzvah, after which some parents allowed their kids to drop out. Looking back on it, our days were pretty full. After public school we would go to the Alliance (Jewish Educational Alliance), about a mile up Capitol

Avenue, and hang around or play basketball. From there we would walk to Shearith Israel for Hebrew school after which we walked home, just over a two mile walk for me.

Shearith Israel's Hebrew School was run and taught by Rabbi Hyman Friedman, the assistant to Rabbi Tobias Geffen. Aside from learning *Chumash*, the five books of Moses, we also learned to *daven*, to say the prayers, and even to lead the prayers at Junior Congregation which took place on Saturday morning. Junior Congregation was an extension of the Hebrew school and we had elected officers just as did the adult congregation. The only difference was that we elected a *chazan*, or cantor, to lead our services while the adult congregation hired their *chazan*. For our first election, I was running for *chazan* against Irving Borstein, the son of Reverand Paul Borstein, who owned Kaufman's kosher butcher shop and delicatessen. Irving had a great voice and was liked by everyone and, had I known that he wanted the position, I never would have agreed to run when Rabbi Friedman asked me to do so.

I had been prepared to concede when Irving made a tactical mistake. For some reason he felt the need to ingratiate himself with the electorate. To achieve this, he gave every potential voter, myself included, pieces of "Candy Pulling," a viscous type of stringy molasses candy that can be pulled to any length. "Candy Pulling," (which had to have been invented by a dentist looking for more patients), was a popular fund-raising vehicle for PTA and other non-profit groups.

As it turned out, this gesture backfired on him. The voters felt that the candy was a form of a bribe and that giving it away had been an unfair tactic since I could not afford to compete. I was convinced that I never would have won had Irving not resorted to overkill by giving out the candy. I thought about the time I had doled out little pieces of the chocolate bar that my brothers had given me for my eighth birthday in France. I suppose if I had been running for a political office, my gesture would not have been as appreciated as it had been.

Hebrew school was only three afternoons a week, which left two afternoons for me to try and find some work that would put a little spending money in my pocket. The first job that several of my friends and I had was stuffing envelopes for Citizens' Jewelers on Mitchell Street. We went straight after school, were set up at long tables, given boxes of folded flyers and of addressed envelopes and instructed to stuff the envelopes. Speed was of the essence since we were paid a dollar per thousand envelopes stuffed. It wasn't much, but for someone who got twenty-five cents a week allowance, the dollar or so a day we earned made me feel a little more affluent. Saving was not a word in my lexicon. As soon as I received my pay, I would walk up to the Peachtree Arcade and into the stamp store. There, after extensive browsing, I would spend my hard-earned money on stamps for my collection.

The school threw a Halloween party and everyone was told to come in costume. I decided to come dressed as a girl. Flo lent me some of her clothes and even offered to put make-up on me to make me look more authentic. I guess she did too good a job. As I was walking up Ormond Street toward James L. Key, Sybil Gilman, one of Flo's friends, saw me from across the street and apparently thought I was Flo, even though I was walking with two boys my age. She waved at me and hollered Flo's name, demanding recognition. I had no intention of responding to her and just hurried along as if I didn't hear her. After all, I was with my peers and it was embarrassing enough that I was dressed like a girl; I didn't want to be caught talking to one. The next day, Flo caught hell from Sybil, who refused to believe that it wasn't she who had snubbed her.

I guess my best friend, after Paul and I went our separate ways, was Charles Berner. His mother had died when he was very young and although his father was still alive, he and his two older brothers lived with a foster family on Atlanta Avenue. We had similar interests and he was as precocious as I was. What I remember most was the way Charles and I used our imaginations to invent games that didn't require expensive toys or equipment. We kept ourselves busy for weeks after school hours, digging a cave on an empty lot at the end of Connally Street and when it was completed, we made it our private hideout. We were both emotionally fragile, although we each tried to project our macho exterior and we tested each other often in the early years of our friendship. Charles and I remained buddies long after I left Atlanta Avenue.

Donald Kessler lived in the same apartment project as the Berner boys. He was actually a little older than my brother Jack, but he chose to hang around with me and decided that he was going to show me the ways of the world. I was not even eleven when he thought it was time for me to learn how to smoke. Somehow, he got hold of a pack of Lucky Strikes and a box of matches. Cigarettes were expensive and hard to come by. They were rationed in wartime and they cost about twenty cents a pack if you could get them. Lucky Strikes were really special cigarettes. Their slogan, that was heard all over the radio and plastered on billboards all over town, was "Lucky Strike has gone to war." That slogan, indicating that our soldiers fighting overseas smoked Lucky Strikes and the fact that Lucky Strike was the sponsor for *The Hit Parade*, a very popular radio show that played and rated the top songs in the country every week, made them the cigarette to smoke. Donald took me to an empty lot, which was an entire block between Grant and Rawlins Streets going east and Atlanta and Kendrick Avenues going south. The block was a big clump of earth rising up as much as six feet from the sidewalk on the Atlanta Avenue side, and had a lot of scraggly dried up undergrowth.

We sat on the elevated, undeveloped site made of red clay, smoking one cigarette after another. I, unfortunately, was a quick learner. Half way through the pack, I was no longer coughing. I don't remember how long it took us to finish the pack, but it must have been a better part of the hot summer morning. When we did finish the cigarettes we wondered what to do with the remaining matches. Not to let anything go to waste, we started lighting matches and throwing them over our shoulders, not knowing or caring where they landed. Some of the lit matches fell into the dried patches of weeds surrounding the site, starting little fires. Much to our surprise, a light breeze came and spread the little brush fires into bigger ones. Before we knew it, the entire block was on fire.

We quickly descended the mound and ran toward Donald's apartment. We met his cousin along the way and she told us that she had already called the fire department and told them that she saw two kids running away from the fire, but that they would be long gone before the fire trucks would get there. Two fire trucks came and quickly put the fire out. The firemen commented that it was a lucky thing that the fire had been contained on the empty block and that it did not spread to any of the nearby homes across the streets. We fully agreed, and vowed to ourselves never to do anything as stupid as that again. I don't know if the firemen suspected us, but they didn't let on if they did.

You would think that my first experience with cigarettes would have been enough to discourage me from making a habit of it, but that wasn't to be. There were several boys at James L. Key who smoked. To some it was considered a badge of manhood, but to Mary Thomas and others, it was a sign of juvenile delinquency. Most of us couldn't afford cigarettes and couldn't get the ration coupons anyway, so Dicky Bradshaw suggested that we roll our own. A bag of Bugle tobacco with cigarette paper was only five cents. We pooled our pennies to buy the stuff and would go into the crawl space of a house near school to make our cigarettes and smoke them.

Just as I was getting proficient at rolling my own cigarettes, someone snitched to my brother Asher that I was seen smoking. Asher was not happy. He pulled me aside and sternly told me that he did not want to hear of me smoking again until I was fifteen years old. I wondered where that came from since Asher was seventeen at the time. As a bribe, he gave me a brand new deck of cards, which, not surprisingly, led to another vice. More out of respect than fear, I listened to Asher and didn't smoke again until I was almost fifteen.

Before I was fifteen I had become quite proficient at gin rummy, hearts, casino, and poker. Playing cards, at least at this level, was less of a health risk than smoking and definitely more lucrative.

No one at James L. Key, after the first six to twelve months, talked to me or asked questions about my experiences in Europe. As if I weren't self-conscious enough as it was, the bullies served to keep me aware that I was different. Peggy Milam was one of the prettiest girls in my class. She was into tap dancing and other performance arts for her extra curricular activities, sort of the Jon-Benet Ramsey of our school, fortunately with a better future. She was really very nice and somewhat shy herself. I remember the evening that I was walking home from a program at school with a bunch of guys on Ormond Street. Peggy's parents stopped their car as they were driving by to offer me a ride.

I would have loved to go with them and Peggy, but I was so self-conscious and embarrassed that I did not even respond. I kicked myself mentally for not being able to seize the moment. I had assumed that Peggy's parents just wanted to talk to me about my background in Europe, as did most people. I didn't like being put in a situation of responding to questions about my family in Europe, especially when my answers often made me sad and occasionally brought an involuntary tear down my cheek. In retrospect, it may not have hurt me to talk about Europe, in spite of my misgivings, particularly since I might have had a chance to get to know Peggy a little better. Although D-Day, June 6, 1944—the day the Allied Forces landed on the beaches of Normandy, France after crossing the English Channel, did not occur until after I had graduated from James L. Key elementary school and had moved on to my next foster home, I remembered that this turning point of the war on the European front occurred on Peggy Milan's birthday. Her's is one birthday I never will forget.

Watching newsreels in the theaters and listening to the radio kept me informed of Allied victories in North Africa and of the pending Allied invasion of the European mainland. Speculation as to where in Europe the invasion would take place seemed surprisingly low key to me. Apparently the motto of "loose lips sink ships" was even adhered to by the media, after a fashion. In the meantime, it had been over a year since our last letter from Mom, and I was beginning to lose hope that we would ever hear from her or Dad again. While news was coming in from the war front, very little, if any, about Hitler's war against the Jews was being reported.

We heard that German troops had even occupied its ally, Hungary, in March of 1944, to round up Hungary's Jewish population. I wondered if that meant that all the Jews from other occupied countries had already been deported to concentration camps and murdered. In January, 1944, President

Roosevelt finally responded to public pressure and created the U.S. War Refugee Board. It focused much of its work in 1944 on rescuing Hungarian Jews, and while it was credited with saving over 200,000 lives, in the eyes of its director, John Pehly, it was "too little, too late." It was most definitely too late to save my parents and siblings.

I had been told on more than one occasion that Mrs. Hershberg was getting exasperated with me. I was told that I had been disrespectful, that I had a mind of my own and wouldn't listen to her and, worst of all, that I would not be home at the hours that she felt I should be. It's funny how a child sees his behavior toward adults as opposed to how adults see that behavior toward them. I truly loved and respected Mrs. Hershberg, yet I apparently persisted in behaving badly. I had never considered my behavior as being bad, but then I never looked at my actions through Mrs. Hershberg's eyes. She hardly ever scolded me. She just reported any behavior that she didn't approve of to my case worker. By the time the complaint got back to me, it was too late to do anything but apologize. Each time I was confronted by my caseworkers and offered an opportunity to move to another foster home, I told them that I really wanted to stay in Mrs. Hershberg's home. It got to the point that she could not tolerate my behavior anymore. The timing was right for her to initiate the break. She needed to have an operation and she did not want to have the burden of caring for me while she would be recuperating.

Flora and Asher had been no trouble to place. I, on the other hand, was considered to be unmanageable. In desperation, Mr. Armand May, President of the Hebrew Orphans Home, at the request of my caseworker, wrote to General Beaver of Riverside Military Academy, giving him my complete history since arriving in Atlanta, and asking if the boarding school could take me as a student. General Beaver responded, "Regarding Benjamin Hirsch, he cannot fit in here until after Victory is won. We are now operating on an accelerated schedule, which means that we are covering three semesters in one calendar year; and, in order to do this, we are teaching six days a week and having only three vacations, of eight days each, annually.

The fact that the youngster is of the Orthodox school will not permit him to attend classes on Saturday—thus preventing him from keeping up with his work." In response to the General's letter, probably addressing the last sentence, Mr. May scribbled a note, "In the event there is any change in this I will let you know." I shudder to think what he meant by that. Undaunted, my caseworker, Edna Backer went to visit Georgia Military Academy as a possible alternative placement for me. She later wrote to Colonel Brewster that shortly after her visit to the Academy, she had been able to obtain a very fine foster home for Benjamin. That was in June of 1944.

All in all, my experience at James L. Key elementary school had been a good one. I made friends and an occasional enemy. Over and above the lessons learned from the required curriculum, I learned the language and I learned about living in a different society. It's hard to predict what information of all that is dispensed to elementary school children will stay in their minds throughout the years. Who would have thought that would I still remember the states and capitols that I had learned in fifth grade. As it turned out, this was information that I had to teach my children at home because it, along with other geographical information, was not a part of their curriculum. With few exceptions, I respected and liked all of the teachers there. I still remember how good I felt when Ms. Cates, the school principal, along with Ms. Brooks and Ms. Brown, my fifth and sixth grade teachers, showed up at Shearith Israel for my Bar Mitzvah, which took place several months after I had graduated from James L. Key Elementary School.

V

THE SUMMER OF '44

I had felt very much at home at the Hershbergs' house. Granted, they were older and spoke with a heavy accent, leaving no doubt that they were from Europe. For me, that was a comfort zone. Their two older sons, the younger of whom was Martin, had been away in the U. S. Army for some time, and their youngest, Harold, had just been drafted before we moved in. Mr. Hershberg was not very communicative except to let me know when I had done something he did not approve of. Mrs. Hershberg was, to my mind, an ideal mother and I had thought, in spite of my shenanigans, that I would be living with her until I was able to be on my own. I had been in complete denial about how my behavior was affecting her, and I was totally unaware of the attempts that had been made to place me in a military boarding school. In retrospect, of all the foster mothers I had, she was the only one I felt comfortable calling "Mamma" and she may have been the only one that had not asked me to do so. This might explain my sadness in the spring of 1944, when I found out that Mrs. Hershberg was ill and that she would no longer be able to keep Flo, Asher and me as foster children after the end of the school year.

Asher had made plans to live with Mrs. Ida Goncher, on Ormond Street. Flo moved out and had gone to live with Mr. and Mrs. Sam Unger on Emory Drive in the general area of Emory University. It was decided by the Children's Service Bureau that as soon as I completed my final school year at James L. Key in June that I would join Flo at the Ungers'.

I had trepidation about moving in with the Ungers, even though Flo would be there with me. It was way on the other side of town, away from all of my friends. It was not near any synagogue or the Jewish Alliance where I played basketball and was used to hanging around with my peers. I was told that they kept a kosher home, but that they did not observe the Sabbath. However, the choice was not mine to make and I knew that I would have to adjust and make the best of the situation.

My first impressions were quite positive. The house was luxurious compared to those I been used to on the South Side. The Ungers were a nice enough family. Sam Unger was a slight man with some kind of brace on one of his legs. Mrs. Unger was an attractive lady, larger than her husband. She left no question as to who was in charge of running the house. The Ungers had two sons, Pat and Joe. Pat was about three years older than I. He was very quiet and studious and was a genuinely nice person. Joe was less than a year younger than I. He was also smart and never missed an opportunity to display it. He was more outgoing than Pat and was very much into competitive games. He didn't care a lot for sports; he was more interested in any game that would be a match of wits. This was exciting for me since I too enjoyed games that challenged the intellect of the players. The *coup de grâce* was that they had a wonderful dog and a pool table.

As it turns out, the summer of '44 was the longest summer of my life. The Ungers entertained often, but seldom with more than two or three couples. Whenever they had company, the evening would somehow turn into a quiz show for their whiz kid, Joe, who liked nothing better than to show off the plethora of information he had stored in his head. Occasionally, the guests would turn and direct questions to me as well. It was unclear to me whether the guests did this to keep me from feeling left out or whether their action had been intended to create a relative scale by which to judge Joe's brilliance. To Joe's surprise as well as his mother's, I was able to field virtually all of the questions that he could and even some that he could not. The only ones that seemed to be enjoying the turn of events were Mr. Unger and Pat. They both found it hard to contain an occasional snicker. To avoid angst within the family, I was ready to excuse myself from these gatherings, or at least leave the room when the "Quiz Kids" game was about to start. As competitive as Joe was, he would have no part of my excusing myself. It became a game that I probably lost as many times as I won. Joe was not a good loser. We were both such game people that we probably engaged in every non-sports game imaginable. Of all the card games and board games, chess was his forte. I was as competitive as he was, particularly at chess. It riled Joe that, over a period of time, I was able to beat him at chess more often than he was able beat me.

At first the competitive games were fun. At the pool table, we played eight ball and rotation with equal skill, winning some and losing some. Ping pong was Joe's game. No matter how much I improved, I was no match for him. Occasionally I would squeak in a win, which only underscored how much he hated to lose. So what started out as two kids enjoying the same types of games and thriving on competition, ended up as a nasty rivalry in which more than once I was reminded that I should be mindful of my place in the house. Joe would tell tales, which seldom had any validity, about me to his mom. For the most part, they were either exaggerations of my behavior and occasionally outright falsehoods. Flo would be brought in to keep me in line. She would remind me that we were living in this home through the generosity of the Ungers, and that, accordingly I should be on my best behavior. Although they received compensation to be foster parents by the Children's Service Bureau, Flo made me realize that being a foster parent was hardly a profitable venture and that it took a special type of family to share its home with parentless children. Nevertheless, I would plead my case, saying that while I never pretended to be an angel, the continual charges that were brought against me by Joe were not representative of my behavior. Neither Mrs. Unger nor my sister were ready to believe that Joe would be untruthful about me. After all, he did not have my reputation for mischievous behavior. The only one who believed me and took up for me was Joe's brother, Pat, who apparently had not found his brother's behavior to be out of character.

In mid-1944, the Nazis temporarily beautified Theresienstadt to deceive the visiting Red Cross and to make a propaganda film that pictured the ghetto, as they called it, "Hitler's gift to the Jews." Terezin, or Theresienstadt in German, was a walled military garrison town in Czechoslovakia where the Nazis began to ghettoize Czech Jews in the autumn of 1941. It also became a concentration camp and transit camp for German and Western European Jews who were eventually deported to Auschwitz. This may have been the place where my mother, with Werner and Roselene, spent most of their days between their deportation from Frankfurt and their ultimate demise shortly after they arrived in Auschwitz, in the fall of 1943. Theresienstadt was also the camp to which many Jewish children with special talents in the arts were sent. In June, 1942, twenty one year old Pavel Friedman finished a poem about the last butterfly he ever saw. Friedl Dicker-Brandeis, a Jewish Bauhaus artist and architect, was interred at Terezin and taught art to the children there. She was an enormously gifted person and I fantasize that my brother and sister had been privileged to learn from her. Among her many students was Petr Ginz who led a group of talented young boys in publishing *Vedem* (In The Lead), a secret magazine that was distributed throughout Theresienstadt. In 2003, one of his pictures was taken into outer space by Israeli astronaut, Ilan Ramon, who, sadly though ironically, was incinerated on re-entry along with the entire crew of the shuttle, Columbia, forty-nine years after Petr was gassed and incinerated upon arrival at Auschwitz. Pavel Friedman, Friedl Dicker-Brandeis and Petr Ginz were among the 2,499 prisoners deported from Theresienstadt in September, 1944, Petr was one of the 1,000 immediately gassed, as he was deemed too short to work by Dr. Josef Mengele.

The Ungers were members of the Mayfair Club, one of the three Jewish social clubs in Atlanta. The Mayfair, along with the Progressive and Standard Clubs, had been a major force in the Jewish community during the 1940s. Two or three times a week, Mrs. Unger would load Pat, Joe and me in the car and drive to the club where we would spend the day at the swimming pool. Except for summer camp, where we swam daily, my only opportunities to go swimming in the summer had been the rare occasions that I was invited by a member to the Progressive Club swimming pool. Although none of my friends from the South Side was ever at the Mayfair and I knew no one other than the Ungers, getting to go swimming so often was a real plus. Of course, all good things often have a bad aspect to them. The first Saturday morning that Mrs. Unger wanted to leave us at the club pool for the day was the turning point of my sojourn at the Unger household. Up until that time I had never ridden in a car on the Sabbath and, after having remained Sabbath observant through so many trials and tribulations in my young life, I was not prepared to start violating the Sabbath to go swimming. It was bad enough that we lived in an area that was not in walking distance to a synagogue, but now was I going to be forced to ride on *Shabbat*?

I was annoyed that I had even been asked to ride in a car on the Sabbath, but I tried not to show my feelings, assuming that Mrs. Unger just did not understand what it meant to be a Sabbath observant Jew or how deep my convictions were. I calmly offered to stay home and play with the dog and to read a book while they enjoyed themselves at the pool. I certainly did not want to keep them from doing what they normally do on *Shabbat*; I just didn't want to be forced to lower my standards of Sabbath observance. A heated argument ensued after which I was told, in no uncertain terms, that staying home alone was not an option for me and that my archaic views of observing the Sabbath were not going to keep them from spending their day of rest as they saw fit. Flo was unable to help me since she no longer strictly observed the Sabbath and felt it would be hypocritical for her to argue on the side of religious observance over obeying the rules of the household. Defeated and deflated, I got in the car and spent a most uncomfortable day at the Mayfair Club swimming pool. The saddest part of this saga, in hindsight, was that after several weeks, I became used to spending my Saturdays that way, swimming at the Mayfair Club and enjoying it.

So here I was, living the life of a suburban kid in a nice two story, light brick, ten-room house with a beautiful lawn, backyard and more amenities than I could ever have imagined. There were no streetcars or busses. We were able to go where we needed by car. My sister was with me though she really wasn't around very much. I had companions in Joe and Pat, even though Joe and I didn't always get along. Then there was the dog, whose name I thought I would never forget (I think it was Rascal), that seemed to love me unconditionally. Still, I missed the South Side, I missed my friends from James L. Key and from

DSI. I missed hanging out at the Alliance, going to Hebrew School and attending services at a synagogue. I even missed Sunday school which I had always thought was a monumental waste of time.

It was a different way of life, much quieter than the city life of the South side. There did not appear to be any gangs roaming the streets looking for trouble, which up to this time had been my middle name. In retrospect, while there were many nice things about living with the Ungers, somehow I felt like a fish out of water. Nevertheless, I was appreciative of the suburban pace even though I was often bored silly, and was intent on going along and making the best of the situation. That is, except for the ridicule I was experiencing because of my need to strictly observe the Sabbath. To that I couldn't adjust. Not that many of my peers at Shearith Israel had been strict in their Sabbath observance, but those that had were not made to feel out of place, at least not in their own homes.

In the meantime, on July 31, 1944, less than a month before the Allied liberation of Paris, another 1,300 Jews were deported from the transit concentration camp at Drancy, France, just northwest of Paris, to Auschwitz. Two hundred and fifty-eight of the deportees were orphans, seized in and around Paris a week earlier. Throughout France, many of the OSE homes had been shut down after raids by *Gestapo* units and French collaborators. Most notable of these raids was the one of the children's home at Izieu, France, near the Swiss border, by a *Gestapo* unit headed by Klaus Barbie. Ten nurses and forty-three orphaned children were arrested and sent to Drancy, from where most of them were later among the 1,300 deportees on July 31. Upon arrival at Auschwitz, all five hundred children who were deported from Drancy at this time and three hundred adults were gassed. This was the last large transport of Jews from Drancy to Auschwitz to be murdered by the Nazis in their zeal to kill as many French Jews as possible before the Allied victory. In all, 73,853 Jews had been shipped from Drancy to their deaths at Auschwitz and Sobibor. I venture to say that the Jewish souls that perished at those two death factories are not comforted by the Carmalite and Capuchine chapels and monastaries that now grace those horrific sites.

I was prepared to go to Druid Hills High School at the end of the summer to once again be the new kid on the scene, but that was not to be. On an overcast Friday in August, Joe and I had gotten into an argument which probably started over some game we were playing. We had gotten into arguments and even fights before, but never like this one. I don't remember the details of how it started or of what finally set me off. It was one of those situations in which

Joe decided to run to Mommy with a concocted story after things didn't go his way. I do remember that, after once more feeling outnumbered and unjustifiably accused, I eventually blew my cool and resorted to all the four letter words I could muster from what I had learned from the streets of the South Side. Mrs. Unger, not knowing all the facts of what had transpired before I blew up, rushed to tell me that the kind of language I was using would not be tolerated in her house. She also invited me to leave if I could not desist from expressing my anger in such a vociferous and "vulgar" way. I couldn't remember ever using that degree of off-colored language before, but then I had never been quite so frustrated, at least, not since I had come to this country.

I felt totally set upon. Flo was not there to hear my side of the story. Pat was not around to calm things down and let his mother know that Joe was capable of making an inactive volcano erupt. Meanwhile, Joe sat smugly with his arms folded, knowing that once again he had instigated an altercation and that this time he had made me go over the edge. I was so totally disgusted and hurt that I decided to take Mrs. Unger up on her suggestion to leave. My thought was to walk to the South Side to Maishie Epstein's house on Washington Street, and spend *Shabbat* there. It was early enough in the morning that I felt that I could complete the walk long before sundown. I slammed the door shut and started walking. I'm not sure if anyone could have stopped me at that point, but no one tried anyway. It seemed as if no one cared if I left or not, that is, except for Rascal. She decided to follow me and keep me company.

I was so angry that I didn't even notice her until I had walked for several blocks. She had been walking, seemingly with trepidation, about ten feet behind me. I happened to turn around for no particular reason, and noticed her there looking sheepishly up at me with her tail feverishly wagging. I was really happy to see her even though she should not have been there. I squatted down and put my arms out to greet her. The little dog lunged at me and started licking my face like it was a bowl of dog food. Instantaneously the depth of my anger dissipated. I stayed there for a few minutes, hugging that cute little gray, black and white mutt, enjoying the effusion of love that could only come from a dog. As much as I would have liked to take her with me, I knew that it was not the right thing to do. I turned around and walked her back to the house and put her inside. I closed the door as I left, making sure that she was still inside, and said nothing in response to the blank stares I was getting from Mrs. Unger and Joe.

As I started walking again, I heard Rascal whimpering and scratching on the door. I hated leaving the little dog locked up like that, especially since it had been thanks to her that I had been able to be much more in control of my emotions. Nevertheless, I knew that I had to get out of there. I picked up my pace, not having any idea of how long a walk it would be from Emory Road to Washington Street near Ormond Street. In my mind, the south side of town seemed so far away that I imagined it would be at least a twenty miles walk. As it turned out the distance was closer to eight to ten miles. I was pleased with my pace and felt confident that I could reach my destination on time. I borrowed a phone along the way and called Maishie and told him that I would be coming and asked if I could spend *Shabbat* with his family. His mother, who had always liked me, asked no questions about why I was coming and said that I was welcome.

By the time I had reached Ponce de Leon Avenue, I knew that I almost reached the half way mark of my marathon walk. I saw Gold's Kosher Delicatessen up ahead, where all of my siblings had worked at one time or another, and figured it would be the perfect oasis. I crossed over to the south side of the street to say hello to the people I knew at Gold's. I waved as I approached the Deli and before I could come in for a drink of water, Jake Goldberg ran out to give me a message from Mrs. Unger. She had called to tell me that Rascal had gotten out of the room in the house I had locked her into and run after me. She hadn't gone into detail as to how the little dog had achieved the escape, or why she and Joe had not bothered to stop the dog from running after me. The rest of her message was in the form of a warning. I better find Rascal and bring her back home or, Mrs. Unger threatened, she would call the police and accuse me of stealing her dog. If I had had any thoughts that she was concerned about my welfare, those thoughts were quickly dispelled.

I explained to Jake that I had brought the dog back long ago, put her in the house and locked her in a room so she couldn't follow me again. As soon as I finished the sentence, I noticed her standing behind a tree near the corner of Parkway Drive. Whoever named that dog Rascal knew what they were doing. I didn't know when or how she got away, and wondered if Joe hadn't opened the door for her, but there she was not twenty feet behind me, wagging her tail. I wanted to call Mrs. Unger and tell her to come pick the dog up in her car, but Jake told me that he had made that suggestion to her and that she replied emphatically that she would not waste the time or gasoline to relieve me of my responsibilities. She intimated to Jake that in her mind, I had enticed Rascal to follow me. After I bring the dog home, she had added, she didn't care where I went as long as I went without the dog. I looked at the clock in the store and it was already 11:00 am. Sundown would not be for another nine hours. I let out a sigh, scolded Rascal for following me and after letting her lick my hands clean, turned around to take her back to Emory Road.

I was becoming very familiar with the real estate between Ponce de Leon and Emory Road. It seemed like I knew every building along the way. Rascal walked with me this time instead of following. It was bittersweet walking with her. I felt like she was my best friend and this was probably the last walk we would ever have together. Mrs. Unger was waiting for me. I waited as she put a leash on Rascal and took her inside. I still wondered how Rascal got out after I had put her inside earlier that morning, but I decided it was useless to broach the subject. Mrs. Unger came back and told me that she had called the Children's Service Bureau and suggested that they find a place for me on the south side of Atlanta. I agreed that it was a good suggestion and asked her to keep an eye on Rascal. I couldn't quite get up the nerve to ask her for a ride to Washington Street. I figured if she had not offered to do so, she would not have been inclined to waste the time or the gasoline on that either.

It was a long walk but I found it exhilarating. Aside from wondering if I had qualified for a hiking merit badge, I had time to gather my thoughts. It appeared that I would soon be finding out if and when I would be moving back to my old stomping grounds. I thought about Pat. He was such a nice guy, so smart and, in his own quiet way, a real friend. Under the right circumstances, I thought, I could have learned a great deal more from him than I had done in the little time I did have with him. I figured that, from time to time, I might see Pat but I had to wonder if I would ever see Rascal again. In spite of the back and forth trips to and from the Unger house, there was a vigorousness to my walk as I breathed the fresh air with every stride. I was very fortunate, even though it was the end of summer, that the weather had been more like a fall day. The relief that I felt as I was walking made me realize how stifled I had felt that entire summer.

By the time I reached Maishie's house, it was after six in the evening. There was plenty of time to bathe, relax and get ready for *Shabbat*. That evening, I mentioned that I might be moving back into the neighborhood and that Children's Service Bureau might be looking for another home for me. Mrs. Epstein volunteered that she would call the Bureau and offer to take me in. That was a nice gesture, but I didn't take it seriously. The Epsteins had a house full with five children ranging from the oldest, Aaron, who was away in the Navy, to Yasee (Joseph), who was a year or two younger than me. I had brought the family name up once before to one of my caseworkers. The response given had been that the Bureau had found the family dynamic was not conducive to adding a foster child.

I spent a pleasant *Shabbat* at the Epsteins, going to synagogue and reconnecting with my peers. When asked, I chose not to mention what precipitated my walking from Emory. I just said I needed to be among my friends for this *Shabbat*. Saturday night, Flo called and told me that I would be moving in with Mrs. Goncher at 22 Ormond Street, where Asher was already staying. Flo was going to be moving in with the Bogart family, her friend Marcia's parents. Flo said that she would pack up all of my stuff and bring it to Mrs. Goncher's house. I apologized to Flo for ruining her chances to stay with the Ungers. She told me not to worry about it, as she had been wanting to move out and had only stayed there because of me.

We had heard the news that on August 25, 1944, Paris had been liberated by Western Allied troops. It was going to be only a matter of time until the thousand-year Third Reich would go down in defeat and we would hopefully hear good news from our parents, Werner and Roselene.

VI

FRANKFURT MEMORIES, September 1932–December 1938

How I would love to have more memories of my mother and father and the first six years of my life. As it is, I will have to settle for the vignettes of memory that I do have and be thankful for them. I remember my father as a stern disciplinarian who ran a tight ship and cared greatly for his family. I've been told that he was a very religious man and that was borne out by the exhortations he had given to my brother Asher in the last letters we had received from him after we were already in the United States. I've also been told of his devotion to the Frankfurt Jewish community and that, after we had left, he ran a soup kitchen for the elderly in our grandparents' old house. He also took in Jewish children from neighboring small towns, where there were no Jewish schools, so they could receive an education in the Jewish school in Frankfurt. But, these are not personal memories.

My father was a dentist. He didn't have a very large practice but it was lucrative enough to support our family well, that is—-until Adolph Hitler and his Nazi party came to power in 1933. I was the fifth child and had been just seven months old when the new Chancellor enacted a law in April 1933 that forbade Jews who had not served in the German army during World War I from receiving any compensation from the government's department of health services. This meant that my father, who had been too young to serve during that war, could not receive compensation for treating patients under the government's health system. Overnight, Dr. Hermann Hirsch lost all of his non-Jewish patients who had made up a large percentage of his practice. Shortly thereafter, to ease the financial burden of feeding five children and two adults on Dad's greatly reduced income, my oldest siblings, Flora and Asher, were sent to live temporarily with relatives in Holland. Until my father went to The Hague a year later to visit them, he had been unaware that these relatives had been running an orphanage. Instead of having Flora and Asher stay in their home with the family, these relatives had put them in the orphanage as if they were no kin. Becoming aware of Flo and Asher's living conditions had been a shock to my father. Figuring out how to deal with the sticky situation posed problems for him because of his limited financial resources. These relatives were, in their own way, helping him out in very pressing times, yet he had never dreamed that relatives would treat his children as if they were orphans off the street. Once Dad's dental practice started producing more income from its now totally Jewish clientele, after 2½ years in Holland, Flora and Asher came back to Frankfurt. Since virtually all of the other Jewish dentists had either packed up and left Frankfurt or were incarcerated by September, 1935, and the newly enacted Nuremberg laws forbade Jews from having any dealings with non-Jews, my father's dental practice became the only game in town for Jews.

This temporary good fortune brought about a more positive attitude in our home. Not only did Flora and Asher come back home to live, but our parents decided that the hiatus in the growth of our family, brought on by the devastation of anti-Jewish laws, could be reconsidered. Werner, (*Shmuel Moshe* in Hebrew), was born March 10, 1937 and Roselene, (*Shoshanah* in Hebrew), was born March 13, 1938. Things weren't exactly back to normal; our family had simply adjusted to the situation hoping that the worst was behind us.

I remember a time, while Flo and Asher were still in The Hague, that Jack and I were staying temporarily at the Jewish orphanage in Frankfurt. I think it had been because our sister Sarah had a highly infectious disease and, as a result, our house had been quarantined. It was the first night of *Chanukah*, either 1934 or 1935 and I had cried myself to sleep because our father had not visited us and we had not received any *Chanukah* presents. My father had come while I was asleep and put cookies and candies and other presents in my crib. I woke up early the next morning and found the cookies floating in my bed. I was so happy that our father had not forgotten to bring us presents for *Chanukah*, that I sat in my wet bed with a big smile on my face as I proceeded to eat the soggy and somewhat weird tasting cookies.

Then there was the time that Sarah and Jack decided that their little brother should be taught to swim. Even though they didn't know how to swim themselves, teaching little Benny had become a priority. I'm not sure how old I was then, but I think I was still in diapers. The playroom had a sink in it and was directly above the kitchen. Sarah crumpled up old newspapers and stuffed them under the door and the stage was set. Jack stopped up the sink and turned on the faucets letting the sink fill and overflow. Apparently, the idea was to make a pool out of the playroom, but alas the wood construction could not contain the water without leaking into the kitchen below. Mom ran up the stairs, pushed open the playroom door and was greeted with a gush of water which cascaded down the steps and flooded most of the main floor. When she caught her breath, she looked around and I was the only one in the room, sitting in the middle of a puddle in my diaper, with a smile on my face, unaware that there had been a disaster. Sarah and Jack had jumped out of the second story window and luckily landed without breaking any bones. Mom turned off the water and, much to Sarah's and Jack's surprise, did not blame the incident on me. It did not take a brain surgeon to figure out that I wasn't even tall enough to turn on the sink faucet. The way I was told, Sarah tried to blame Jack and he said it was all her idea which had seemed to be correct to my young and limited ability to comprehend. Mom apparently did not care whose idea it had been to teach me to swim, she summarily punished both of them equally. That experience had no effect on my desire for aquatic sports. I finally learned to swim, but not until about eight years later after we had escaped to the United States of America.

I have fond memories of going to the park as a little boy, sitting on a bench and watching the white swans and the geese swim in the lake. That was what I missed most when the Nuremberg Laws came into effect in September 1935. I was three years old and my family and I could no longer sit on the benches facing the lake. The one bench for "*Juden* only" did not have a view of the water. I had begun to learn to deal with the bands of little storm troopers, the younger contingent of Hitler Youth, ever present on the streets. However, the fact that the entire Jewish population was only permitted to use one bench in the park and from that bench one could not see the lake or the ducks, geese and swans, saddened me greatly. Of all the restrictions placed on us as Jews, not being allowed to enjoy the beauty of swans gliding on the lake in the park left the biggest impression on me. I had accepted so many of the other restrictions as part of life. But this one had affected an enjoyable experience, I had always taken for granted, and that etched an indelible impression in my young mind.

The little storm troopers, in retrospect, were almost comical. They wore the same uniforms as their adult counterparts and they came in all sizes. The ones that used to chase me when I wandered away from our house on Grünestrasse, ranged from the ages of five or six to nine or ten years old. They would roam through the streets looking for little Jewish boys or girls to harass and beat up. I actually don't remember ever being caught by any of them. Whenever it looked like I was going to be caught, I would stop in front of the nearest house and yell for my "Momma" at the top of my lungs. Invariably, that would be enough to make them run away. As rough and tough as the uniforms made them look and probably feel, they still had a fear of mothers, at least before 1938.

The *Hitlerjugend*, Hitler Youth, was established in 1926 and by 1934 it reached a membership of 3.5 million. Early in 1934, interestingly enough, Hitler Youth members were turned loose throughout Germany to intimidate members of Catholic youth groups. Of course, they didn't need to officially be told to intimidate Jewish children. It was the natural order of things in Germany that even the younger uniformed kids, the Hitler Youth want-to-bes, took great pleasure in.

By 1939, membership in the Hitler Youth and its companion organization, the *Bund Deutsher Madel*, League of German Girls, became compulsory and its numbers rose to almost 9 million Germans between the ages of ten and eighteen. In 1945, as the fall of the Third Reich became imminent, the naive Hitler Youth was among the few Nazi groups that remained loyal to their Fuhrer. Thousands of Hitler Youth died fighting to that end.

I was sent to Switzerland for a summer, but I can't remember which year, probably 1936 or 1937. I remember very little about that summer except that I thoroughly enjoyed waking up to the brisk cool mountain air while snuggling under a fluffy down feather quilt. That I had been waited on, hand and foot, by my hosts, the Meyers family, was equally memorable. Max Meyer was my father's first cousin; he later had been the one who ransomed my father out of Buchenwald after his arrest on *Kristallnacht*. I don't remember playing with any boy cousins; they must have been too young or not born yet. Henrietta and her sister were both older than I, but to my recollection they spent a lot of time with me. Who would have thought that one of them would become my sister-in-law? My brother Asher had met the family in 1947, while serving in the U.S. Army and visiting Basel to find out more about our parents. Following over a year of transatlantic correspondence, Henny and Asher were married in Basel, in 1949. I had always thought of my trip to Switzerland as a summer vacation but, in retrospect, I probably had been sent there for other reasons, but I was never told what they were.

People who knew my mother told me how beautiful she was and what a pious woman and devoted mother she had been. I remember her as the purveyor of love and tenderness in my life for those few short years I had with her. I remember one incident that brought out her uncanny wisdom. She walked into the kitchen one day and found Jack and me helping ourselves to some sugar that was in a container in a wall cabinet, supposedly out of reach to children. We had climbed on the kitchen counter to make the sugar more accessible and were sitting on the counter enjoying our ill-gotten gains when she walked in. We were both scolded and sent to bed, and for the next few dinners we were not allowed to have dessert. We thought that was the end of that incident until the first night of *Chanukah*. It was time to open our presents and the anticipation could be felt in the air. To our surprise, Jack and I each had received a one kilo bag of sugar, about 2.2 pounds, as our *Chanukah* present.

Not at all disappointed, we dove into the bags of sweet stuff. I had gone through barely a third of the bag before I was totally nauseated and had to stop. From that point on I began using sugar sparingly and limited my intake of sweets to pastries, avoiding overly sweet candy and the like. Jack, on the other hand, finished his bag and asked if he could have the rest of mine which I gladly handed over. For the rest of his life, until his doctors intervened, Jack put three teaspoons of sugar in each cup of coffee or tea while I still prefer to have mine without any.

I don't have many memories of my father. I know that I inherited his artistic talents and he took an interest in the development of my drawing ability. I remember once showing him a drawing of a field of grass and flowers with trees. Under the green grass, in my drawing, I had drawn brown soil. Dad pointed out that you don't see the soil when you look at the grass and I argued that the soil was there and, therefore, had to be shown. I remember the argument because neither of us had given in. If I knew then what I learned in architectural school, I could have explained that I had been drawing a cross section of the field. That was one of the few times that I argued with my father. He was a strict disciplinarian and was not known for taking back-talk from his children. Jack never learned to refrain from talking back to our father. The rest of us had learned to avoid contradicting Dad, even if we might have been right. Dad had gastric problems, which seem to run in the family, and had been known to emit gas or belch frequently. He had a habit at looking at one of us and jokingly asking if we had done that, after he had freed himself of gastric gas. Only Jack would insist on confronting Dad and insist that he had done the deed. He was invariably rewarded with a slap for his insolence.

I remember that one of Dad's prize possessions was a set of two red hardbound volumes of Hans and Fritz, the Katzenjammer Kids cartoons. I loved to look at them, but could only do so when he was present. I developed a great appreciation for cartooning from them. I also remember that we only shared meals with our father on *Shabbat* and on Holy days when we ate in the dining room, and that was where the two red volumes were kept on a shelf. For all other meals, we children ate in the kitchen. Reading the Hans and Fritz volumes became my *Shabbat* treat if I behaved during the meal.

I don't remember my grandparents at all. Only two of them were alive when I was born. My father's father, Anselm Hirsch, after whom Asher was named, died in 1922 before any of my siblings were born. His mother, Hermine Fuechtwanger Hirsch, died in 1934. The only thing I remember about her funeral is that I was too young to attend. I was just over two years old, but I do seem to remember watching some kind of procession from an upstairs window at Sandweg 2, which was the address of the house we were living in at the time. My mother's mother, Helen Posen Auerbach, died in 1930.

Asher has told me about our mother's devotion to her father, Aaron Auerbach, and about how she prepared a place for him to live in our house when he retired from his business in Hamburg. She was so looking forward to being able to take care of him in his waning years. Unfortunately, he died before he had a chance to make the move. Asher recalls how, in her disappointment and grief, Mom confronted God. It had been a one way conversation, with hands raised in the air and eyes looking heavenward. She pleaded for an answer from God, wanting to know how He could have taken away her opportunity to perform the *mitzah* of *Kibbud Av* (the commandment of honoring ones father), after she had prepared so meticulously, and with such anticipation, to perform this *mitzvah*. She didn't expect an answer but she wanted to register her complaint, and she did so with great fervor. Aaron Auerbach, my grandfather, died on July 7, 1938, on the second day of the infamous Evian Conference, which was held in the French resort of Evian-les-Bains on Lake Geneva. I can only assume that his funeral had been in Hamburg and that the younger children didn't go, because I have no memory of it.

The Evian Conference was an international meeting convened by the president of the United States, Franklin Delano Roosevelt. From July 6 to 14, in 1938, delegates from thirty-two nations of the "free world" and representatives of thirty-nine private relief agencies met at the luxurious Hotel Royal. They gathered to discuss the dire straits of the Jews of Germany and Austria, and to try to find them safe haven, should Hitler allow them to leave. All thirty-two nations and other countries as well, had closed their doors to Jews attempting to flee from Germany and Austria. Hitler's response, on hearing of the conference, was to offer Jews at $250 a head to any country that would take them with just the shirts on their back. The main purpose of the conference was to convince the countries present to each allow as many Jews as possible to enter their country. Hitler chose Dr. Heinrich Neumann, a world famous Viennese neurosurgeon who had already been incarcerated by the Nazis, to present the case for providing refuge for the Jews of Germany and Austria. He was brought to Evian from his imprisonment to plead in front of the delegates, on behalf of his fellow Jews. During the conference, he made it very clear that these Jews were otherwise in grave danger and would most likely be killed if they remained in Germany and Austria. To sweeten the pot, the United States offered to match the number of visas allowed by each country.

The records show that all of the delegates availed themselves of the many amenities offered at the Hotel Royal, including tennis, sailing, golf and horseback riding. Only one nation was represented at every session. Nazi Germany, though not invited to the conference, was interested in attending and monitoring the proceedings. As it turned out, no burden would be put on the closed-door immigration policy of the United States. Every nation was willing to take in the eloquent Dr. Neumann, but only the Dominican Republic and Costa Rica, both of which wanted enormous sums of money, agreed to take in any other Jews. This paltry showing by the countries of the "free world," was evidence of their total lack of concern or compassion for people in fear for their lives. Dr. Neumann declined all offers and opted to go back and share the fate of his fellow Jews. To the world Jewish community, who when they first learned of the conference had considered it a godsend, the outcome was devastating. To the xenophobic opponents of America's offer to take in as many Jews as all the other countries combined, the end result of the conference was a blessing. A July 14, 1938 Nazi newspaper headline "JEWS FOR SALE AT A BARGAIN PRICE—WHO WANTS THEM? NO ONE," summarized the results of the Evian Conference. An elated Adolph Hitler announced in a speech that the world had shown that it agrees with his plan for the Jews. The way had been paved for *Kristallnacht* only four months later.

Kristallnacht was an attack on Jews and Jewish institutions, sponsored and coordinated by the Third Reich. It erupted on the night of November 9, 1938 and continued throughout the next day. The Jews in all of Germany and countries under German control, including Austria, were affected. Jewish stores were looted and their storefronts were shattered, thousands of Jews were arrested, some were murdered and more than two hundred synagogues were destroyed in that orgy of violence. I still remember standing along the *anlage*, the park across the street from our synagogue, the *Friedberger Anlage Synagoge*, which had been the most architecturally celebrated synagogue in all of Germany. I was standing there with my fourteen-year old cousin, Arno Horenczyk, along with a group of nearly a hundred spectators. Arno's mother was my father's sister and the family had lived next door to us on Grünestrasse. We were watching in utter amazement and bewilderment as hoodlums, some in Hitler Youth uniforms, were running in and out of the synagogue. They ran in with incendiary devices similar to Molotov cocktails in an obvious attempt to torch the building, and they ran out with ornamental items of silver, such as Torah breastplates and crowns. Eventually, they carried out some of the Torah scrolls, unrolled them and hung them on the metal picket fence in between the arches surrounding the courtyard in front of the synagogue. They pierced the parchment of the holy scrolls with the fence pickets and let out triumphant cheers as they completed their deed.

I was dumbfounded and I imagined that most of the other spectators were too. There had been armed policemen there, but we quickly learned that they were not there to protect anyone other than the hoodlums who were trying to destroy the synagogue. I was aghast at what was happening before my eyes and looked around me at the other spectators to gauge their reaction to this carnage. It was somewhat comforting that about half of the spectators seemed as stunned as Arno and I, but it was equally discomforting that the other half were cheering on the hoodlums as if they were at a soccer game. Arno suggested that we had better leave while we still could. It was good that we lived so close to the synagogue. We had decided not to run, but to walk fast so as not to draw attention to our departure, and breathed a sigh of relief after we reached Grünestrasse. I was only six years old at the time, but the memory of that horrendous sight has stayed with me, and probably will, until the day I die.

Later that day, the Nazis came to our house to arrest my father. I have no memory of this event but, have been able to piece together the story from accounts given to me by some of my nieces and nephews, the children of my siblings. My only thoughts as to why my siblings would not talk about this story to me is that they either had no idea that the incident had been totally blocked from my memory, or as with so many other stories, they chose not talk to me about unpleasantness because I was the youngest of those of us who had escaped and they may have felt the need to be protective of my psyche.

From all accounts, three armed men came to the door. Two of them were wearing S.S. uniforms, and each had a German police dog on a leash. The other man had on plainclothes, a trench coat and a hat with the front of the wide brim pulled down almost over his eyes. It was pretty obvious that this man was in charge. He confronted my mother, who answered the door holding my seven and a half months old sister in her arms. He ordered Mom to have "Dr. Hirsch" present himself. Fearing for my father's safety, she calmly told the man that her husband was not at home and suggested that he leave his card, so that her husband could call him when he returned. Apparently, the *Gestapo* had been watching our house all day and knew that my father was home, which may account for what happened next. The plain clothed *Gestapo* quickly grabbed my baby sister from my mother's arms and threw her to the floor. He then pulled out a pistol and pointed it at Roselene and in a dry, matter-of-fact tone told my mother that she had 30 seconds to make her husband appear. If not, he continued, he would first shoot the baby, then he pointed his pistol at my younger brother and said he would shoot Werner next, then me, and so on until he shot all of her seven children by age. He pointed his gun at each child as he made this threat. Then, he concluded, he would kill her after she would have watched all of her children die. Within seconds, and before the words were completely out of the *Gestapo's* mouth, my father appeared from his hiding place and gave himself up. He was immediately arrested and, as we later found out, taken to Buchenwald concentration camp. My older siblings and I never saw our father again.

With my father in a concentration camp, my mother suddenly was left with the sole responsibility of seeing to our welfare and safety. If any German Jews had been under the illusion, as my father had been, that they and their families would be safe in the Third Reich, *Kristallnacht* dispelled that fantasy. In her new role, Mom decided to immediately find a way to send us, at least those who were old enough to travel, to a safer place. My guess would be that she had not thought this would be a permanent separation, but only until the anti-Semitic violence in Germany subsided and Jews could live their lives without fear. Someone told her of *Kindertransports* that were being organized by the head of the Jewish Orphans' Home in Frankfurt. She found out that there were six transports contemplated going to major cities in six different European countries. The first one of these would be going to Paris, France within a month. Mom had an aunt and Dad had two brothers living in Paris with whom, she felt sure, she could place us. She then made arrangements for all seven children to be passengers on that *Kindertransport* which was scheduled to leave on December 6, 1938 for Paris. To play it safe, she booked all of us on all six *Kindertransports,* in case the first one did not materialize. Flo was actually too old, having turned thirteen in October, but was allowed to go so she could take care of me, since I was a very small six year old. It wasn't until the day before we left for Paris that Mom changed her mind and decided that the babies, Werner and Roselene were too young to travel or to be away from their mother for an extended period of time.

The decision to split the family up, even temporarily, was a brave one to make, knowing that our father had always expressed his strong conviction that the family unit should not be separated. The next couple of weeks were spent preparing for the trip. When Mom told us we would be going to Paris, I could hardly hold back the excitement that I felt. I was too young to grasp why we would be going to Paris. Actually, I had thought we were preparing for a pleasure trip from which we would return soon. I remember being impressed at the care that my mother took in packing my suitcase for me. Everything was so neatly placed. With every item she would put in, a teardrop would fall from her face. Her sadness, and that of my oldest siblings, was apparent and, at the same time, very confusing to me. Going to Paris seemed so exciting to me, yet Mom, Flo and Asher were so sad. I simply did not know what to make of it.

When the day finally came, Mom found someone to take care of Werner and Roselene while she took us to the *Banhoff*, the Frankfurt train station. She saw to it that each of us had our own luggage and the little lunch bags she packed for us. There was a lot of hustle and bustle. Younger kids were running around while the older ones, from nine to thirteen years of age, were clinging to their parent or parents for that last bit of parental affection. I still had no clue as to what was going on. I saw Asher, Flo and Sarah holding on to Mom, all of them weeping, yet I still was unable to fathom a reason for all the sadness, especially since we would be embarking on a short pleasure trip to Paris, the "City of Lights." Actually, no one told me the trip would be a short one; I must have assumed that on my own. We boarded the train, waved and blew kisses to our mother and we were on our way. It was a blessing that I didn't realize that we wouldn't see Mom or the little ones for a long time or, as it turned out, forever. I don't think I would have been able to handle the separation.

In New York, ten to fifteen years later, while visiting a lady who had been from Frankfurt am Main, my brother Asher, was shown an article from a college newspaper, written by her son. It turned out that her son, who had been on the same Paris-bound *Kindertransport* as all of us, had been the editor of that newspaper while he was in college. The article told about the most unforgettable experience of his life. He wrote of how he, at twelve and a half years, had been one of the oldest children on the train and how he boarded the train early so that he could watch and take notes about the reactions of the mothers who were sending their children, out of harm's way. He mentioned seeing one woman who had been sending off five of her children and decided to focus in on that family dynamic and, specifically, to study the reactions of that mother. After her children had boarded the train, he watched her as the train was pulling away from the station. The last thing he saw was the woman passing out on the platform. Asher told me that he had gotten chills reading that article. He realized that the woman in the article had to be our mother, since she was the only one that had sent five of her children on that transport. We were not aware that Mom had fainted on the platform. We knew that she must have recovered because of the letters she had written to us, first in France and later in the United States, until they stopped coming at the end of summer, 1942. Not one of her letters ever alluded to that fainting incident. I can only assume that she must have had an inkling that we would never see each other again.

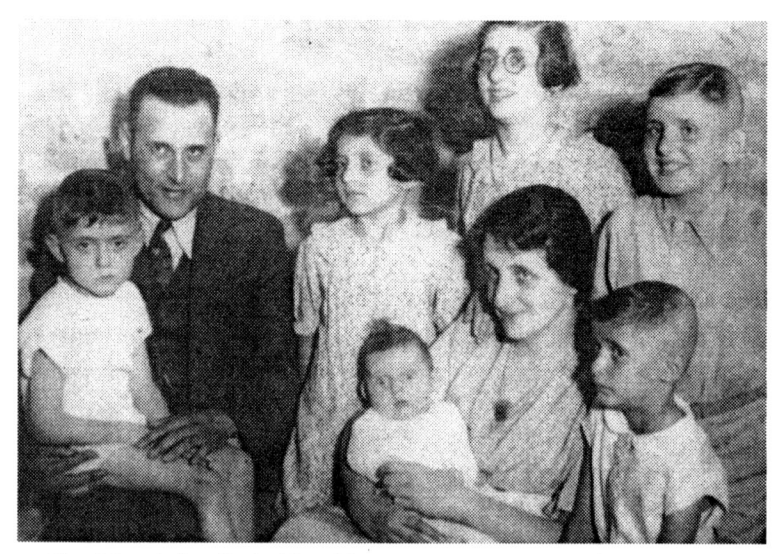

The Hirsch family in Frankfurt, c.1937. L-r: Ben (on father's lap), Dr. Hermann Hirsch, Sarah (standing), Werner (baby), mother Mathilda Hirsch, Flo (standing behind Mathilde), Jack, and Asher.

Werner (Shmuel Moshe) Hirsch, my brother as I last saw him. *Photo from Ben Hirsch.*

Roselene (Shoshanah) Hirsch, my sister as I last saw her. *Photo from Ben Hirsch.*

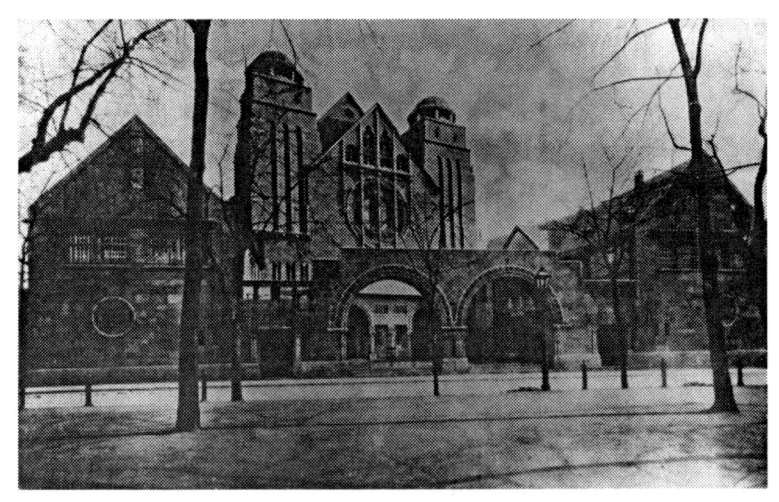

(above) The Friedberger Anlage synagogue, destroyed on Kristallnacht, November 10, 1938.

(below) The sanctuary of the Friedberger Anlage synagogue.

(at left) Ben with the current owner at 30 Grünestrasse, the home he left in December 1938. Photo taken November, 1995.

(below) Monument at the site of the Friedberger Anlage synagogue, destroyed on Kristallnacht and dismantled through August 1939.

VII

MRS. GONCHER—JUNIOR HIGH, September 1944– August 1947

Mrs. Goncher's house, my fourth foster home, was to be a temporary home while the Bureau was in the process of finding another place for me to stay. I was no stranger to her. She was friendly with Mrs. Bregman, her daughter, Goldie, had been going steady with Martin Hershberg for years, though she did not marry him, and of course, I had visited Asher several times at her house. My case worker, Miss Backer, was working diligently to find a permanent foster home for me, even while she was getting mixed messages from Mrs. Goncher. On one hand, Mrs. G. kept asking her if they had found a home for me yet, while on the other hand, she "expressed fondness for the child and said that he has been a pleasure to have in her home." She spoke of the fact that she was getting older and feared that she could not give the proper care and attention to a child as young and as mischievous as I. At the same time, she stated that I had certainly fitted into her household nicely and had become one of the family group. This family group included Alex Zomper, a teenage refugee from Belgium, Abie Flitman an adult boarder, Alice Goncher and my brother Asher, who was making plans to move to New York and study in a *yeshiva*, a school of higher Jewish learning.

    I was so happy to be back in the Jewish community on the south side of Atlanta. Of course I had missed my friends, but I also missed the Jewish milieu that was unique to this neighborhood, and did not exist in the suburban areas. I began to appreciate all the Jewish amenities that were available within a one mile radius. There were three Ashkenazi synagogues, Ahavath Achim, Shearith Israel and Anshe S'fard, and one Sephardic synagogue, Or VeShalom. There were at least five meat markets that were either butchers or delicatessens or both—Stein's, Siegel's and Kaufman's—on Washington Street, Gold's on Capitol Avenue and Merlin's on Georgia Avenue. The Jewish Educational Alliance on Capitol Avenue had Siegel's kosher restaurant across the street. Manhattan Bakery was on Georgia Avenue and another smaller kosher bakery was across the street. Outwardly, these were all the trappings of a viable Jewish community. In retrospect, what had been missing to make it sustainable was Jewish education beyond Hebrew school three days a week and Sunday school, both of which were seldom attended after Bar Mitzvah age.

Late in September, Miss Backer came to visit Mrs. Goncher to advise her that they had selected a new home for me. She did not want to make the transfer, however, without first talking to Mrs. Goncher, who had expressed some feeling that she might want to keep me after all. Mrs. G. asked what home had been selected and was told that it was a Sephardic, Spanish-Jewish, family that lived on Capitol Avenue. Mrs. Goncher immediately expressed concern, although she said that she knew the family well and that they were lovely people. While she was confident that they would be nice to me, she was concerned about differences in religious practices between Ashkenazi and Sephardic Jews. She referred to the Unger family where she felt that my efforts to maintain my level of religious observance had been misunderstood. She then said that she, "…..hates to think of Benjamin going from one home to the next just because he is making an effort to hold on to this religion." That being said, Mrs. Goncher agreed that I would stay with her as long as she was physically able to properly take care of me.

Mrs. Ida Goncher lived right around the corner from James L. Key elementary school, on Ormond Street between Capitol Avenue and Crew Street. She was an old pro at taking care of foster children. Years ago, she had taken in a young orphan whose name was Abraham Lincoln Stein, and continued caring for foster children from then on. Lincoln, as she lovingly referred to him, was serving in the U.S. Army at the time I moved in, but he kept in touch with her even though he had moved to Virginia and married some years before he enlisted. I got to meet him when he came to visit about a year later. He was still in the army and cut quite a dashing figure in his uniform. I had heard so much about him that I probably showed my admiration for him. He had been an orphan boy in Mrs. Goncher's house, went on to make a life for himself and was doing what I had aspired to do, serving in the army of the United States. He spent more time with me than I had anticipated. He even walked to synagogue with me on *Shabbat*, even though he professed to not being religious. While walking, he told me that I reminded him a lot of himself when he was my age and proceeded to give me advice on how to stay out of trouble. There was no doubt that he was a favorite of Mrs. Goncher's, which may have been because he was close to the same age as her son, Meyer. Meyer was killed a year or two earlier in a plane crash during a training mission in Texas while serving in the U.S. Army. Lincoln visited one more time, a year or so later, and we continued on where we had left off. Mrs. Goncher bemoaned that he was not much of a letter writer, but the few times that he did write, he would occasionally put in a note for me.

Mrs. Goncher was a widow. She had three daughters and Meyer had been her only son. Her oldest daughter, Lottie, was married with three sons and lived in Wilkes-Barre, Pennsylvania. I don't remember whether Goldie was already married when I moved in, or just engaged. She married Joshua Stampfer who, along with his brother, was still a rabbinical student at the time. I had heard that the Stampfer brothers were exceedingly bright and became a believer when I witnessed them playing a game of chess without a chessboard, while waiting for a streetcar. It was mind boggling to watch. Alice, the youngest, had graduated high school and was still living at home.

It didn't take me long to feel comfortable in my new home. The first month at the Gonchers, I was so preoccupied with getting used to our new school setting at Hoke Smith Jr. High, walking to Shearith Israel Hebrew School three times a week and home from there, not to mention Asher's pending departure for New York, I found little time to obsess on when we would be hearing from or about our family in Europe. Although Paris had been liberated by the Western Allies and Soviet troops were closing in on the Germans from the East, liberating camps along the way, the gassing of Jews in Auschwitz/Birkenau was continuing at an accelerated pace. I had seen no newsreel reports that large numbers of Jews were being deported from Theresienstadt to Auschwitz on a regular basis, and that a large percentage of them were being gassed upon arrival. Yet even if we had heard this news, we would have been unable to make the connection that this may have been the transit camp at which our mother, along with Werner and Roselene had been before they were transported to Auschwitz. I guess not knowing somehow made it easier for me to go on with my life.

After a couple of postponements, Asher finally left for New York on October 10, 1944. The postponements were for logistical reasons, but each one left Asher feeling that things were working against this move that he was so anxious to make. He no longer felt that his presence in Atlanta was necessary. He saw that his siblings were well settled in their respective foster homes and thought it was time for him to pursue the life he wanted for himself. Max Lieberson and Mr. Heffler had been paying for Asher's private *Talmud* lessons and they were willing to help foot the bill to send him to a *yeshiva* in New York. The move came barely a month after I moved in to the Goncher household, but I was prepared for it. Asher had been talking about it for quite a while.

Among the instructions Asher gave me before he left was the admonition to refuse any offer to sing in the Ahavath Achim choir. This was a little strange since it had never come up before, either from the synagogue's side or mine. Even though it had been a while since I had attended A. A. Hebrew School or services at the synagogue on any regular basis, Asher was convinced that Cantor Schwartzman was going to try to get me to join his choir. I knew that Asher and Jack had sung in the choir and received money for their services and I may even have been a bit envious of them at the time. I figured that since I was never asked, the Cantor did not feel that my voice was good enough. All of this made Asher's insistence on my promise not to accept an offer I never expected to receive a bit ludicrous to me. Though I had no problem going along with this request, my curiosity was piqued. Asher explained he had felt for a long time that Rabbi Harry Epstein was guiding his congregation toward the Conservative Movement and that our father would not have approved of my taking part in enhancing the services of a non-Orthodox synagogue. Only after this explanation, did Asher finally let me know that Cantor Schwartzman had been asking him for permission to contact me about singing in his choir for some time and, each time, Asher told him that I was too committed to leading the junior congregation services at Shearith Israel.

After Asher left, Alex Zomper became the closest thing to a role model in the Goncher household. He was no Lincoln Stein; in fact, it had been obvious that he was jealous of the fuss everyone made over Lincoln on his visits back to Atlanta. Abe Friend also lived there, but he was a boarder, probably in his late thirties, who shared few interests with young refugees from Europe like Alex and me. He did, however, have a flair for drawing and painting and often used the plight of the Jews in Europe as subject matter for his art work. He made a point of sharing those drawings with both Alex and me. Alex was a year or so older than Jack and was highly critical of my brother as well as all other European children who had come to Atlanta without parents. He had come to America with his older brother from Belgium before we did, and he gave the impression that anything other refugees did was open to his criticism. When the Zomper boys first came to Atlanta, both of them stayed with Mrs. Goncher, but his brother had moved out of town before I moved in. Alex had fanciful adventure stories of growing up with his brother in Belgium. He enjoyed telling me of sexual exploits that they both had experienced before either of them was ten years old. From what I could tell, most people thought Alex was a grumpy and unfriendly guy besides being a braggart with quite an imagination. Maybe because he found a good listener in me when he spoke of his exploits and criticized everyone around him, he kind of took me under his wing. It wasn't that I was particularly interested in his seemingly exaggerated stories, I just didn't want to be rude. That he took me under his wing did not keep him from ridiculing any and all of my religious practices, making fun of me when I would show serious remorse for any of my own misbehavior. He was a good student, in high school at the time, who worked hard to do what was expected of him, but he just did not appear to be a people person, or to be a happy person, for that matter.

Hoke Smith Jr. High was a new experience for me. I remembered hearing about how my brother Jack had once been pushed into his locker by a couple of boys who then locked him in. He wasn't let out until he had missed part of his class. When I first heard about that incident, I was very angry and wished for an opportunity to get back at those bullies. By the time I attended Hoke Smith Jr. High, Jack had moved to the other side of town and was attending O'Keefe Jr. High. I had no idea who the bullies were and, with the passage of time, thinking of that incident just made me wary of hanging out in the halls. I was very excited about starting a new school year. I still look back, when fall weather is in the air, and think of the excitement I used to feel at the start of every new school year, especially shopping at the little store across Hill Street, for new school supplies. I liked the challenge and I always looked forward to meeting new people. My homeroom consisted of a lot of students from grammar schools other than James L. Key, which made for instant new acquaintances. I was anxious to leave my reputation for getting into fights behind and was glad to see that none of my regular combatants were in my homeroom. Unfortunately, one homeroom does not an entire school make and, after the summer hiatus, it wasn't long before I was challenged to duke it out in the schoolyard. At first, I couldn't tell if I was still being accosted for being a Jew and a foreigner, but when the inevitable ethnic slurs were uttered, it was clear that, at least to some, I had not yet become an accepted member of American society. Fighting during recess seemed to be more acceptable in junior high. No one ever came to stop a fight unless it looked as if someone was going to get, or already was, seriously injured.

    I made new friends quickly. The girls were more developed and getting prettier and the boys, including myself, were feeling awkward at the realization that we were all of a sudden interested in the opposite sex. Frances Tiller was the *femme fatale* of the class and her sidekick, Betty Meadows, was not too shabby herself. Several DSI members who had not gone to James L. Key were now at Hoke Smith. Jack Rosenberg was in my class, Leon Tuck was a semester ahead of me, and Sam Pinsky was at least a year ahead. Sam was the only guy, for many years, who ever expressed a real interest in my life before coming to Atlanta. I wasn't that comfortable in talking about what preceded my coming to America. I had not felt the need, or the desire, to think about it enough to know how to respond to Sam's questions. The fact that he seemed genuinely interested stuck with me. The only stories I remember telling him were about my brother and sister's antics involving me while we were still in Frankfurt.

Having a different teacher for each course was a new experience. Aside from math, English, and history, there were courses like wood shop, electricity shop, mechanical drawing, and even art. Jack had told me stories about the shop courses. He told me they were not hard if you just listened to the instructors and followed their directions. I prepared for and even looked forward to doing just that. I knew that the main project in electricity shop was to build a crystal radio and I couldn't wait to learn how to do that. Mr. Icenogel, the electricity shop teacher had different ideas. He too had come from Germany to America, albeit many years before and, at first, he wanted me to spend each class period speaking German with him. When he finally realized that my German was virtually non-existent, he switched to reminiscing about the Old Country with me. Not only was I not comfortable talking about Germany to a non-Jewish German who was also my teacher, but I was also looking forward to learning how to build a crystal radio. When I broached that thought with Mr. Icenogel, he said there was nothing to building a crystal radio and that he would give me one along with an automatic B in the course if I would continue to talk to him every shop period. I didn't know all of the details of the concentration camps and killing camps at the time. The atrocities that I had been aware of were, in Mr. Icenogel's mind, anti-German propaganda. I got my grade and my crystal radio, but electricity shop was a horrendous non-learning experience for me. The most important thing I learned was restraint.

Mechanical Drawing had turned out to be another problem. While I was relatively proficient in art, I had no experience at drawing with instruments. Mr. Martin was well thought of as a Mechanical Drawing teacher and I was looking forward to learning from him. However, Mr. Martin had heard that I was a good chess player and he loved to play chess. I was no Bobby Fisher but then he wasn't either. I actually enjoyed playing chess with Mr. Martin every class period, although I was supposed to be learning mechanical drawing. I finally got up the nerve to tell him that, while I enjoyed playing chess with him, I really wanted to learn with the rest of the class. His response was that, with my artistic abilities, I was far ahead of the rest of the class and that I would ace the course no matter what. I decided against going to the principal, accepted my A in the course and enjoyed playing chess. Years later, when I enrolled at Georgia Tech, I wished I had learned more about mechanical drawing. In contrast to the two required shop classes above, in Mr. Casteel's Wood Shop I was allowed to learn with the rest of the class, with only a few interruptions for obligatory conversations about Germany. I made the classic Mickey Mouse bookends and other required knickknacks and managed to get a C out of the course.

Ms. Mary Beacom was an art teacher par excellence and she took an immediate interest in utilizing my talents wherever possible in school. She introduced me to Mrs. McKee who was the faculty advisor for the Hoke Smith school newspaper, *The Vanguard*, and I was drafted to do artwork for the paper. Ms. Beacom was an interesting person. One would never have guessed that she was a handwriting expert and was often called upon to be an expert witness in criminal trials. She occasionally went on assignment with the Georgia Bureau of Investigation when a big case requiring her full attention would come up. She was a pioneer in areas having to do with design. She was the only person I knew who had bought a Studebaker in 1946, the automobile model that had such a revolutionary design that, while it had been considered an oddity when it came out, eventually would pave the way for almost all automobile design for the next 40 years. When the '46 Studebaker was first produced, the joke in all the media was that one couldn't tell if the car was coming or going. Mary Beacom had been impressed with the innovative design and had the guts to show her approval by buying the car. Ms. Fuller was the other art teacher at Hoke Smith. Between the two of them, the art department presented opportunities for any student to become proficient in various media and to learn to appreciate art. I took full advantage of it.

Mrs. Goncher was very proud of my aptitude for art and she not only praised me to her friends in various women's organizations, she also found herself offering my services to do artwork for these non-profit groups. This was a good way, she pointed out, for me, to repay the community for the support it had given to my siblings and me. At first, I was enjoying drawing up flyers and making posters for the various ladies' groups. No one had ever taught me that it was okay to say no when asked to do something for an adult. It did not take long before I had a long waiting list for the various drawings that I had agreed to do. Yehudis Friedman, the Rabbi's wife, came to me with a special project. She asked if I could design a poster advertising the Sisterhood's *Chanukkah Latke* (potato pancake) party and she wanted it in color. Since she was Rabbi Friedman's wife and she was in a big hurry, and since it was going to be a one of a kind piece of artwork, I agreed to put everything else aside. I submitted the final product to her and she was ecstatic with the design and execution. Then she then reminded me, as if she had mentioned her need for more than one poster before, that she needed seven more just like the one I had just completed. I was taken aback. Had I known that her need was for multiple posters, I would have made a simpler design. As a way out, I suggested that she find a printer to reproduce the design, but she had no budget for professional lithography or printing. She reiterated how crucial it was to the success of the Sisterhood event to put posters in the kosher marketplaces as quickly as possible, and was taken aback when I showed her the waiting list that had preceded her request. For her ace in the hole, she pointed out that those on the waiting list were not paying for my artwork, while the Sisterhood was prepared to pay me fifty cents per poster if I would do them first.

Since everyone on the list had come through Mrs. Goncher, I turned to her and asked her for guidance on how to resolve this issue fairly. Rebetzin Friedman had already been in touch with her and Mrs. Goncher seemed to agree that paying customers come first. I put everything else aside and worked on the posters every spare moment I had. I dreamed of a technology that would allow me to make one poster to perfection and then make as many copies by some method of photocopying. If only we could have put the Sisterhood's request on hold for 40 years, we could have taken that first poster to Kinko's and called it a day.

When the posters were finished, I had Mrs. Goncher call to let her friend know the work had been done. The Rebetzin picked up the posters and seemed to be delighted with the work, but she did not offer any payment. After all the work I had put in, I decided not to be shy and reminded her that I was due the money I had been promised. Apologetically, she admitted that she had only mentioned the money in order to get the work done as quickly as possible. She stressed the point that Sisterhood was a non-profit organization and did not have money in their meager budget for this type of work. Mrs. Goncher had overheard the exchange and intervened, saying that it was not fair to promise payment and then not give it. Mrs. Friedman agreed, reached in her pocketbook and gave me fifty cents for my efforts. I reminded her that the agreement was for fifty cents per poster and that I was due $3.50, which had been representative of the hours of work the project demanded. She expressed appreciation for the hours and talent I put into the posters, but insisted that there must have been a misunderstanding and that a total of fifty cents, which she pointed out was more than I was getting from the other groups, was all that she had agreed to. Since I didn't have our agreement in writing, and Mrs. Goncher was not willing to intervene further in my behalf, I had no leg to stand on. That incident made me shy away from non-profit organizations and kind of put a damper on my aspirations of doing artwork for a living.

While Asher was in Atlanta he often took me to visit the Heflers on Washington Street. He had become very friendly with them. Mr. Hefler had been one of the men responsible for Asher's going to *yeshiva* in New York and for his *Talmud* lessons while he was still in Atlanta. About a month after Asher left for New York, Mrs. Hefler called Mrs. Goncher and told her that I was "a tramp." When pushed to explain the accusation, she said that she had not been feeling well a day or so earlier, and had been lying down when her doorbell rang. She had gotten out of bed and went to the door, but she found no one there. She did, however, see me with a friend walking down the street and had made the assumption that my friend and I had rung her bell and run off. She felt that I had done this on purpose, possibly as a prank. She continued that this disturbed her so, that she was going to call Rabbi Hyman Friedman to report my behavior, but she had hesitated to call him without first talking to Mrs. Goncher.

Much to her credit, Mrs Goncher asked me if I had done what Mrs. Hefler had accused me of and I honestly told her that I did not go to Mrs. Hefler's house or ring her doorbell and that I was very surprised at the phone call. Mrs. G. not only believed me, but she took up for me, something I had not been used to. Needless to say, I had very little desire to visit Mrs. Hefler again and made it a point to stay away from her house.

Asher had left Atlanta right after the *Sukkot* holidays, on October 10, 1944. Max Liberson had been wanting to sponsor Asher to go a *yeshiva* in New York for some time, but Asher had said that he was afraid to go without the consent of the Children's Service Bureau, for fear that the Bureau might "take it out on the remaining Hirsch children." The real issue had been that he would not have been able to move to New York without the Bureau's permission, because he was still classified as an enemy alien. Rabbi Hyman Friedman spoke to Mrs. Wyle at the Bureau on Asher's behalf and convinced them to give him permission to leave Atlanta.

When Asher arrived in New York City, he moved into the dormitory of Yeshiva University High School, with the intention attending school there toward getting his high school diploma. To his chagrin, Y.U.H.S. would not give him credit for the commercial courses, such as bookkeeping and typing that he had taken at Commercial High School in Atlanta. This was quite a setback to his plans, as it would put him one year behind in graduating high school. After trying unsuccessfully to get the registrar to make an exception, he suggested that Y.U. allow him to attend George Washington High School at night which would allow him to graduate with a General Diploma in one semester, while taking Yeshiva University's teacher training courses in the morning. From his response, it was apparent that the registrar totally misconstrued Asher's motivation to enroll in a school of higher Jewish learning.

Fully confident that Asher's reason for wanting attend Yeshiva University was to avoid being drafted in the army, the registrar remarked "Mr. Hirsch, you're seventy and a half years old now. In another two months, your case will come before the draft board. It will look mighty peculiar that in the morning you're studying to be a rabbi and in the evening you're studying to be an accountant." Asher took great offense to the registrar's insinuation and responded, "If you think for a moment that I came to Y.U. to dodge the draft, you have another think coming!" With that, he got up, slammed the door behind him and left Yeshiva University. He found a job stuffing toys for a toy manufacturing company, left the dormitory, boarded with the Katzenstein family in Washington Heights, and lived there until he was drafted in November. While waiting to be drafted, he visited the draft board several times to check on the status of his call up to duty and he attended *shiurrim*, classes, at Rabbi Breuer's congregation at night, to keep up with his Judaic studies.

Mrs. Goncher had a younger sister, Khaike Klein, who lived on Haygood Avenue near her grocery store. Khaike was a widow with a daughter a little older than Flo and a son, Aaron, who was around Jack's age. Haygood Avenue was just a few blocks south of Mrs. Goncher's house. I went there often on days we had no Hebrew school and occasionally even helped out a little in the store. Mostly, I would hang out with Aaron. Among the weird things Aaron involved me in was volunteering for a political candidate. I don't remember the year, but a man named Roy LeCraw was a candidate for mayor of Atlanta, running against the incumbent, William B. Hartsfield. I knew absolutely nothing about politics or either candidate, but Aaron had been actively stumping for LeCraw and he decided to enlist me to help. I took his word for it when he told me that Roy LeCraw was what Atlanta needed. I dutifully became his trusted assistant in distributing leaflets door to door and stuffing mailboxes. Our efforts were for naught; the race wasn't even close. Mundane and uneventful as it was, it was my introduction into the world of politics.

 The sad thing about our candidate not winning was that I would not be able to bring to the Mayor's attention the request that had been made to the city traffic department so many times before by the residents in the area of the intersection of Ormond and Crew Streets. Mrs. Goncher's house was at 22 Ormond Street, between Capitol Avenue and Crew Street. In the six months or so before the mayoral election, there had been an average of one accident every two weeks at the corner of Crew and Ormond and the neighbors were pleading for a traffic light at that corner before someone might get killed. The only ulterior motive I had in working with Aaron on LeCraw's mayoral campaign was the hope that, if our candidate won, we might be able make him aware of the need for a traffic light at that treacherous corner.

The fatal accident finally did happen only a few weeks later. I had been in the house when I heard the crash and went running to the corner, as I had done on so many times before. I was one of the first on the scene. It was grotesque. A man in his twenties had been driving an open top sports car at high speed south on Crew Street. He collided with a car on Ormond Street driven by a middle-aged woman who was thrown from her car by the force of the collision. The man was dead by the time I got there, with a huge hole on the top of his head. The woman was alive and pleading for help. One of the neighbors had already called for the police and ambulance. Instinctively, I knelt down to ask her if there was anything I could do to help her. She was so frightened and in pain. I sat down on the curb and put her head on my lap and listened as she started to tell me about her family. She needed someone to talk to and I felt fortunate to be able to be there to listen to her last words. She died with her head still on my lap a few minutes after the ambulance came. Though I didn't feel traumatized at the time, I had bad dreams for many months after that accident. I actually felt that I should have been inured at dealing with death by that time. Having someone die, albeit a stranger, with her head on my lap had been among the more traumatic experiences of my young life and no prior experiences could have blunted the effect it had on me.

A few months later, I had another learning experience on Ormond Street that was somewhat less traumatizing though it left its mark. Five of us were walking home from Shearith Israel Synagogue one Friday evening. We had just left Maishe Epstein and Murray Schatten at their homes on Washington Street and continued on to Ormond Street where Burton and Arthur Clein parted company with me as I turned onto Ormond by myself and they continued on Washington toward their house. I wasn't alone for much more than a minute when a man drove his car to the curb, stopped the car, leaned over to the open passenger side window and called me over as if to ask for directions. As I approached the window, he invited me to get in the car. I responded that I couldn't do that, not mentioning that it was my Sabbath, but offered to give him directions if he was lost. He then suggested that I allow him to do some perverted things to parts of my anatomy because, he claimed, he needed to do these things for me. I had heard about this type of behavior in dirty jokes, but I never thought that people actually did that sort of thing. The directness in his approach startled me and I stood there speechless for a few seconds, though the time span seemed much longer. My instincts told me to get away from him as quickly as I could. Not wanting to be rude, I blurted out "No thank you!" and took off like a bat out of hell.

I ran as fast as I could, all the way home, which happily was less than two blocks away. I didn't slow down until the front door slammed shut behind me. Alex saw me and wondered what had frightened me so. After I caught my breath, I recounted the incident to him. He burst out laughing and told me that I should have taken the pervert up on his offer. Abe Friend, the other border, had been listening to the exchange and scolded Alex for belittling the potential danger of the situation. It was a frightening experience, but at least I learned that there were men in this world who seek out boys for their own sexual pleasures, and that they were dangerous and should be avoided at all cost.

Khaike, as she preferred to be called, was a beautiful middle-aged woman. She worked very hard to serve her customers, most of whom were black, and all of whom were treated with courtesy and respect. I had been aware, at the time, that there were supposed to be differences between whites and blacks but whatever those differences were, beyond appearance, they did not register with me. I suppose I could not remain oblivious to the segregation of the races around me forever. I had been a naïve twelve-year-old boy when the day came that I was introduced, quite rudely, to some of the prevailing laws and customs that had been enacted in order to facilitate and maintain the separation of the races.

One of the reasons that I tended to gravitate to Khaike's store was that "Jellybean" worked there. Jellybean was a black man, tall and husky, jovial and very friendly. He helped out in Khaike's store, making deliveries and doing any chores that needed to be done. I don't know exactly what drew me to him. He seemed interested in whatever I was talking about, and he was fun being with, even when there was nothing to say. One day, I boarded a trolley on Capitol Avenue to go the Jewish Educational Alliance. I looked up after paying my nickel fare, and saw Jellybean sitting in the back of the streetcar. While there were several empty seats, I noticed that the one next to Jellybean was free. I rushed to the back to make sure that no one else would take the seat first and sat down next to my friend. I was just in the process of telling him how happy I was to see him when all hell broke loose.

I truly had no idea that I had done anything wrong. I had noticed that black people sit toward the back of streetcars and buses, but I did not know that a white person could not exercise his option to sit in the back with a black person. Since I was a young boy and Jellybean was so large, they accused him of taking advantage of me and kicked him off the trolley along with threats of having him arrested. I wanted to get off too, but someone grabbed me and forcefully insisted that I stay on. I was totally unnerved at the unfairness of the situation, not to mention the discrimination. I was the one who sat down next to Jellybean. Why was he the one who was being punished? I didn't get any playing in when I arrived at the Alliance, because I was so full of guilt.

I saw Jellybean a few weeks later and I apologized profusely. It turned out that he was arrested and charged with child molestation, but Khaike had come to his defense and he was let out of jail after a couple of days. He didn't blame me, saying that he should have told me not to sit down. I cried when I found out that he had to spend time in jail. He tried to comfort me by telling me that he was used to "special treatment." I had been in this country for over three years, but it took this incident to make me realize that the unwritten laws of segregation were for real and that there were definite limits to freedom in my new country.

In the newsreels, we saw American soldiers entering the Ohrdruf slave labor camp, near Gotha, Germany, on April 4, 1945. It was the first liberated by the Western Allies, although Soviet troops had already liberated several camps, on the Eastern Front, including the Auschwitz death camp which was liberated on January 27, 1945. Even though Ohrdrof was not designated as a killing center, the American soldiers found mass graves containing thousands of corpses.

Everyone speculated that the war was coming closer to an end. By April 15, the British had liberated Bergen-Belsen, where Ann Frank had died just a few days before and where they discovered tens of thousands of unburied bodies abandoned by the fleeing Germans. By that time, the entire world could see the evidence of atrocities that hallmarked the absence in humanity of the Third Reich.

On V-E Day, May 8, 1945, the day of victory in Europe, men and women danced in the streets of American cities to celebrate the Allied Forces' victory over Nazi Germany. I found it hard to celebrate. The newsreels I had seen of the camps being liberated left me with anger and despair. Had I been watching the fate of my family? We still held on to hopes that they somehow survived and would be reunited with us as soon as the smoke would clear. But even if that were so, the incontrovertible evidence of Nazi Germany's genocidal assault on my people left me with little to celebrate about.

I had been studying for my *Bar Mitzvah* when I heard of the victory in Europe. My graduation into manhood was a little over four months away. Hopefully that would be enough time to prepare me for my part in the big event, and the passage of time would allow me to feel like celebrating. I had started studying for my *Bar Mitzvah* with Rabbi Friedman before school let out for the summer. Selecting a Saturday for my *Bar Mitzvah*, which, among other reasons, had to be done to define which *Haftorah* portion I needed to study, was not cut and dry. There were three of us who had been born four days apart, and I was in the middle. I don't know how he figured it out, but Rabbi Friedman scheduled my *Bar Mitzvah* for *Shabbat Shuva*, which was a good two weeks after my Hebrew birthday and is the Sabbath between *Rosh Hashanah* (the New Year), and *Yom Kippur* (the Day of Atonement). Since I had experience at leading the *Mussaf*, the additional service after the *Torah* reading, in Junior Congregation, for my *Bar Mitzvah* the Rabbi suggested that I take on that responsibility at the adult service along with reciting the *Haftorah* and a short speech that Rabbi Friedman had written for me.

Asher was unable to attend my *Bar Mitzvah*. He was to be drafted in the U. S. Army at any moment, but Flo, Sarah and Jack were there to cheer their little brother on. The congregation had been invited to a *Kiddush*, light refreshments, after the services, and it wasn't until I had thanked Mrs. Goncher for having provided the *Kiddush* that I found out that Flo had arranged and paid for all the refreshments. In spite of all of my shenanigans, Mrs. Goncher let it be known that she was very proud of me.

Flo not only paid for the *Kiddush* reception following the services at my Bar Mitzvah, she, along with Sarah and Jack also gave me a basketball. Basketballs were expensive, especially an indoor type, such as this one. At first I was a little disappointed since most of my playing was outdoors and some of the guys made fun of the ball since it was not as sturdy as an outdoor ball. Then I realized how lucky I was to have my own ball. I carried it with me to Hebrew school and played on the half court behind the synagogue. My right wrist was in a cast from a fall shortly after my *Bar Mitzvah*, but that didn't stop me from making full use of my pride and joy. I taught myself to shoot left handed and actually developed a good left handed hook shot. I had the ball less than two months when a couple of us were playing catch on the sidewalk on our way home from Hebrew school and somebody missed a pass. The ball rolled into traffic on Washington Street. Car after car swerved to miss my ball and just as I had run to get it, a car came speeding, from out of nowhere and ran over it without ever stopping. I was devastated at loosing the present that my sister paid so much of her hard-earned money for and I chose not to tell Flo, partly because I didn't want her to spend the money for another one and partly because I felt guilty and embarrassed. I did not say a word to her about it until she asked about the ball a year later.

After my Bar Mitzvah, I was approached by a man whom I later found out was Max Lieberson, the same man who helped finance Asher's *yeshiva* schooling in New York. He told me that he had been so impressed by the way I had led the service that he thought I should go to New York and study to be a cantor. He offered to pay my way and see to my room and board as well. It didn't take long for me to respond to the offer. I told him that while I was gratified and very flattered by his offer, I did not want to move again. I explained that I had been on the move virtually all of my life and since I had finally begun establishing some roots, I did not want to pick up and move again. For years, I had thought that he made the offer because he was enthralled with my voice. I found out later that Asher and Dr. Möller had been making behind the scenes efforts to get me to move to New York, for fear that if I stayed in Atlanta, I might lose all of the religious training I had received from my parents.

The Bureau gave me a 14-carat gold ring for my *Bar Mitzvah* and I was cautioned to take special care of it. I was very proud of the ring, which had my initials etched on it, and didn't hesitate to show it off in school. One afternoon, several of us who had been doing extra-curricular work after school were hanging around in the hall. Among the group were Frances Tiller, the prettiest girl in our class, and her friend Betty Meadows, an attractive girl who had tried to make me feel that she had a crush on me. I liked her, but flirting in school was about as much as I could imagine. Betty noticed my new ring and, after fawning over it, asked to try it on. Reluctantly, I took the ring off and, before I handed it to her, I expressed my trepidation by explaining where the ring had come from and why I would have to get it right back. She put it on her wedding ring finger, 'oohed' and 'aahed' and informed me that we were engaged. If she had said that to fluster me, it had worked, in spades. Maybe I should have been flattered, but I was so concerned about what would happen to me if I came home without the ring, that I couldn't enjoy the moment.

I pleaded with her to give me back the ring. I told her that it had nothing to do with how I felt about her, and reiterated that I would be in big trouble if I came home without the gold ring. She started crying and ran into the girl's bathroom. I knocked on the door pleading with her to come out, while Frances was cracking up. I waited for Thirty minutes and she still wouldn't come out. Frances was my only hope and I begged her to reason with Betty. It took another Twenty minutes, but I finally had the ring back. After that short engagement, Betty and I were never that close again.

Concentrating on schoolwork in eighth grade was becoming a challenge. It wasn't that I had just become aware of girls overnight. Probably like most teenagers, I found girls to fantasize about and even engaged in flirtatious repartee. I wasn't quite prepared for girls being aggressive and I found myself unable to walk away from advances, even when they could have been considered inappropriate, partly for fear of hurting the girl's feelings and partly because I was curious as to where the banter could lead. Jean and Ann were a couple of good looking girls who were considered physically mature for their age. They made teasing an art form and always, so it appeared to me, as a twosome. At the end of the day, it was all strictly in fun, although often at the expense of some poor schnook who took them seriously.

A new girl came into Ms. Hertzka's history class a few weeks after the semester had started. For whatever reason, she decided to latch herself on to me. She was not particularly pretty, but she was persistent, and she made no bones about wanting to release me from my virginity. I was both intrigued and scared. Fortunately for me, Ms Hertzka pulled me aside after she had noticed the interaction and asked that I stay after class and have a talk with her. She warned me against getting involved sexually with any girl, but specifically told me to stay away from that girl. To make her point, she informed me that the reason that the girl had come to school after the start of the semester was that she just had a baby. Ms. Hertzka had been aware of how strong this girl was coming on to me and said that she overheard the girl talking to her friends and saying she was looking for a vulnerable Jewish boy to help support her and the child. How misled could this girl have been? I had no wealthy parents and I was only getting twenty-five cents a week allowance. When Ms. Hertzka first started this conversation, I resented her for putting her nose into my private life. That resentment was short lived. I was grateful to her and relieved to be out from under the pressure this girl had been putting on me, and I am still ever grateful to her for saving me from messing up my life. It became evident in ensuing weeks that this girl was pregnant again, and might well have been when she was pursuing me.

It had been many months since Dr. Marvin Goldstein had put braces on my upper teeth and I hated them with a passion. I was so happy when he decided to take them off, although my two front teeth were not yet straight. He gave me removable braces. The instructions were not to wear them during sports activities, to definitely wear them in bed at night and, of course, not to lose them. I was in the eighth grade and conscious of my appearance, so they stayed in my pocket at social times such as recess.

The fact that I had worn braces never stood in the way of whoever wanted to pick fights with me, and they also didn't seem to care that I no longer sported railroad tracks on my teeth. I survived a few tussles at recess with my new braces sagely ensconced in my pocket. Then one recess as I was going into the yard, I was attacked from behind by Latrell, a classmate who couldn't get enough of fighting with me. Anticipating a light tussle, I quickly put my braces in my shirt pocket and proceeded to defend myself. It turned out to be one of the most vigorous fights of the year with plenty of onlookers until a teacher broke it up. I asked for permission to look for my braces before reporting to the principal, and was denied that opportunity. After school, I returned to the scene of the fight and my braces were nowhere to be found. I didn't know what to do. I was afraid to go back to Dr. Goldstein for fear that he would put permanent braces back in my mouth and I didn't want to tell Mrs. Goncher, fearing that she would make me go back to the dentist. To avoid the issue, I didn't go to the dentist for two years and suffered the consequences. When I finally went to the dentist, I had twenty-one cavities.

The challenges to fight at school were coming less frequently and I felt I was beginning to see a light at the end of the tunnel, that is, I hoped that soon I would be known as a student without the reputation of always fighting. Then one afternoon, as I was walking home from Shearith Israel Hebrew School with Stanford Firestone and Jack Rosenberg, three boys who were active at the Atlanta Boys' Club on Pryor Street stopped us before we reached Georgia Avenue. They were Grady and Billy Walker and Joe Johnson, who were all ranked Golden Gloves' boxers in their respective weights. Joe was the younger brother of Hildegard Johnson, one of the most popular ladies in the neighborhood. I had known Joe from school and he had been quite friendly in the past, so I didn't feel threatened before he had started to speak. I couldn't believe what I was hearing from him. He told Stan and Jack to step aside unless they wanted what was in store for me. They were only interested in me, the "Jew-foreigner." I wondered what that was all about. After all, the war in Europe was over———. I didn't have time to give it a lot of thought; I had to prepare to defend myself

Joe put up his fists and started jabbing at me. He was no bigger than I and he was wiry to the point of being skinny. I knew he was an experienced boxer at the Club, but I had hopes that I would be able to hold my own. I had forgotten the lesson that I had learned about confronting gangs and I proceeded to duke it out with Joe. Under normal circumstances, the fight might have been called a draw, but the Walker boys, not happy with the way the fight was going, decided that Joe needed their help. The result was not pretty. I had been beaten to a pulp by the time they decided to leave us. Not too many words passed on the way home. Jack turned off at Georgia Avenue and Stan accompanied me to Washington Terrace, where he turned off. Mercifully, I walked the rest of the way home alone, trying to piece together what had just transpired. By the time I arrived, I had composed myself, wiped the tears and straightened my clothes, as much as possible. I decided against telling Mrs. Goncher, but I did confide in Alex who, in his contrary way, offered that I must have brought it on myself.

The threesome of Grady, Billy, and Joe had become my regular tormentors. We had Hebrew School three days a week and they would show up on any given day at an average of once a week. With two exceptions, each time they had been able to convince whomever was walking with me to step aside while they offered their punishment for the double crime of being a Jew and a foreigner. As for me, I had learned my lesson well and refused to fight back. At each confrontation, I remained standing as the fists flew and occasionally asked, "Are you done yet?" The hardest thing for me was to keep from crying, but I preferred enduring the pain without allowing them to see me cry.

One of the two exceptions was when a group of at least six of us had been walking toward Shearith Israel Hebrew School and were approached by the unholy trio less than a block away from our destination. As usual, they told everyone else to step aside while they performed their ritual on me. Bobby Tuck had never encountered these three bullies before and he refused to step aside. He challenged the biggest of the three and went toe to toe with him until Grady decided to call it quits. The other two wouldn't dare jump in, seeing that numbers were not in their favor. A few months later, Paul Muldawer was in the same situation and he gave Billy Walker more than he could handle. In spite of those two encounters, the three musketeers continued to seek me out and try to change my facial features.

I don't remember how long these encounters went on, but it seemed to have been for well over a year. Eventually, I decided to randomly change my route home in an attempt to avoid them. I found that by walking on Crew Street, one block east of Washington Street, if I could get past Georgia Avenue and would virtually be home free. Then one day, as I crossed Georgia Avenue at Crew Street, they were waiting for me on an empty lot across from the Empire Theater, along with several other goons. I thought that day would never end. They all had to get their licks in and they so wanted me to either fight back or cry. I didn't give them the satisfaction of doing either. I stood there for a long time after they left, writhing in pain and too angry to cry. I finally pulled myself together and walked home, sobbing all the way. When I arrived home, Mrs. Goncher was talking to my caseworker. He took one look at me and wanted to know, "What the hell happened to you?" This time, I decided not to hold back. I described what had been going on in detail and I gave him names. I was too angry to worry about the consequences of ratting on these goons, and I figured there was nothing more that they could do to me anyway. As it turned out, Grady, Billy, and Joe were sent to reform school for three years. I figured that I would be in major trouble after they were released but, much to my surprise, when I finally saw them again years later, they acted as if we had been the best of friends. Go figure?

Most of my would-be assailants at Hoke Smith either approached me in the halls or at recess. One interesting exception took place as a result of my coming late to P. E. class. Mr. Cook was the P.E. teacher and he seemed to have no love for me. He also had no tolerance for students who came late and he would never listen to any excuse for tardiness. He had the entire class standing in formation as I ran in several minutes late, having been held up in the hall by the faculty advisor to the school newspaper. He stopped me in my tracks and told the class to get a good look at the Jewish kid who was responsible for his, yet to be announced, collective punishment for the whole class. The class's schedule had called for volleyball that period, but due to my tardiness, the class would have to run wind sprints until ten minutes before the hour. At that time, he would leave the class alone and said that anyone who felt he had a grievance against me could handle it in any fashion he saw fit.

It was an open invitation to mass mayhem. Fortunately, only one boy felt the obligation to come and hit me. It was almost like he felt duty bound to do so. He hit me in the face and I didn't bother to hit him back; after all, I did cause the whole class to do wind sprints. He looked as if wanted to hit me again, but I just looked at him. He wasn't one of the "tough guys" who aspired to rankings in the pecking order. I knew him to be a decent boy and didn't want to fight with him. After giving me his one best shot, he turned around and walked away.

Ever since I moved back to the South Side, Rabbi Hyman Friedman had been my mentor, except in Hebrew school, where I was just another student finding it hard to be serious after a full day at public school. While waiting for Hebrew school to start, we used to play a game that was sort of a cross between handball and tennis. Joe Arnold gave it the name of '*Shtup* Ball.' Other than Joe, none of us understood *Yiddish* and we innocently accepted his name for the game. I had an inkling that the name was not appropriate when Rabbi Friedman came out one afternoon and asked what game we were playing. His face turned red when we told him it was '*Shtup* Ball' and he threatened to punish us all until he realized that we had no idea that the word, which literally means 'push', was commonly used to mean 'fornicate' in *Yiddish* slang. Joe was cracking up during the whole scene. He was lucky to not be expelled for his part in the naming of the game.

There was a basketball backboard and hoop at one end of Shearith Israel Hebrew School's back yard, but after my ball had been run over, there was seldom a basketball with which to play. It was easier to improvise with football, so until dusk or as long as one could see the ball, we played that game a lot after Hebrew school. Actually, no one had a football either, but we improvised by using a handkerchief stuffed with gravel, grass and straw and tied in a bundle. Missing a pass was not an option for a player who did not want to chance facial injury or losing a couple of teeth. The players who wanted to be pass receivers had to become very proficient at catching and holding on to the ball, while those with butterfingers became the linemen protecting the passer. The few times that someone brought a football, it inevitably ended up in the yard of the woman next door. This woman appeared to be older than God and seemed to relish making us plead to get the ball back. These exchanges with the elderly neighbor took up much available daylight and influenced many of us to opt for stuffed handkerchiefs over actual footballs.

Everyone has funny stories about Hebrew school. One of my favorites has to do with the time we had been translating a sentence from the *Torah* portion of the week and had just come to the words that translated as "sweet smelling stones." Just as those words were uttered and translated by Rabbi Friedman, Leon Tuck emitted some flatulence. Without missing a beat, Leon turned around, pointed his finger at me and disapprovingly yelled "Hirsch!" The Rabbi took the cue and kicked me out of class. At first, I felt violated for once more being punished for something I did not do. Then I started laughing out loud. The Rabbi heard me, opened the door and asked me what was so funny. "I'm being punished," I answered, "but I'm in the fresh air while all of you are stuck in the classroom with that putrid smell." While he appeared to see the irony in the situation, he did not realize that Leon had pulled a fast one. He started to wonder, however, when I declined his invitation to come back into the smelly classroom.

For Passover of 1946, I moved temporarily in with Rabbi and Mrs. Friedman while Mrs. Goncher went to visit her daughter Lottie's family in Pennsylvania. That was about the same time that my sister Sarah started writing to Dr. Hermann Hirsch, a dentist in Berlin, hoping that he might have been our father. Mrs. Copelan of the Bureau had written to him in February through the chairman of the Atlanta Section Council of Jewish Women, Service to Foreign Born, after learning from the National Council of Jewish Women that his name was included on the list of five hundred sixty Jews found in Berlin. Mrs. Copelan had yet to receive a reply. Passover is the holiday of deliverance and liberation. With the war in Europe over, my siblings and I were getting anxious about our parents and younger siblings. Flora and Sarah had been making inquiries through every agency they could find, and Asher, who had been serving in the U.S. Army in Germany, was not going to rest until he located our family.

We had no idea what was going on in the D.P. (Displaced Persons) Camps. Until the D.P. Camps were finally emptied in 1957, nearly 250,000 displaced Jews who had nowhere to go, had gone through these camps that didn't physically vary much from the concentration camps in which the Nazis had imprisoned them. The D.P. Camps were, however, where forlorn Jews tried to find each other, their families and their friends. Somehow, they managed to develop an intelligence network that spread from camp to camp, to help each other to find surviving loved ones or, as in too many cases, information about those who did not survive. There were many successful reunions and just as many disappointments. As a G.I., Asher tried his luck at the D.P. Camps in his area with no success. He did manage to convince his commanding officer that it was just as important to make collections for supplies for the Jews in the D.P. Camps as it was for Christmas gifts for the German citizens of the town near the base.

Flora had heard from Asher that our parents, according to reports of a refugee organization, had been found at Thereisenstadt, a concentration camp near the German-Czechoslovakian border. She informed the director of the Bureau of this and told Mr. Cohen that the information had been given to Asher by the Joint Distribution Committee. Mr. Cohen strongly suggested to Flo that she should not build up any hopes based on this information and cautioned her not to excite Sarah, Jack or me until, and if, the information was verified. In August, Mrs. Copelan received a response from Dr. Hirsch in Berlin, dated July 16, 1946:

> Best thank for your letter from February 25,'46, which arrived me before some days. I will answer your questions, though I must say, that you will not find in myself, or in my wife, those you are asking for. I was born in 1897 in Plau (Mecklenburg), my wife was also born in Plau, in June 16, 1906. My date of Native was February 24. We have been married in 1927. I, myself, am dentist (Sahnarzt). As we have no children, I am sorry of the poor children you have in your care.
>
> Some months before, the same questions we had to answer at the "American Joint Distribution" in Berlin—Zehlendorf, Kronprinzenallee, 247 and I think it will be the same purpose.
> Best Regards, yours
>
> Dr. Hermann Hirsch,
> Kathe Hirsch, born Wagner.

On September 30, 1946, Mrs Copelan had written a letter to another Dr. Herman Hirsch, this one at Schaidswalstrasse #4, Frankfurt am Main, Germany, making the same inquiries about him and his wife and telling him about the Hirsch children in her care. I found no record of a response. All of this correspondence had been going on while I had no knowledge that efforts were being made to find my family. The idea must have been to spare me and probably Jack from the anxiety of waiting for responses. In retrospect, while I can't speak for Jack, it didn't shield me from the anxiety of wondering when we would hear any news about the whereabouts of our family.

In the meantime, there were enough diversionary summer activities to keep me from obsessing about the unknown. I finally signed up to take a summer course at the High Museum of Art. It meant not going to Camp Daniel Morgan, as I had done for at least one session for the past three summers, but this was something that my case worker and Mrs. Goncher had been pushing for a long time. The chance to take lessons at an art school without having to attend on Saturdays was an opportunity that I was not about to pass up. The class consisted of boys and girls my age or younger, all of whom had attended classes at the High before. Even though I was the only newcomer, the other students helped keeping me from feeling out of place. The first day, the teacher had us experimenting with different media. I had drawn with charcoal and pastels before in Ms. Beacom's class, but I had never been introduced to drawing with conte crayon, sort of a cross between the two, but more fun than either of them and not nearly as easy to smudge. I enjoyed the class and was friendly with several of my fellow students, though somehow in the spite of everyone's efforts, I felt out of place. I felt as if I was a kid from a needy part of town attending an art school for high society children. While this was the case, I could not put my finger on why I felt that way since none of the budding artists could have been accused of putting on airs. It may have been my own self-consciousness about being out of my element.

 Our final project was to make a clay object and the subject matter was of our own choosing. I chose to sculpt a large dog lying down. I had seen a photograph in *Life* magazine of such a dog in repose and remembered how graceful its lines had been. Our teacher chose to not grade our work. For the final project, she announced that all of our work would be put on display and the students would judge each other's work by voting for the best three pieces, in order of preference. The winner, she continued, would be awarded a certificate and receive a five dollar prize. The students decided that the vote should be by secret ballot. From the scuttlebutt that I couldn't avoid hearing, my piece had been in contention along with the piece of the undisputed best student in the class. I liked his piece, but I truly thought mine was better. I was torn. The feeling I had gotten from some of the students was that it was not gentlemanly to vote for your own work, even if you think it is best. I finally reasoned that I should vote for the best work, regardless of who created it. I won and my closest competition said he voted for mine because he thought it was best. It was a bittersweet win. Justifiably or not, I had pangs of guilt for voting for myself.

I was ready for school to start again. There's something about fall being in the air that promotes the excitement of a fresh start. Mrs. Goncher told me that Rabbi Tobias Geffen's wife was going out of town for a couple of days and that I would be staying with the chief rabbi of Congregation Shearith Israel so he would not be alone in his house. I was under the impression that I had been asked to stay with the elderly rabbi to keep him company and take care of him. Later, Asher explained to me that there is a *halacha* (Jewish Law) which states that a righteous man is not allowed to be alone in his home at night, lest he be tempted by the evil inclinations that are in all of us. Not that I had a choice, but I was glad to get to know Rabbi Geffen better. His sermons at the synagogue's *Shabbat* morning services had always been in *Yiddish*, as were his daily *Talmud* classes, so I was surprised to find that he was quite fluent in English. He had a long, bushy white beard not unlike Santa Claus. He had been brought to Atlanta from Lithuania in the 1920s to become the rabbi of Congregation Shearith Israel, where he had been revered by his congregants and respected by the entire Jewish community. All of the Geffen children had long since been grown and out of the house on Washington Street across from Siegel's Meat Market & Delicatessen. This formidable man, whom I had thought I would be catering to, turned out to be a gentle and kind man who catered to my every need. He had even made my school lunches and they were so good that I looked forward to the next time his wife left town.

Between staying with Rabbi Geffen whenever his wife was out of town, staying at Rabbi Friedman's when Mrs.Goncher was out of town and baby sitting for the Friedmans' children, Shaina Esther and Lippa, one could have thought that more of their religiosity might have rubbed off on me. As it turned out, I seemed to have been more influenced by my peers than by my rabbis and teachers.

Rabbi Friedman received a telephone call from my brother Asher, while he was still serving in the U. S. Army and stationed near Frankfurt am Main, Germany. At Asher's request, he had called my other siblings and me to come to a meeting at his house on Sunday, December 1, 1946, at 3:30 P.M. I think we had all figured that the meeting would be about our parents, and that it most probably would be what we had been dreading to hear. Everyone was punctual. I came early and sat very quietly and nervously while waiting for the meeting to start. Rabbi Friedman did not mince words. He told us of Asher's telephone call. Mom, Dad, Werner and Roselene had been murdered by the Nazis. According to what Asher told him, Dad was killed on November 5, 1942 in Oranienburg, outside of Berlin, while Mom, with Werner and Roselene, had been seen going to the "showers" in Auschwitz, some time in the fall of 1943. After offering each of us condolences, Rabbi Friedman suggested that some form of *Shiva*, the seven day mourning period, would be appropriate, if for no other reason than to create closure to the years of living in the limbo that had been our experience. As it was, my closure did not come until 1995, when I visited Auschwitz-Birkenau forty years later.

Many years later, Asher told me of the worst day of his life, the day that he finally confirmed the fate of our family. Asher had been drafted on November 28, 1945 into the U.S. Army. After serving for six months, he was given the opportunity to re-enlist for thirteen months, which would consist of one month of leave time and twelve months of service. He had wondered how he could get leave to celebrate the *Shavuot* (Pentecost) holiday and saw this re-enlistment opportunity as the answer to his dilemma.. Shortly after reporting back from his leave, Asher was shipped overseas and in September 1946 he arrived in Germany, two weeks before *Rosh Hashona*, the Jewish New Year. Probably because he was fluent in German, he was stationed at the U.S. Army Intelligence Base at Oberursel near Bad Hamburg. He was there only a few days when he got his first pass to leave the base and he seized the opportunity to go to Frankfurt am Main to see if he could find our house at 30 Grünestrasse and, hopefully, find some information as to the whereabouts of our family.

Somehow he knew which *strassenbahn* (streetcar) to board to get him to Grünestrasse, our street. There he saw, in what had once been a long block of row houses, only one house left standing—and that was number 30, the house in which we had last lived in Germany. His adrenaline was flowing as he rang the bell. A tenant came to the door and before he could say a word, Asher asked him, in German, "To whom does this house belong?"

The tenant responded, "Dr. Hirsch."

Asher then asked, "What happened to Dr. Hirsch?"

The woman indignantly responded, "Why should I tell you that?"

At this point, Asher could hardly control his anger as he responded, "First of all, I'm an American soldier! Second, I am Dr. Hirsch's son and I deserve to know what happened to my father."

The tenant decided to be cooperative and offered: "A telegram came from the German Government to Mrs Hirsch after she had been deported, stating that Dr. Hirsch died of natural causes, November 5, 1942, in Oranienburg."

Asher took a moment to compose himself after hearing that devastating bit of news before asking, "To whom do you pay rent?"

"The government appointed a landlord to collect rent," she replied, giving Asher a name and telephone number. He immediately called the landlord who, in response to Asher's questioning, said he had heard that Mrs. Hirsch lived in Bad Hamburg.

Totally drained, Asher went back to his base and related his experiences of the day to his barracks sergeant, who sent him to a social worker, a German who had been assigned to the base. The social worker went with Asher to Bad Hamburg to help him find our mother. They first went to the synagogue and then to the Jewish old age home. They then went to the hospital to check the records and finally tried the continuous care institution. He knew he had to go on, but this was tearing his insides out.

He called the landlord back and screamed at him, "What kind of a man are you!? You hear that the owner's wife lives in Bad Hamburg and you don't bother to look her up!? It's a good thing that a telephone separates us! Do me a favor. If you ever see me on the street, walk away before I see you, because I don't want to spend the rest of my life paying for killing you."

Later that day, on the 28th of *Cheshvan*, November 22, 1946, Asher called Uncle Philipp Auerbach, who was then in the British Zone of Germany, as State Commissioner for the Rights of those Persecuted on account of Race, Politics and Religion. Uncle Philipp told Asher that while he was an inmate working as a chemist in Auschwitz, someone (possibly a secretary) had shown him the list of the latest transport that had arrived and was scheduled to be gassed and cremated. The list included a Mathilda Hirsch, nèe Auerbach, along with Werner S. Hirsch and Roselene Hirsch. All of the dates and places of birth were the same as those of our relatives. Recognizing the names as those his sister, her son and daughter, he ran out of the building where he worked, toward the barbed wire fence that separated it from the rest of the camp. He went as far as he could, without trying to scale an electrified fence, and saw them in the distance, preparing to enter the "showers", that was, in fact, a gas chamber. He looked at the crowd of naked souls, each awaiting their turn to be deloused as they had been told, in the infamous "showers." Although they were far away, he recognized his sister, niece and nephew among the crowd and stood there until he saw them enter to their demise, without being able to do anything but bear witness. In what was supposed to have been some consolation, he told Asher that he was confident that none of those unfortunate souls had any idea that what awaited them was Zyklone-B gas instead of water.

Uncle Philipp was a chemist before the war and had used his talents and experience to stay alive in Auschwitz. By his own words, he had been one of several who made soap from human remains while in Auchwitz and later, at the behest of his captors, in Buchenwald. I found it strange that Uncle Philipp could not remember the date or even the month when he had seen his sister and her children walk into the "showers" to their death. After poring through much testimony from camp survivors, I became aware that simple things, such as knowing what day or month it was, were not relevant in places like Auschwitz. He had only been sure that it was the autumn of 1943.

Although I had little memory of my parents and even found it difficult to remember how they felt or what they looked like, I was deeply affected by Asher's report. I think, after all this time, we had all half-way anticipated the worst, yet I was crushed at the news confirming our parents' demise and beyond consolation that my brother and sister had been included in their fate. Truth be known, in spite of Uncle Philipp's detailed testimony, I really could not accept that Werner and Roselene had been killed. I believed without reservation, the reports of the murder of my father and mother. I just could not accept the reality that those two adorable children, who were twenty-one months and nine months old when I saw them last, had also been systematically killed. For many year, in the back of my mind, I harbored the hope that someday I would go to Europe, find Werner and Roselene and bring them back with me.

While the laws of *Shiva*, the week of mourning for a departed loved one, did not officially apply in our situation, Rabbi Friedman told me to refrain from frivolous activity for a week. He also instructed me to attend daily prayer services at the synagogue for thirty days and recite the *Kaddish*, the praise of God for the merit of the deceased that is traditionally recited by a mourner. One afternoon toward the end of the *Shloshim*, the thirty days mourning period, I was delayed and arrived at the synagogue after the evening services had been completed. I felt so guilty that I ran home and confessed to Mrs. Goncher, who scolded me for disrespecting the memory of my parents and sent me straight to bed. Alex Zomper came into my room and asked why I was lying on my bed crying. When I explained, he burst out laughing and said I was ridiculous to put so much emphasis on prayer and reciting the *Kaddish*. I had been able to laugh off his cynicism in the past, but this time he really hurt me.

Among my other activities, I joined Boy Scout Troop No. 27 at the Alliance. Sidney Kaplan was our first scout master and later Josiah Benator took over in perpetuity. I had tried to keep as busy as possible so as not to think about my parents' and siblings' fate. Being a ninth grader in junior high was, in essence, being a senior. I was enjoying working on the school newspaper. I had been doing artwork for *The Vanguard* since seventh grade, and I was finally given the opportunity to do some writing. Our sports editor had resigned and when I was asked, I gladly took over. The timing couldn't have been better. As sports editor, I was invited to go to a high school journalism conference in Athens at the University of Georgia campus. I had never been to Athens, but had heard a great deal about it, and especially about Effie's, probably the state's most well-known bordello. One of my friends, who was also going to the conference, suggested that we sneak away and go see what Effie's was all about. I mentioned the conversation to Alex, who insisted that I would not be a man if I did not go. It had never dawned on me to reply that I was only fourteen and a half and not yet a man.

My friend and I sneaked out between sessions of the conference and hailed a taxi, figuring that any cab in Athens would know where Effie's was. I got in the cab first and all of a sudden my friend decided to change his mind. He turned to go back to campus and I was stuck with a taxi driver who expected to get paid whether or not I went. It ceased being a moral dilemma and turned into a financial one. Since I had to pay for the cab anyway, I decided to go and see what the place looked like and take it from there. It seemed no more than three to four blocks from where we had hailed the cab. Effie's was a simple wooden house with a porch. Two fairly attractive, buxom ladies were sitting on the porch and invited me to come in. The moment of truth had come. Did I really want to go through with this? As I was weighing the pros and cons in my mind, the ladies were getting more and more persuasive. It must have been a slow day for them. The rite of passage was not what it was cracked up to be. Though I was much too nervous to complete the task, I still had to pay. Somewhat confused about how I felt about what had just happened, I got back to the campus in time for the last session, and no one except for my friend was the wiser. I only missed one session and he had taken copious notes for me, out of guilt for abandoning me with the cab driver. He also wanted details, which I declined to offer.

One spring afternoon, I stayed late for a meeting of *The Vanguard* staff. I missed Hebrew School and was walking home along Georgia Avenue approaching the intersection of Capitol Avenue when I noticed that Jimmy Bloodworth, whom I had known since my arrival in Atlanta, was waving at me to come where he was standing, catty-corner from where I stood. I had not seen him in a while, but I remembered how interested his family had been in me and the plight of the Jewish people in Europe after I first entered James L. Key elementary school.

I waited for the traffic light to change and went over to see what Jimmy wanted. As I approached him, he pulled out a switchblade, grabbed me by the ear and told me to do as he said or he was going to cut off my ear. I had not seen him for a while and I never saw him so visibly distraught. I was completely caught off guard and was scared to death. He was ranting and raving about how my people killed his Lord and, the more I tried to reason with him, the more agitated he seemed to get. After a few minutes that seemed like hours, he decided to start walking down Capitol Avenue with me, all the while holding the switchblade to my ear. He insisted that I say nothing. I was really afraid he might kill me and kept my silence, while crying to myself and shivering. He pulled me along for a full block as we passed Bass Street and he threatened that at Love Street, the next corner, he would cut off my ear. My heart was racing as we reached the corner of Love Street and Capitol Avenue. He stopped momentarily, saw me trembling while the blade was touching my head by the ear, and blurted out that he would wait one more block, at the corner of Little Street, to exact my punishment. That may have been the longest half-hour of my life. By the time we reached Little Street, he lowered the blade and said I should go quickly before he changed his mind. I ran the block and a half home, and sat on my bed shivering for a long time. In retrospect, I wonder what made him change his mind. At the time, all I could think of was to thank God that he did. I didn't see Jimmy again for many years. The last time I saw him, he was a bible-thumping preacher at a little park one block south of Five Points. I saw him there often, when I used to work at Beck's Shoes not far from the park, but I doubt if he remembered me. He was so wrapped up in his preaching and focused on converting the world to Jesus Christ that he never noticed I was trying to make eye contact with him.

By the end of the semester, it was announced that we would not be graduating Hoke Smith Jr. High. We had been asked earlier to select between the available City of Atlanta high schools, Boys' High, Girls' High, Tech High, or Commercial High Schools. Without a lot of notice, all of that changed. The Board of Education had made the decision that seventh through ninth grades junior high schools and tenth through twelfth grades high schools would be done away with and changed to eighth to twelfth grades high schools, while seventh grade would be added to elementary schools. All we had been told was that we would be going straight into Hoke Smith High for the tenth grade. No other details as to the disposition of the various existing schools would available until later in the summer. At least confirmation from Sunday School had not been changed. According to tradition of the community, bible school confirmation was held on *Shavuoth*, the Pentecost holiday, which was on June 1 that year. None of us who graduated were sad to have this part of our Jewish education over with.

That summer, I decided not to go back to the High Museum for art classes. I wanted to just hang around and go to the Progressive Club swimming pool as often as possible for swimming and gin rummy. But, my caseworker had other ideas. She scheduled me for Camp Daniel Morgan starting the first week in July. In the interim, swimming at the Progressive Club was limited to no more than three times a week. Mrs. Goncher was going to visit her daughter for the whole month of August so plans were made for me to move in with the Tuck family for a couple of weeks after I came back from camp.

Asher came back to New York in June in preparation for his discharge from the U.S. Army. Apparently, he and Dr. Möller had never given up trying to get Jack and me to move to New York. He called Rabbi Friedman and asked him to talk to both of us about moving to New York to live among a newly-settled group of refugees from Frankfurt am Main in the Washington Heights area of Manhattan. Rabbi Friedman's task had been to get our reactions to this idea and to call Asher back with our response. Jack and I responded separately, but our answers were virtually the same. We were both happy with our lives in Atlanta and neither of us wanted to move to New York or any place else. Asher did not ask the rabbi to talk to Flora and Sarah, saying that they had "Americanized too rapidly" and in the process had lost most of their religious beliefs. Apparently, he still had hopes for Jack and me.

Camp was a lot better than I had anticipated. Being one of the older kids for a change, was fun. I tried to sign up for two more weeks but I was too late with my request. I moved in with the Tucks on the last day of July. I knew Leon, Bobby, and Elsie from Hebrew school, Junior Congregation and the Alliance, plus Leon was a semester ahead of me at Hoke Smith. He Bobby and I were going to be attending Hoke Smith High School, which was changed to go from eighth to twelfth grades, come September. Changes in the high school scene in Atlanta, details of which had finally been made available, were a topic of discussion in the Tuck household. Over the summer, Bass, O'Keefe, Joe Brown, and Hoke Smith Junior High schools had been transformed into new high schools. The Girls High campus became Roosevelt High, the Boys High & Tech High combined campus became Henry Grady High and the Commercial High campus, to the best of my knowledge, became a night school for high school dropouts.

When I returned home to Mrs. Goncher's, letters and phone calls from Asher were waiting for me. The gist of what he wanted was to convince me to move to New York, to live with him and, as he put it, to quit taking charity from the Atlanta Jewish community. His main agenda was for me to get an intensive Jewish education. After giving his request a great deal of thought, I responded that I did not want to study for the rabbinate. I was confident that I had been getting a good education in Atlanta and while I was appreciative of the help that the Bureau had been giving me, I did not think of myself as a charity case. What I did not tell him was that I had felt he would not be able to take care of me and would end up placing me with one of the newly-settled Frankfurt families. I hated to burst his bubble, but I felt that it was too late for me start my education over as a yeshiva student.

Mrs. Goncher rightfully complained that I had too much time on my hands over the summer. I called Gold's Delicatessen and asked if they had a summer job for me. All of my siblings had worked, at one time or another, for Dave Gold, but he did not have an opening for me at the time. He did say he would call me as soon as there would be a job. I bought art supplies so that I could do artwork at home and not waste so much of my time. Toward the end of the summer, the job at Gold's Delicatessen came through. It was for Sundays, so I would be able to continue working past the summer.

Ben's *Bar Mitzvah* picture, September, 1945.

120	Home Is Where You Find It

Scout Troop 27 on a camping trip, c.1946. L-r: Joseph Epstein, Sonny Copeland, Nace Varon, Charlie Copeland, Ben Hirsch, and Johnnie Benator. Courtesy Josiah Benator.

Commercial High, 1947. Jack Hirsch, 2nd from right, Alex Zomper, 3rd from right, and Alvin Minsk, far left. Courtesy Malcolm Minsk.

VIII

NEW LABELS, NEW BEGINNINGS, September 1947–August 1948

For fifteen-year-old teenagers, labels often define who they are. My status as a student officially changed at the beginning of the school year. Even though, we were in the same building, where we had been junior high school students for three years, the facility was officially changed to Hoke Smith High School. The classes would be from eighth through twelfth grade, which automatically gave my classmates and me upper class status to the freshman and sub-freshman, eighth and ninth grade, classes. As of December 1, 1946, I officially become an orphan, a status change that didn't have any outward implications. I was not so macabre as to wish to be labeled an orphan; I just privately experienced what could be interpreted as a graduation from a state of limbo, of not knowing if I would ever see my parents again. Along with this change, I experienced only partial closure. There was no physical validation of my parents' death. There were no graves to visit to say a prayer for the souls of my loved ones, just an acceptance that my siblings and I were officially without parents. Having lost Werner and Roselene was another matter, at least for me. I had the previous nine months to let the report of their demise sink in, but for some reason I could not accept it, even though there was no doubt in my mind that the reports of our parents' demise was true. The label that I wore proudly, however, was that of a tenth grade high school student. This label gave me the focus to go on with the rest of my life with all the excitement of discovery, as well as disappointments, inherent in the high school experience.

Starting a high school from scratch presented challenges across the board. Mr. Shirley Watkins had been the basketball coach at Commercial High, which was closed as part of the new Atlanta high school system. His first job as basketball coach at Hoke Smith High was to recruit players for a team that would be competitive in the newly formed City League. He brought W. A. "Slats" Skelton, his star player from Commercial High, but he had to build a team around him. Burton Clein approached me, saying that the coach told him to round up all the Jewish boys who play basketball at the Alliance, and have them try out for the team. Since I was only on the D.S.I. B-team, I had no illusions of making a high school team. Burton promised to deliver and I thought it might be fun, so I came to the tryouts. As it was, five players from the Alliance made the varsity squad the first year. They were Bobby and Leon Tuck, Burton Clein, Herb Mendel (the only one over 6 feet tall), and Stan Firestone. Also on the team were W. A. Skelton and Doyle "Whitey" Kugler (both very good big men), Sid Bonner and a few others that I can't remember. I was happy to make the B-team along with Conrad "Tank" Moon, our star fullback from the football team.

There was no such thing as too much basketball. There was always a mad rush to be the first ten boys out at recess to play in the first pickup game. I seldom made the first game and when I didn't, I would sit on the steps and watch the game as I ate my lunch. One such recess, I was sitting about ten steps up and three girls were eating their lunch a couple of steps below me. As they were eating, they were watching the game and rating the players based on which one they thought was the cutest. I tried not to pay attention to their giggling and to what they were saying, focusing on eating my lunch so that I could get into the next game. I even made a point to appear to ignore them when I heard them talking about my friend Burton. One girl mentioned that he had the most beautiful blue eyes and black hair, but it was a shame that he was a Jew. As soon as she got the words out of her mouth, one of her cohorts pointed to me and said that I was his best friend and a Jew too, and that I had been eavesdropping on everything they had been saying. Suddenly, she threw her lunch at my head. I was too startled to duck. I went to pick up her lunch bag which was so heavy that I thought she might have a rock sandwich in it. Without commenting on its weight, I offered the lunch bag back to her, though I did express surprise at her actions. Before I could finish my remarks, the three of them pounced on me and started beating on me with all their might. Mr. Kimbal, the track team coach was standing within twenty feet of the action, but he didn't seem interested in putting a stop to the attack. They were hurting me and it seemed like no one was going to come to my aid, so I hauled off and swung at the strongest of them, hitting her body but not her face. At that point, Mr. Kimbal decided that it was time for him to intervene. He pulled the girls away from me and tried to find out what terrible thing I had done to set them off. When they were not forthcoming, he asked me what my provocation had been. After I told him, he suppressed a laugh and suggested I sit out the rest of recess in the detention room, a blessing in disguise. I did not want to stay in the school yard and risk taking a ribbing from everyone about getting beat up by girls. Whoever said that girls were the weaker sex, never had the misfortune of being hit by those three amazons.

Shortly after my brother, Asher, left for New York I had taken up smoking again. At first, I made a point of not smoking in or around school. Now that I was in high school, where smoking students were not that uncommon, students no longer considered the school grounds off limits for smoking. I was one who felt grown up and important with a cigarette hanging out of my mouth, but I only indulged my nasty habit outside of the school building. Eventually, Mr. Keith, the principal, called me in and requested that I not smoke anywhere on school property. I would have been better off to take that admonition as an opportunity to stop smoking. That would have to come later, at a much higher price.

My Sunday job at Gold's Delicatessen was not what it was cracked up to be. All of my brothers and sisters had worked for Dave Gold at one time or another, so I was told that I had big shoes to fill. When I first went to work there, I did odds and ends, restocked the shelves, swept the floors and anything else I was told to do. Between Dave and Ida Gold and Jake Goldberg, who worked behind the deli counter, I was kept busy all day long. After a month or so, Dave decided that the most effective use of my time would be to stay at the cash register, to ensure that customers would never walk up to an unmanned register. His concerns were two-fold. Customers had been complaining about waiting for someone to check them out and some people had been walking without paying for merchandise when they found no one at the register.

The first Sunday the new strategy seemed to work fine, that is until there was a lull in the number of customers ready to be checked out. Ida saw that I was not busy and grabbed me away from the register to restock some shelves. Dave saw that I wasn't at the register and was not happy. He found me and proceeded to chew me out. To no avail, I tried to explain that his wife had pulled me away. He demanded that I stay by the register, even if it meant twiddling my thumbs between checking out customers. I went back to my post and, as if she had been waiting for it, Ida came rushing to me at the next lull at the checkout line and started screaming that I wasn't earning my pay. I tried to explain that the boss, her husband, insisted that I stay by the register, but she countered that, as far as I was concerned, she was the boss and that I had to obey her orders. She dragged me toward the dry produce section to replenish some of the depleted stock. Within minutes, Dave saw me and blew a gasket. He didn't care why I was not at the register; the fact that I didn't heed his orders was inexcusable. He told me that the next time I was not at the register, I would be fired.

    The next hour or so was very busy and the checkout line was quite active. As soon as things slowed down, Ida demanded that I come with her for some more chores. I steadfastly refused and told her she would have to take it up with Dave. She confronted Dave and told him that I was not worth the twenty-five cents per hour they were paying me, if I were not going to be busy all of the time. He countered that he wanted me at the cash register at all times. They went to the back of the store to hash out their differences. They came out twenty minutes later and told me to pack up my things because I was fired. I took off my apron, got my things and was out the door in less than five minutes. Jake came running out to stop me. He overheard all of the back and forth, all day long, and said he could intervene and get me my job back. I told him that if he did, I would never forgive him. He gave me an understanding look, a pat on the back and wished me luck. It was a relief to be out of that loony bin. The down side was that I needed to earn money and Sunday jobs were very hard to come by.

Several of my friends had started selling colors at college football games. They would go to Max Markales's newsstand and get a board of pins representing the two teams of a particular game, along with pennants for both teams. Max would let them have the material on consignment and they would sell the merchandise at three to four times the cost. The more enterprising guys, like Charlie Copeland, ordered the materials wholesale and made their own buttons in competition with Max. At first, I resisted the temptation to join them because the games were always on Saturday, and I did not work on the Sabbath. However, I ended up being left with no one to hang around with on Saturday afternoon, when all of my friends were off to sell colors. After a while, the feeling of being left out and the potential of making as much as $6.00 on a very good game made me waiver. I discussed the situation with Rabbi Hyman Friedman and his solution was to offer to pay me $6.00 to wash his car every Sunday, if I would not succumb to working on Saturday. I realized what a very generous offer Rabbi Friedman was making. It was obvious that he could get his car washed professionally for much less. I didn't feel right taking advantage of him in that way, but that wasn't the only reason I didn't take him up on his offer. I was no longer willing to be the only boy refraining from work on the Sabbath, the grass seemed so much greener on the other side. I was fifteen years old, no longer putting on *Tephilin,* (philactories), every morning and no longer observing the Sabbath by doing no manner of creative work. At least for the moment, I was still only eating kosher food.

It seemed as if the more money I made, the more money I spent. When football season was over, I looked for other ways to make money. After Thanksgiving, Charles Berner and I were among several teenagers who were selling shopping bags in front of Rich's department store on Broad Street. We got them from Max, on consignment, for a nickel apiece and sold them for fifteen cents to a quarter. I needed to earn some money in order to attend the Southeast Regional Young Judea convention in Birmingham, Alabama around Christmas time. Our club, D.S.I., was affiliated with Young Judea and all of the members were going to try to go. Selling shopping bags wasn't as lucrative as selling colors, but I was able to net $6.00 over a weekend and, with what I had saved from selling colors, that was enough to make the trip. Now all I had to do was get permission from immigration to go out of state.

The convention in Birmingham was a new experience for me. It was a weekend with programs that focused on teenage Jewish boys and girls from all over the region, meeting one another. There were all sorts of planned activities including a basketball tournament and a final banquet at which almost everyone paired up with a date. The basketball tournament was memorable. My club, D.S.I. was not among the teams considered to be a contender for the regional championship. We had a good team, but S.O.Z. (Sons Of Zion), also of Atlanta, was better and more experienced, their players being an average of one or two years older than our players. The team from Birmingham was the tournament favorite. Their star players were the Faigelson twins, who were both all-state high school basketball players. D.S.I., on the other hand, had hustle, speed, and determination.

The hustle and determination paid off. To the surprise of the odds makers, D.S.I. not only reached the semi-finals but ended up beating arch-rival S.O.Z. in the semi-final game to gain a championship berth against the vaunted Birmingham team.

The championship game was exciting, to say the least. I, along with a handful of D.S.I. fans, was in a tiny minority among the spectators. Being the underdogs took the pressure off of the D.S.I. team. They could play hard to win and not lose face if they didn't succeed. The game plan was to play aggressively and to bottle up the Faigelson boys, who were both taller than anyone on our team except for Bert Saul, who was 6'-4". By 1947 standards, D.S.I. played the roughest game ever seen at the Birmingham Jewish Community Center. Bert Saul fouled out with four minutes left to play, but we were still holding on to a slim lead. With less than a minute to play, one of the Faigelson twins caught a long defensive rebound and was off on a fast break to an uncontested lay-up, which would have given his team the lead. At least it appeared to be that way.

Seemingly, from out of nowhere, Paul Muldawer caught up with him, ran into him from behind, smashing him into the wall, which was less than ten feet behind the goal. Paul was kicked out of the game for the flagrant foul and Gene Faigelson was awarded two free throws for the foul and one for the technical foul. Paul's ejection left the team with only four players and, to make matters worse, the refs would not allow either Sam Pinsky or me to go in and play in our socks and street clothes for the remaining seconds of the game. The outlook was bleak. An 85% foul shooter was at the free throw line for three shots and we were only one point ahead. Faigelson was so woozy from his collision with the wall that he missed all three shots. D.S.I. got the rebound and held on to the ball until time ran out. It was a dubious victory but it got the team invited to the upcoming tournament for the national championship at the Young Judea National Convention in New Hampshire.

The banquet was billed as the main event. I had a date with one of the Roth twins and Stanford had a date with the other. At our age, there weren't too many kids with cars. I don't remember who was driving or whether there was another couple in the front seat, but I'll never forget being crowded in the back seat of a 1946 Buick, three fifteen year-old boys with dates on their laps. The only thing I remember about the banquet was triple dating in the back seat of a car and, after the girls were taken home, cruising around looking for Buick rings to snap off and use for bracelets. I went along for the ride, but refused to take part in that caper for fear of endangering my status as an immigrant in line for citizenship.

There was plenty of free time, enough to allow for some card playing and individual liaisons with girls we met at the various activities. I had my choice of card games. Burton Clein acted as my self-appointed manager. He gave me such a build up that kids were lining up to take me on in gin rummy and poker. Luck was with me and I lived up to my new-found reputation as a card sharp. I came home with more money than I left with, after paying all the fees and still having a good time. I found out later that my sister Flo had given our club leader five dollars for my use in case I ran short of money.

I met a girl from South Georgia at one of the functions and we seemed to hit it off. Testing her interest, I asked her to go to an afternoon movie with me. I think we saw "*My Wild Irish Rose.*" I remember enjoying the movie but remember enjoying her company even more. I thought she was so pretty and nice and couldn't believe she could be enjoying herself with me, but she seemed to be. We spent an entire afternoon together. I even gave up a card game to be with her, and I was feeling so good that I didn't know what to do. I had very little experience at dating. It was the last afternoon of the convention and before we parted, we swapped addresses so we could keep in touch. She did write to me once and I procrastinated responding for so long that, by the time I decided to respond, I lost the letter with her address.

While I was busy trying to be a typical Jewish-American teenager, I paid little attention to what was going on with the Jews of Europe who had survived attempts at annihilation. I still wondered about the fate of Werner and Roselene and clung to belief that they were alive and well, somewhere. I believed that the Allied victory over the Nazi Axis put a stop to the mass murder of European Jews, made it easier for survivors to find new lives, and wherever possible, reunite with their loved ones.

The movie theater newsreels, that I had relied on as a source of information did not make a point of showing details of life in the D.P. camps. There was mention of the "illegal" Jewish refugee ships trying to smuggle Holocaust survivors into Palestine. In September, I remember seeing how British troops used tear gas on the survivor passengers to prevent the landing, in Palestine, of the *Exodus*, the Jewish-refugee ship that was later immortalized in a movie of that name.

The Nuremberg Trials had been receiving a great deal of media coverage, but little was said about the secret network of organizations that facilitated the escape of many Nazis and furnished them with new identities. Among the many high SS officials that escaped prosecution using the secret network known as *Odessa*, Adolf Eichmann, Josef Mengele and Franz Stangl reached safety in South America, while others found haven in Egypt and Syria. There had been much speculation as to the leadership and financing of the secret organizations that made the escape of these war criminals possible. Evidence suggests that high ranking members of the Vatican were actively involved in these escapes. I remember being irate in 1948 upon hearing that Pope Pius XII requested mercy for all Nazi war criminals condemned to death by military tribunals. His appeal was duly noted, but turned down by General Lucius Clay, the Deputy Military Governor, and I breathed a sigh of relief.

My behavior was again the subject of Mrs. Goncher's complaints to my sister Flo. I had been coming home late a lot, I was hanging out at the Alliance too much and she had heard that I gambled a lot. She had also been concerned by my diminishing orthodoxy. Flo felt responsible for my behavior and offered to take me in to live with her after she got an apartment. After much discussion, including a conversation with me, Flo realized that she would not be able to take the role of a mother to her teenage brother. In spite of her unhappiness about my behavior, Mrs. Goncher was still the most qualified parental figure to try to keep me in line.

My case-worker suggested that if I had a weekend job, I might not be so focused on gambling to earn money. The facts were that I enjoyed gambling because I was good at it and I got a thrill out of winning money. Nevertheless, Mrs. Goncher got me a Saturday job at Tannenbaum's Grocery Store on McDaniel Street. Since I had already broken the religious barrier by selling colors at football games on Saturday, the transition to having a job that required me to work on *Shabbat* was no longer a problem for me. She fixed me a kosher lunch to take with me every week so that I wouldn't have to compromise that religious tenet as well. The lunch was almost always the same, thick slabs of yellow cheese sandwiched between two very thick slices of *challah*, special bread usually baked for *Shabbat,* and not enough mayonnaise to overcome the dryness of day old *challah*. I lasted for at least two months at that job. It was long hours and hard labor and the pay was not commensurate with the effort, which included getting up very early to catch a streetcar to get to work by 8 am. Before quitting that job, I took a job at the Big Apple Store on Memorial Drive. It wasn't as far away, the hours were shorter and I earned $7.00 for a Saturday, a dollar more than at the last job.

My case worker, Mrs. Gertrude Fink, called me in to discuss the results of the vocational testing she had sent me to take at Emory University, the week before. She stood out, among the fine case workers who had been assigned to me, as being truly compassionate and making me feel that she cared about me while being tough when she needed to be. On the one hand, she was very pleased with the scores that indicated a mental age of 18.6 years and an I.Q. that could be considered superior. On the other hand, she could not reconcile my poor performance in school with the results of the tests. I was interested at what the tester termed as a high percentile rating on the interest inventory, one which indicated aptitude in fields akin to music, art, or other creative areas, or public performance occupations. Actually, when the tester spoke to me after I took the tests, he mentioned so many different fields that I could choose from that I left more confused than before I took the tests.

The bottom line was that I had no excuse for not doing better in school. I admitted to Mrs. Fink that lack of interest and poor conduct on my part were the main reasons for my poor performance in school. Some of that had to do with sheer boredom. The results of the tests boosted my self esteem and I promised that I would quit fooling around and work harder to live up to my newly discovered potential, even if it meant bringing books home from school. I realized that I had to start thinking about my future and, that without better grades, I would never get into a college of my choosing, but I was also interested in getting a nod of approval from Mrs. Fink. As soon as I left her, I went to a shoe store to see about getting a job.

Clerking in a grocery store was not the kind of work I wanted to continue doing. Even though I was still somewhat small for my age, I decided to check out the shoe stores on Whitehall Street to see if I could find a job. Kinney's Shoes was the smallest of the line up of shoe stores that started south of Alabama Street and went north past Five Points, so I chose to go in and to ask for the manager. I was told that Mr. Tatum was not in and was asked if anyone else could help me. Having been advised not to speak to anyone but the manager, I said that I would wait until he came back. As I waited, I made a point of watching the salespeople's approach to customers as well as their sales techniques.

Mr. Tatum came in after about an hour and was told that a little fella had been waiting for an hour to see him. With a quizzical look in his eyes, he approached me, introduced himself and asked what was on my mind that would warrant waiting an hour to see him. I introduced myself and came right out and asked him for a weekend job. Although the sales personnel were snickering in the background, he managed to smile as he asked what job a twelve-year-old boy would be capable of doing at a shoe store. Stretching the truth, I told him that I was actually fifteen and a half years old and that, although I felt I could be a good salesman, if there were no sales positions open, I would be willing to accept a starting position as a stock clerk.

To my surprise, he said he liked my spunk and that I should come in on Tuesday and Wednesday afternoon to learn the stock, start on Friday afternoon, be prepared to work until closing and to work all day Saturday. I started out in the stock room and quickly learned the system well enough to locate any shoe requested in a matter of minutes. The Easter season had started and the store was so packed on Saturday that Mr. Tatum asked me if I thought I could help out on the sales floor during the busy hours. I jumped at the chance, took off my smock and ran to the sales floor. I ended up having such a good day that he offered to put me on commission in addition to my forty cents per hour salary. Several customers specifically requested that they wanted to have "the little boy" wait on them. That annoyed a few of the sales personnel, but most of them were appreciative of getting some relief on the sales floor and thought it was kind of cute, or even funny, to see customers waiting to be served by the little stock clerk.

My size did not exempt me from "initiation." My second Friday, Mr. Tatum told me that we were getting in a large shipment of shoes and did not have enough space in the stock room for them. He asked that I go next door to Burt's Shoes, and see if they had a wall stretcher that we could borrow. Dutifully, I went to Burt's and was told that they had lent it to Butler's, who in turn had lent it to Beck's, who sent me two blocks north to Chandler's. The people at Chandler's asked how many shoe stores I had been to in search of the wall stretcher. After a good laugh, they decided to have pity on me and let me in on the joke, making sure that I knew that they usually would have sent me on to Davison's shoe department and then to other stores from there. So I wouldn't feel too stupid, they told me that all new, first time personnel in shoe stores were given the same initiation and that virtually all, regardless of age, fell for it. I still felt stupid, but grateful that they cut the initiation short for me.

I was very conscious of my eventual need to become totally self-supporting. Earning spending money became my responsibility when I started working and I hoped to be able to save enough to start buying my own clothes. Even though I was working at Alterman Brothers' Wholesale grocery warehouse on weekday afternoons and at Kinney's Shoes on weekends, I still found it hard to make ends meet. Ms. Fink met with me to help me work out a budget in line with my resources that would allow me to meet my obligations.

Ms. Fink was surprised to find that my largest source of financial pressure was paying back my share of birthday presents that Sarah and Jack had bought for our siblings. They both had good taste and the ability to spend money for good things, and they did so without thinking about how difficult it was for me to pay an equal share. Sarah, on her own, started buying clothes for me, but she kept a record of what she spent so that I could reimburse her when I had the funds. Ms. Fink met with Sarah and Jack and suggested that my share of joint presents should be considerably less than their share. They told her that they just wanted me to feel as if I had an equal part, but they never really expected me to pay an equal share. Of course, they had failed to share that little bit of information with me, and they had no idea how I was being affected by the pressure of owing more money than I could afford to pay back.

The Alliance engaged Mr. Healy as a boxing instructor and coach to those who chose to enter the Golden Gloves tournament. Quite a few of my friends were involved in the new program, especially those from Or VeShalom, who lived in the vicinity of the Atlanta Boys Club, where boxing was a major activity. I found myself gravitating to Mr. Healy's workout sessions, at first, mostly to hang out with my buddies. Then I found that I was getting more than exercise out of the workouts. Healy was a good teacher. As much as I enjoyed it, I wasn't disciplined enough and couldn't commit to the program with its very rigid schedule. At first I was excited at the thought of developing skills that could help me in the many street encounters that seemed to be my lot. I soon realized that boxing, as noble as a sport as it might be, had very little to do with duking it out with a gang of toughs in a street fight—the operative word being gang.

I liked Mr. Healy a lot and I thoroughly enjoyed the workouts and sparring with my friends to help them prepare for their bouts. Healy tried to talk me into fighting in an upcoming tournament, but I saw no glory in getting my brains beaten out in front of a lot of people. That was happening enough already, albeit in the streets and in front of small crowds. I got a lot of vicarious pleasure out of watching the Benator boys, Asher and Johnny, Nace Varon, Archie Merlin, and Herb Mendel win their first bouts. Then there was Charlie Copeland who lasted less than a round, much as I would have done. Asher was amazing to watch. He went in like a buzz saw and decimated boxers much bigger than he, most of them with TKOs in the first round. He was definitely on his way to winning the championship in his weight category.

Tenth grade was the year that I was going to apply myself. After all, I had to start thinking about my future and making a living. The first time I brought books home to do homework, which before then I had always done during study periods, was when my English teacher in Ten Low, Ms. Respess, gave us assignments that mandated taking books home. At first I was angry with her for being so demanding, but it was very hard to stay angry with a teacher with such amazing legs. She would sit on the edge of her desk with her legs crossed and actually expect the boys to pay attention to what she was saying. As it turned out, taking home the books and doing the assignments made up for the lack of concentration on the subject matter in class. I also found it to be a good work ethic for my other classes and soon my grades began to improve.

Mr. Harrington was my English teacher in Ten High, and his focus was on creative writing. I was told that he had retired from being a college professor before coming to teaching high school. I learned a lot from him, but most importantly, he instilled in me a love for the written word and made me aware that I had the ability to write creatively. Aside from the daily in-class essay assignments, he assigned two major essay projects for each of us to write at home. The first major piece was fiction. I chose to do a Mickey Spillane-style detective story and had a lot of fun doing it, which is probably why I got an A on the paper. When it was time to turn in the second major essay, a non-fiction assignment, I found that I had totally mismanaged my time. I allowed deadlines for the artwork I had been doing for the school paper and the yearbook to take precedence over my class assignments. I had not even selected a topic and I was getting frantic. Then I remembered that I had read a really good article, in *Life* magazine, on the evolution of man which debunked theories of the racial superiority of Caucasians over Negroes, and decided to use it as a basis for my article. Before I knew it, my lazy streak and that bit of larceny in me took over. I decided to copy the article verbatim and turn it in as if it were my own. I was not aware of the penalties for plagiarism; in fact I had never heard the word before. Luckily, Mr. Harrington was not as punitive as he could have been, and he had a marvelous sense of humor. He returned my paper to me with a C- and a note that said that it was a shame that I did not write this myself, since I had proven to him that my writing was better than what I had copied from *Life* magazine. What a wonderful way to teach a student that cheating is not the proper road to success. He could have flunked me for that indiscretion, but he allowed me to salvage a B out of his course.

Extra-curricular activities, especially cartooning and art work for *The Senator*, the school newspaper, and the *Smithsonian*, the school yearbook, kept me busy, occasionally at the expense of school work. Catherine Mckee was the faculty advisor for the paper as she had been for *The Vanguard* at Hoke Smith Jr. High. When I advanced the idea of a comic strip of a boy and girl called Hoke & Smitty, she loved it. The strip had a three-year run, and never missed an issue. There were times when I barely made the deadline, because Ms. Mckee's censorship caused last minute changes to the strip. It seemed that I patterned Hoke after some of the more well-developed girl students and the advisor felt that Hoke should be more like a fashion model, svelte, and flat chested. That may have been the only thing that she and I ever fought over and, of course, she always won. Frances Messer took over the yearbook when Hoke Smith became a high school. She asked Ms. Mckee if she could recruit me to do artwork and was granted conditional permission. The condition was that no work for the *Smithsonian* could keep me from meeting deadlines for *The Senator*. Miss Messer was always complimentary and very appreciative of the work I did for the yearbook, and there was never a cross word between us—that is, until I was a graduating senior.

Because Hoke Smith was in its first year as high school, the student body had no officers, but there was a student council consisting of delegates from each homeroom. The faculty advisers of the student council announced there would be a general election for president and vice president of the school on May 19 for the 1948-49 school year. Using the school colors, the Purple Party and the Gold Party were created and we were told that candidates for each party were chosen in party conventions that took place May 12 and 13, by delegates that supposedly were following the wishes of the homerooms they represented.

The word around school was that the nominees had been pre-selected by the faculty advisers and the delegates just followed the recommendations of the faculty, without being told that they had a choice to do otherwise. While I heard no derogatory comments about any of the candidates, I heard widespread complaints that the candidates of both parties, while excellent students, were equally lackluster choices.

The Purple Party candidates for president and vice president were Thomas Armstrong and my friend Sue Peek while the Gold Party offered Teddy Frankel and Eleanor Howard. All had leadership ability but not enough name recognition among the majority of the student body, not to mention gravitas, to give interest to Hoke Smith High's first general election.

Besides being the cartoonist for the school paper, I was also a reporter on occasion and I saw the makings of a good story. I approached Conrad Moon and Leon Tuck and suggested that they run for president and vice president on an independent party ticket. Both were well known sports figures in the school and could bring excitement to the elections. I didn't think they could win with such a short election campaign, but they could get a lot of votes and have loads of fun in the process. Assuming we could get approval to run, I would make all of the campaign posters and, along with an enthusiastic group of student volunteers, try to get out the vote.

The student council told us we would be required to get signatures of five hundred Smith High students in order to qualify as an independent party. The challenge was to get this done in the short time available. We called ourselves the Smithy Party and proceeded to get signatures. The reaction of the student body to our independent slate was overwhelming. In less than two days, we acquired more than five hundred signatures and the student council granted our candidates the right to run in time to make campaign speeches at the assembly on May 19, just prior to the general election.

Both Conrad and Leon had agreed to become candidates on a lark. They never expected to win, but thought they would be sending a message to the faculty to be more open to student participation in choosing candidates for student body leadership. To the surprise of almost everyone, Conrad "Tank" Moon, all-state fullback of the football team and Leon Tuck, high scoring starting guard of the basketball team, were elected as Hoke Smith High's first president and vice president. I was the instigator and their unofficial campaign manager. It was my first real venture into political campaigning and I thoroughly enjoyed it.

Sarah was the first of my siblings to get married. Though she had been dating Harry Shartar for well over a year, she wanted to wait until after her eighteenth birthday before getting married. The date was set for May 9, 1948, which just happened to be Mother's Day. Of all my brothers and sisters, Sarah was the one whom I expected to get a college education. She had often talked about wanting to become a doctor. Instead, she got married just one month after her eighteenth birthday, foregoing, at least for the time being, any thoughts of attaining a higher education.

Harry was six years older than Sarah, and at least a foot taller. He had served with the U.S. Army in China during World War II and was getting his degree in Industrial Engineering at Georgia Tech. He was very optimistic about finding a good job after his graduation. The dean in charge of placement told him that many industrial companies had signed up with the university's placement system to interview I.E. graduates, particularly those who were war veterans and had served overseas. He soon found that most of the industrial companies asking for applicants had restrictions that did not allow hiring Jews. World War II seemed to have changed nothing in the hiring practices of industry in the United States. After a year of rejections, Harry finally found a job with Jewish-owned Atlanta Paper Co. which later became Meade Atlanta Paper Company. He stayed with that company until he retired more than forty years later.

I was really fascinated to hear that Harry had been a medical miracle. When he was twelve years old, he was in a school bus accident that threw him from one end the bus to the other. As a result, he developed spinal meningitis. In the 1930s, spinal meningitis was considered fatal. Miraculously, he survived it, was written up in medical journals, and he went on to lead a normal life.

I wondered if Sarah would regret not pursuing a college education. She was such a good student. Her desire to get married and start a family apparently superseded any other desires she may have had. She also seemed to have a strong desire to become the matriarch of the Hirsch family. She even talked about having me come live with her and Harry after they got settled, but I wasn't sure if she had discussed that idea with Harry.

Jack offered to buy me a suit for the wedding, but Mrs. Fink had already planned to take me shopping and discouraged him from buying things for me that were still the Bureau's responsibility. We went to Rich's basement and I couldn't find anything in my size that I liked, so I suggested that I could get more use out a blazer with trousers and Mrs. Fink agreed and approved of my choice. After all that, Sarah did not let me wear my new outfit for the wedding. She insisted that I wear my winter suit, and since it was her wedding, I obliged.

The wedding was held at the Ahavath Achim educational building on Tenth Street. All five of the Hirsch siblings were there, including Asher who came in from New York. Asher took the opportunity to speak with Mrs. Fink after the wedding to discuss my diminishing observance and practice of Orthodox Judaism and my future. I no longer ate only kosher food outside of the house and I was working on Friday evenings and Saturdays. He found out that for Jack's birthday, the four Hirschs had dinner at a French restaurant. From talking to me, he felt that my future depended on the development of my artistic talents. He was aware that I leaned in the direction of cartooning as a career, although I had no idea how to go about starting such an endeavor. He made the case for me to move to New York, go to an industrial arts high school and pursue my career choice. He was convinced that there were no opportunities to develop artistically in Atlanta. His unspoken agenda was for me to move to an environment that would be more conducive to my returning to Orthodox Jewish practices.

My case-worker let Asher make his case, then told him that, for years, the Bureau had been interested in helping me develop my talent in art. She told him that the High Museum of Art was an excellent school and that I had not availed myself of offers from the Bureau to attend art school, with the exception of one summer. She shared with Asher the progress I had been making, including how well I had done on the vocational and psychological testing. She also mentioned that student aid loans could be available to me if I stayed in Atlanta. Then, for the clincher, she made the point that Asher would not be able to look after me if I moved to New York.

Asher conceded that I was better off staying in Atlanta. He just bemoaned the lack of a religious milieu in Atlanta and the fact that I had gotten completely away from Orthodox Judaism. Mrs. Fink suggested that I should have the right to decide for myself the manner in which I practiced my religion just as Asher had done. That all this conversation about my future and about me went on without any input from me was unfortunately typical where my brother was involved. In retrospect, Mrs. Fink did miss the point that the changes in my religious practices had a lot to do with the fact that I had no Sabbath observant peers or role models in Atlanta. At the time, eating non-kosher food outside of the house was an accepted practice among Jews in Atlanta, who considered themselves Orthodox. It could be argued that I could have bucked the trend, had I enough passion for it.

Sarah and Harry went on their honeymoon and I started to plan for the summer. I applied for a job as junior counselor at Camp Daniel Morgan and the Bureau again offered art classes at the High Museum. Thinking that I might get the job at camp, as an art instructor I turned down the art classes. By the time the rejection came from Camp Daniel Morgan because I was too young, classes had already started at the High. I could have joined the class but chose not to because I wanted to focus on getting summer work, earning some money and being a bit more independent.

I started the summer with two jobs. On Mondays and Tuesdays, I worked for Aaron Lichtenstein as a collector for Morris Lichtenstein Insurance Company. I used streetcars and trolley busses as transportation to reach the widely dispersed policy holders. Invariably, the policy holders felt sorry for me—a little refugee boy traveling long distances to collect premiums they should have already sent. As a result, my percentage of collections per call was quite high and Aaron suggested that I consider the insurance business as a career. On Thursdays, Fridays and Saturdays, I worked at Alterman Brothers Wholesale Grocers stamping cigarettes in the warehouse. Wednesdays and Sundays I was free to swim and hang out at the Progressive Club.

I discussed my desire, with my bosses, to attend a Young Judea convention in July. It would convene in Atlanta and would entail my missing a few days of work. Aaron had no problem with my request and Max Alterman didn't see any problem either. So I called Herman Popkin, who was the regional director of Young Judea in charge of the convention, and told that I would attend and help him in any way that I could. For whatever reason, I seemed to have been more interested in the organizational and planning aspects of the convention than in actually participating in the activities. Herman kept me so busy that I never thought about trying to get a date for the final dance. Among the volunteers helping Herman with the convention was a very attractive and mature young lady, with whom I worked well and whose company I thoroughly enjoyed. Herman mentioned that she did not have a date for the dance and suggested that I ask her. I felt that she was out of my league and told Herman so, but he insisted that he thought she would like to go out with me.

As Herman predicted, she graciously accepted my invitation. Even though I was fond of her and felt that she liked me too, I had the feeling that this date was just the means to an end, so that she would not have to go to the dance unescorted. Nevertheless, as the evening started we appeared to be the ideal couple. I was dancing with her and was thinking to myself that this is as good as it gets. Then guys started breaking in, all of them at least two years older than me. Although I had anticipated that this type of thing would happen, and I realized that I would not be able to monopolize her dance card, I felt threatened. Instead of dealing with my date's popularity, I reverted to the immature behavior of a twelve-year old and started to hang out with friends who didn't have dates. Rather than being there to retrieve my date at the end of each dance, I just left her there with whomever had broken in. Toward the end of the evening, she told me that one of the guys she had been dancing with asked to take her home and she figured I wouldn't mind since I seemed to be so occupied with my friends. I pretended that I was okay with that and so ended my date with a special girl that I didn't have the maturity or self-confidence to handle properly.

After the convention, I went back to my insurance collecting job with no repercussions, but when I returned to Alterman Brothers. I found that Sam Alterman did not agree with Max, that I should have been allowed to take off for the convention and I was fired. I went straight to the shoe district on Whitehall Street and acquired a weekend job at Burt's Shoe Store.

Before the summer was over I decided to submit cartoons to the *Saturday Evening Post* magazine. I wanted to be a cartoonist and figured that I had the talent, so I shot for the top. I had previously submitted some cartoons, which were rejected, to *Parts Pups*, the publication of Genuine Parts Company. A few weeks later, my cartoon ideas appeared in *Parts Pups* redrawn by someone else. I wrote them to get my fifty dollars per cartoon but they just ignored me. I figured that a magazine as classy as the *Saturday Evening Post* would not resort to that kind of chicanery. The *Post*, very professionally thanked me for submitting, rejected my work and encouraged me to keep trying.

Benjamin Hirsch 139

Ben's 10-L homeroom at Hoke Smith High School. Ben, first row, 2nd from left.

140 Home Is Where You Find It

Hoke Smith High basketball team, 1948. Front row, L-r: Bill Blankesnship, Bobby Tuck, Leon Tuck, Burton Clein, unknown, and Sidney Bonner. Back row, L-r: Trainer, Victor Copeland, Leon Cunningham, W.A. Skelton, Herb Mendel, Conrad Moon, Arthur Bartell, Coach Shirley Watkins.

Sarah's wedding, May 9, 1948. From left: Ben, Jack, Harry Sharter, Sarah Hirsch Shartar, Asher and Flo.

Student Body Elects Officers
Moon and Tuck to Lead School

In a general election held May 19 the two Independent Smithy candidates for the Presidency and Vice-Presidency of Smith High were elected. They were Conrad Moon, president; Leon Tuck, vice-president. Conrad is a varsity football player for Smith and Leon was a member of the Smithy five.

The other candidates were the Purple Party, Thomas Armstrong, president; Sue Peek, vice-president; Gold Party, Teddy Frankel, president; Elanor Howard, vice-president. Campaign speeches were made in an assembly May 19. The Smithy Party expressed (1) the desire to have regular campaigns to keep Smith neat and clean, (2) regular assembly programs, and (3) better order in the halls.

The candidates fo rthe Purple and Gold Parties were chosen in the party conventions May 12-13 by delegates from each homeroom. The delegates were sent with instructions to naminate and vote on the people whom the homerooms had elected indvidually.

The Smithy Party was granted the right to run by student Council Representatives signed by more than 500 Smith High students. The other candidates have pledged their whole-hearted support in cooper with Conrad and Leon in giving the student body the best student government possible.

Conrad Moon

Leon Tuck

(on left) Article in the Hoke Smith *Senator*, May 1948. *Courtesy Leon Tuck*

(above) Smith High vs. Murphy High, February 27, 1948. L-r: Herb Mendel, Bobby Tuck, Leon Tuck, W.A. Skelton, and Conrad Moon. *Courtesy Leon Tuck.*

Shearith Israel Bible Class graduation, 1948. Front row, from left: Sidney Rich and Ms. Stern (teachers), Marilyn Piel, Shirley Silverman, Estelle Flax, Rabbi Hyman Friedman, and another teacher. Rear, from left: Jack Rosenberg, Stanford Firestone, Walter Huebner, Leon Tuck, Paul Baker, Jack Horowitz, and Ben Hirsch.

IX

FINALLY, AN END TO FISTICUFFS, September 1948 –August 1949

More than three years had passed since Hitler's Germany had surrendered to the Allied Forces. The death camps and concentration camps had been liberated and at last the world was learning of the Nazi's murder of half of Europe's Jews. During the war, the United States did not allow its existing immigration quotas to be filled by Jews. After the war, despite the conditions facing European Jewish survivors, those quotas were not increased. Thousands of Jewish survivors in the D.P.(displaced persons) camps had to wait years to obtain U.S. visas. Initially, they were required to find relatives in America who would sponsor them and guarantee their financial support.

In 1941, my aunt Martha and cousin Helen were unable to get U.S. visas when they fled France, and so they found refuge in Cuba. Even with the sponsorship of Aunt Martha's brother, Hanz, it took until July of 1943, for them to obtain papers to come to New York. Immediately after the war and through the late 1940s, orphaned child survivors whose parents had been murdered by the Nazis were given visas to immigrate to the United States, and were resettled in various communities throughout the country. Those of us that came to Atlanta before the war's end were few in number, though perhaps more than fifty child survivors arrived from 1946 through 1948. All the while, I kept hoping that Werner and Roselene would be among the next arriving group.

In the meantime, many survivors were finding their way to the British Mandate of Palestine. Although the quotas for Jews allowed into the Holy Land were strictly enforced by British troops, many Jewish survivors, desperate to get out of the D.P. camps and to go to a land where they could live as Jews, risked their lives to get smuggled into the Promised Land. For the most part, Arabs in Palestine were not thrilled to see the influx of Jewish refugees. The British troops who were mandated to protect Jews and Arabs from each other appeared to be decidedly pro-Arab. When, in February, 1948, the news reached us that Arabs had slipped through lax British security and detonated a bomb that reduced the Jewish sector of Jerusalem to rubble, I waited for cries of outrage from the United States, European governments and the world press. It soon was apparent that no condemnation of the terrorist bombings would be forthcoming. Immediately, Pastor Martin Niemoller's famous personal statement uttered in 1945 came to mind—"First they came for the Communists, and I did not speak up, because I wasn't a Communist. Then they came for the Jews, and I didn't speak up, because I wasn't a Jew. Then they came for the Catholics, and I didn't speak up, because I was a Protestant. Then they came for me, and by that time there was no one left to speak up for me." How close to home, I wondered, would a terrorist bomb have to explode, before other nations condemned such acts of terrorism?

On May 14, 1948, Britain's mandate to govern Palestine expired and the land was partitioned, in accordance with a vote taken by the United Nations five-and-a-half months earlier, into the State of Israel and the Kingdom of Jordan. On the same day, the Jewish National Council proclaimed the independent state of Israel and U.S. recognition followed within hours. The jubilation that followed was short lived. The next day, Egypt and Jordan, both of which had armies trained by the British, invaded the one-day-old state. Thousands of Holocaust survivors found themselves fighting in a war for survival, only this time they would not leave their fate in the hands of any one else.

After the Holocaust, nearly one million Jewish refugees were welcomed into Palestine and, three years later, Israel. I had just started high school a few months before the State of Israel was born. I remember my disbelief upon hearing of the U.N. vote for partition, in November, 1947 and later, when the State of Israel was declared, I was conflicted between euphoria and guilt. I was torn between the comfort level that I had developed in Atlanta, of finally feeling that I was establishing roots, and wanting to be with my people in their struggle to create a viable Jewish state. The fact that I was not even sixteen years old and that I was not free to travel as I pleased was not lost on me. It did make me bemoan that, once again, I would be on the sidelines, safely in America, while the Jewish people in Israel were struggling for survival. I harbored these feelings all through the eleventh grade at Hoke Smith High School, though I never found anyone with whom to share these thoughts. Intense as my feelings may have been, they were momentary and did not keep me from acting like a typical eleventh grader, with all the baggage of the personal and physical changes I was undergoing. I was still somewhat of an outsider, but I was doing my very best to change that.

There was always something exciting about starting a new school year. With expectations of new horizons, a new home-room teacher, a fresh start and, of course, the exhilarating autumn weather. Hoke Smith's basketball team was looking forward to a good year. Of the first seven players on the varsity, six of them were Jewish, the seventh was W. A. Skelton. "Whitey" Kugler was still in school, but he had used up his eligibility. To get some more size on the team, Coach Watkins brought up Conrad "Tank" Moon from the B team to sit on the bench in case an intimidator was needed. I was very happy that "Tank" was allowed to be a swing player, so he could still be on the B team, where he was needed, and would get a lot more playing time.

One of Hoke Smith's first away games was at Russell High, a school in Hapeville that probably had no Jewish students. The local spectators were not particularly hospitable to any visiting team, but they were particularly brutal in their response to the players on Hoke Smith's team who happened to be Jewish. As the first quarter went on, what started out with catcalls singling out Bobby and Leon Tuck quickly turned into vociferous anti-Semitic epithets. I was among the few who had come along to cheer for our team, and feared that we might not get out of that gym in one piece.

Emboldened by the crowd, one of the Russell High players started getting physically and verbally abusive with Bobby Tuck. Sensing that things were getting out of hand, W. A. called a time out, asked "Tank" to come with him to Russell High's bench. In an unprecedented move, they approached the opposing bench and addressed a startled team, none of whom were close to the size of the two Smith High visitors, and proceeded to read them the riot act. The rest of the game went smoothly as far as rival high school basketball games go. As the second half started, the home fans seemed to tone down some of the vitriolic epithets that were mixed in with their yelling, cheering and partisan catcalls. Smith won the game and the team made a beeline for the exit, boarded the bus and took off without waiting for the customary shaking of hands with the other team. Everyone breathed a sigh of relief when we passed the "Hapeville City Limits" sign. We were finally home free and we all realized that the team had just experienced a scene that could have easily turned ugly and very dangerous.

Later, on the way home, I asked Conrad what had transpired at the enemy's bench during the special time-out. He said that Skelton did all the talking. He just told them that any one who even appears be to physically or verbally abusing one of the Jewish players on his team would have to deal with him and the "Tank." He thought of holding the team and coach responsible for controlling the anti-Semitic vulgarities and threats to our players coming from the crowd, but he figured that was not something that the team could control. "Tank" added that he had never experienced such race baiting and openly admitted that had he not known his teammates personally, he probably would not have been so incensed and most definitely would not have gotten involved. As it was, he said he was proud of himself that he did.

I was actually surprised that two, albeit pretty tough looking, guys were able to intimidate an entire basketball team, especially one that was being egged on by an anti-Jewish crowd. I felt sure that the suddenness of the called time-out caught them by surprise and the fact that non-Jewish players would stand up for their Jewish teammates totally threw them for a loop. I thanked Conrad for being our "Golem of Prague." His questioning smile acknowledged that he didn't have a clue about what I was referring to. He told me that he knew that I was not dumb enough to say something bad about him. He was right; I meant that reference with gratitude and great affection.

Mrs. Goncher was out of town from mid-September to mid-October so, once again, I was sent to stay with the Tucks on Washington Street. The Russell game with its scary implications was one of the main topics of discussion at the dinner table for quite a while. To me, it was a wake up call; a realization that mob antisemitism was not a phenomenon limited to Nazi Germany or Europe. Since my arrival in Atlanta, I had been, and still was, experiencing anti-Jewish sentiments from individuals and groups,. This, however, was the first time that I, and for that matter, Bobby or Leon, had witnessed a stadium full of spectators reviling Jews with such animosity.

To switch the conversation to less unpleasant matters, at Friday night *Shabbat* dinner, "Mr. Hush" became the main topic of conversation. A national radio network was having a contest inviting listeners to identify the mystery celebrity, "Mr. Hush". This contest had been going on for several months, with new clues added every week, and caught the imagination of the vast, pre-television era, radio audience. Everyone at the large dinner table was conversant with the contest. Between the family and guests, we were able to restate all of the clues and everyone took a turn at trying to guess the mystery celebrity's identity. When it came my turn, I was unable to think of anyone, so I calmly declared that I was "Mr. Hush" and that they had just misspelled my name. For reasons I cannot explain, that brought the house down. Mr. Joe Tuck, catching his breath from laughter, said that was the funniest thing he had ever heard while everyone else at the table was cracking up. Laughter is contagious. As I stopped laughing, I wondered to myself whether it was what I said or how I said it. I had been accused of being a comedian before, but this time I wasn't even trying to be funny. Maybe, I surmised, everyone just needed a laugh to relieve whatever tension they had. Some weeks later, someone in Illinois picked up on the clue that "Mr. Hush would walk again." It turned out that Jack Benny was from Waukegan, Illinois and he, not I, was "Mr. Hush."

I always enjoyed staying at the Tucks'. They had four children, Bobby was the oldest and Leon was slightly older than I, while Elsie and Albert were both younger than me. Leon remembers that the first time I came to stay with the Tucks, he and Bobby confronted their mother wanting to know where I would sleep. There was a single bed and a double bed in their bedroom. Bobby normally slept on the single bed, while Leon and Albert shared the double bed. Without hesitation, Mrs. Tuck said that, as a guest, I would sleep on the single bed and that Bobby, Leon and Albert would share the double bed. Considering the normal dynamics of a family with four young children, it would have taken some major misbehaving on my part for Mrs. Tuck get upset with me. As it was, I worked hard at being on my best behavior that first time, and continued to do so whenever I had the occasion to be at the Tucks. When Mrs. Goncher returned, she was pleasantly surprised with the report of my good behavior while she was gone.

When I came home from Hebrew school one October afternoon, Mrs. Goncher introduced me to a reporter from the *Atlanta Constitution*, It was a fortunate coincidence that no gang or individual had opted to pick a fight with me, either in school or on the way home that day, so at least I looked somewhat presentable. Before I arrived, the reporter, who sought out Mrs. Goncher because, since 1930, she had been a foster mother to more than fifteen orphaned or displaced Jewish children, had already interviewed her. After a few awkward moments, it became apparent that the reporter was waiting to interview me, the latest and youngest of Mrs. Goncher's foster children.

Since I was not told beforehand about the possibility of this interview, my responses to her questions had to be spontaneous. She first asked where I was from and then asked me to name all the different places where I had lived before coming to the United States. I mentioned that I was almost nine years old when I came to the States and that, prior to that, I had lived in Frankfurt am Main, Germany (where I was born), Basel, Switzerland, Paris, Montmorency, Cruez and Vichy, France. Also, while escaping Europe, I had traveled from Marseilles, France to Madrid, Spain, then to Lisbon, Portugal where I boarded the ship to America.

The reporter naively asked why it was that I had lived in so many places in my short life. Thinking that the question was not a serious one, I glibly responded, "I must have been a bad boy—nobody wanted me," and, just that quickly, the interview was over. To my embarrassment, she used that glib response that was an attempt at humor, as the lead sentence for her article that appeared in the *Atlanta Constitution* on October 22, 1948. When I saw the article, I expected to get a lot of ribbing from my peers, but the only comments I received were from "Cookie" Jacobs. He gave me enough of a hard time to make up for all of my friends.

Julian "Cookie" Jacobs was the first boy in D.S.I. to drive a car and at age 15 or 16 he was the first to smash up his parents' car. Fortunately, he was not badly hurt. Very few D.S.I. boys had access to automobiles, in fact, not that many of their parents even owned a car. "Cookie", therefore, was quite the celebrity. When Vic Romano got his driver's license, he became the guy with whom to double date. The first one to buy his own car with money he had earned was Charlie "Amoeba" Copeland, (I actually gave Charlie that nickname, but that's another story.) It was a used sedan from the 1930s, which fortunately held five passengers, the number of people often needed to push the car when it wouldn't start or it decided to stop mid-route. On one of those occasions, I was one of the passengers when the car stalled on Glenn Street almost at Washington Street. We all got out to push, and to try to jump-start it. Just as the car started, my gold Bar Mitzvah ring that I just had enlarged slipped off my finger to the pavement. As I yelled at "Amoeba" to stop the car, he panicked and put it in reverse. One of the rear wheels ran over the 14-karat gold ring and it became part of the pavement, as if a steamroller had run over it. I felt awful about the loss and worse about my inability to protect one of the few items of value in my possession. I didn't have the nerve to tell Mrs. Goncher or Mrs. Fink, so I kept the embarrassing tale of how my Bar Mitzvah ring was lost to myself.

Charles Berner and I decided to go into partnership to sell colors at Georgia Tech football games. Our new source for pins and pennants was Charlie Copeland, who had a good little business working out of his parents' house on Georgia Avenue. Being in direct competition with Max didn't seem to bother him. My partner and I made plans to go to Birmingham for the Alabama-Georgia Tech game which had been sold out for at least a month. Not anticipating a problem, I mentioned our plans to Mrs. Goncher, who was quick to remind me that I had to get permission from Mrs. Fink in order to leave town. Mrs. Fink was not pleased to find out that there would be no adults going to Birmingham to supervise or to be responsible for the teenage entrepreneurs. She told me that even if I had already acquired government permission to travel out of state, a precondition that had completely slipped my mind, she still could not allow me go unsupervised.

She regretted that I had already spent eighteen dollars on a board of colors and pennants to sell at the game and sincerely hoped that I could find a buyer for them. I had really been looking forward to the excitement of the Tech-'Bama game and to the potential of making big money there. I envied the other boys who seemed to have more freedom to move about then I, although I could not imagine that any of them went without getting permission from their parents.

    Charles bought my board and went without me. When he came back, he told me about how much trouble he had trying to find a good sales location. All the corners near the stadium were controlled by local sellers working for Sy Denaburg, the Birmingham equivalent of Max Margoles. Despite having to move every fifteen or twenty minutes, Charles cleared a remarkable amount of twelve dollars over expenses. Four years later, my brother Jack married Sy Denaburg's daughter, Gladys.

The Jewish boys selling colors at Grant Field, home of Georgia Tech, found it necessary to stick together. There was a group of toughs, who ostensibly were selling for Max. These toughs went around looking for isolated smaller Jewish kids to harass and steal their merchandise. Asher Benator and Nace Varon, both golden glove boxers, had become our defenders around the stadium, and after a few weeks, the harassment seemed to tone down appreciably. The week after the Alabama game, the tough guys came back with their own boxing champion and again started picking on the smaller of the Jewish kids selling colors, making them leave their positions and then taking them over.

    Virtually all of the sales of colors and pennants went on before the game. After the game, the remaining merchandise was offered to the throngs of exiting fans at reduced prices. With the crowds streaming in and out of the stadium, and with everyone trying to make the best of the peak periods, there was not much time for harassment between the vendors. This game was different. The tough guys had their own champion and he was a real intimidator. He looked like a miniature Arnold Schwarzenegger, and was wearing a skin-tight tee shirt in 40-degree weather. It was apparent that he was not a vendor since he didn't even have a board. He acted like a hired gun, flexing his muscles as, one after another, he took over established selling positions from the smaller Jewish vendors. My guess was that, aside from taking over the better sales spots, he was looking for a showdown with either Asher or Nace.

    Asher had been selling outside of the West Stands, totally unaware of what had been going on at the South and East Stands, until his brother Johnny came running toward him from North Avenue with the intimidator at his heels, closely followed by his entourage of would-be tough guys. The football game was well under way, there were no crowds left outside of the stadium and it looked like the showdown that had been brewing was about to commence. Johnny was a decent boxer himself, but realized that he was no match for the intimidator, who outweighed him by at least twenty pounds, so he wisely stepped behind Asher. Though Asher was a bantamweight while his challenger was probably middle to heavy weight, my money was on Asher.

The two stood about five feet from each other, each with his group behind him. The intimidator told Asher to step aside so he could get at Johnny, but Asher wouldn't budge. He just stood there, carefully watching and waiting for the muscle-bound bully to make his move. Finally, he drew back to take a swing at Asher while calling him a kike. Then, like someone popped a cork, Asher laced into this guy so quickly that the intimidator never had a chance to get in the first swing. By the time the police came to break it up, Asher had him against a metal grille between the gates, swinging punches so fast that the bully couldn't do anything but shield his face and cry for help. Nace was standing there in case anyone wanted to join the fracas. The police broke up the fight and disbursed the crowd, but not before Asher Benator became a legend in the annals of those who sell colors at Georgia Tech football games.

I had graduated from afternoon Hebrew school at Shearith Israel and started attending Hebrew High School at the Alliance on Monday and Wednesday in the late afternoons. It had been a while since I was accosted on the way home. The Walker brothers were out of reform school, but were no longer a threat. Even though I had grown substantially, there were still a handful of challengers at Hoke Smith. I kept very busy with school work and extra curricular activities, but I was still marked as the man to beat if one was to become a respectable bully.

There was one aspiring bully who had challenged me a couple times during recess and came out on the short end of the stick both times. A few weeks later he approached me in the hall between classes and demanded revenge. I was more interested in being on time for class that acceding to his demands, but he apparently had been working out and felt that he was ready to "whup my ass," as he put it. A crowd started to gather as he kept pushing me and throwing jabs at me. There seemed to be no teachers around to keep me from once again having a fight in the halls. As we started to square up against each other, Doyle "Whitey" Kugler, the 6'-4" Golden Gloves champ, pushed his way through the crowd and stepped in between the two of us. He wrapped his big hands tightly around my challenger's fists and told him that he had something important to tell him and everyone else in the school. A hush came over the once rowdy crowd as "Whitey" started his statement. He told him to pass the word that Ben Hirsch was a friend of his, that he was sick of seeing people pick fights with his friend and that from that point on, anyone who wanted to fight with Ben would have to fight him first.

He released the guy's fists and asked if he had made himself clear. The response was an affirmative shake of the head, after which the assailant took off like greased lightning. I shook hands with my new protector. We had been friendly acquaintances, but after this incident there was a permanent bond. I kept up with Doyle's activities and reveled in his accomplishments. In later years, he became an officer and jet fighter pilot in the U.S. Air Force. In the 1950s, he wrote to tell me that he was being considered for the part of 'Ozark Ike' in a proposed Hollywood movie, but it was going to have to wait until he had finished his obligations to the U.S. Air Force. Unfortunately, my gentle giant friend was killed when his jet plane crashed around 1964, before he had the chance to be immortalized in film as he so richly deserved. I was unable to get any details with regard to the crash. All I knew was that a wonderful man with a promising future and a love for life was no longer alive. My friend had put an end to the attacks and challenges that had plagued me and tested my survival skills from the time that I had arrived in this country seven years before. It was no wonder that I broke down and cried at the news of his demise.

After two semesters of Spanish, I signed up for the third, only to find out that it was not being taught. Since I was required to take a language, I was stuck in a first semester French class. I no longer spoke French fluently, but I could still read it. The teacher introduced herself as Mademoiselle Brooks and it was clear, from the way she pronounced French words with an American southern accent, that she had never lived in or perhaps even been to France. Her Dixiefied French along with her mispronunciations would have been offensive to anyone who had an appreciation for the beauty of the French language. I found myself correcting almost every sentence she uttered. To no one's surprise, Mademoiselle Brooks asked me stay after class. For fear of being sent to the principal, I explained that I had been fluent in French and that, while I intended no disrespect, I had great difficulty in listening to her textbook taught French, without correcting it. She was aware that I had been placed in her class because Spanish was not being offered this semester, so we struck a compromise. I would sit in the back of the class and use it as a study period, as long as I didn't correct her French pronunciation. If I cooperated, she promised that I would get a B in the course. To keep my part of the bargain, I often wore earplugs during the class.

Early in 1949, Mrs. Goncher took in a new immigrant who had recently come from Europe. Alex Taub, who was 25 years old, would share my room. He had received his high school diploma through a post-war program for young survivors whose education had been interrupted by the war. He was very bright and, by his own evaluation, a genius. Eager to go on with his life, he had a job during the day and went to college at night. He was industrious, to say the least, and very enterprising, always coming up with new business ideas. It was no wonder that Mrs. Goncher felt that he was a perfect role model for me and didn't miss a chance to tell me so. Aside from his insufferable sense of self-importance, there was one flaw in his armor of perfection that was major in my eyes, or should I say to my ears? He snored loud enough to wake the dead.

After two nights of no sleep, I approached him and suggested that he have his sinuses checked. He refused to take me seriously, thinking that I was playing a joke on him. He reminded me about all of his wonderful character traits and his intelligence, all of which should have been enough proof that he could not possibly snore.

I tried to take the issue up with Mrs. Goncher, but she felt that I should be able to work out something so simple with my roommate. I tried stuffing cotton in my ears before going to bed, but that too brought no relief. I was barely getting any sleep and was getting in trouble at school for falling asleep in class.

I tried once more to plead with him to take me seriously, thinking that he could see how haggard I was, but he was so much into himself that he couldn't see what was going on with me. He finally told me that I was getting on his nerves, and that if I didn't stop bugging him about his alleged snoring, he would beat me to a pulp. I failed to mention that he was built like a weight lifter. By midnight, I was desperate. I had to get some sleep and he was snoring loud enough to shake the windowpanes. Finally, I went to the kitchen and got a box of matches. I stuck one between his toes, lit it with another one and waited for a reaction. I had never heard of a hotfoot without shoes, but they say that necessity is the mother of invention.

In a matter of seconds, he was screaming bloody murder. If he hadn't been so stunned, he probably would have beaten me to a pulp. His initial reaction, after the shock of it all, was total disbelief that I could do something so hateful to someone as wonderful as himself. Then, as though he had been hit by lightning, he began to think that maybe it was possible that he snored. For the first time in a week, he actually looked at me and saw how worn out I was. After he composed himself, we sat on the edge of our beds and talked for a long time. I assured him that I had meant him no harm, but that I desperately needed to get his attention. I couldn't quite get him to laugh about it, but he seemed to better understand what motivated my drastic actions. I asked Mrs. Goncher, who was awakened by his screams, if I could sleep on the living room couch until other arrangements could be made. In the meantime, while waiting for a resolution to the problem, we took turns sleeping in the living room on alternate nights. It was my hope that Alex would seek out a doctor to help him with his respiratory problem. Instead he chose to move out.

Ms. Beacom told her advanced art class that she wanted to submit some of the better student artwork for Scholastic Art Awards in the State of Georgia Regional Exhibition of the Annual National High School Art Exhibition. She asked the students for permission to submit their work. I thought it would be an honor to have one's work submitted and couldn't understand why she had asked for permission. Once everyone had given her the okay, it was not brought up again until Ms. Beacom announced in class, those who had Placed and those who had been awarded Gold Keys, the two categories of awards. I had no idea that this fine art competition had such stature. I was told I won two Gold Keys, one for a portrait I had done in pencil and one for a clay figure of a dog. I was proud of the awards, especially after I was told that winning two gold keys was a rarity. I was invited to attend the exhibition at Rich's department store and it was suggested that I get a new suit for the awards banquet.

If that wasn't enough to give me a swelled head, I was invited to sit in on some of the judging of the regional winners that would be sent to National Exhibition, for the following year. There was no conflict of interest since I did not win any Gold Keys that year, and the three Places I had been awarded were not eligible for the National Exhibition. The chairman of the judges was non other than Lamar Dodd, one of the foremost artists in the state and head of the Art Department at the University of Georgia. The first time I opened my mouth to express an opinion during the judging, Mr. Dodd made it clear that I was there as a guest, to see and be seen but not to be heard. After I got over the embarrassment of publicly being put in my place, I sat there and listened to the critiques of the judges, taking in every word. As humbling an experience as that was, I actually felt that I could have made valuable additions to the critiques, had I been given the chance.

I had been working at Maurice Rich's grocery store in East Point for a few months. His brothers Sidney, who was our D.S.I. club leader and Joe, who was one of the older members of DSI, had recommended me for the job. The job was for Friday afternoon and Saturday and paid $8.00 a weekend. Joe also worked there, but I think he went in every afternoon after school as well. Joe knew all of the customers and was able to translate for me when I couldn't decipher what a customer wanted. There was one little black child, younger than ten years old, who ordered the same thing every day. The first time I encountered him, I couldn't for the life of me understand a word he was saying. Joe just smiled as he watched me try to figure out what this cute little guy wanted. He asked for, what sounded like, a "squawbey beywash ana moo pa." After I asked him to repeat his order for the fourth time, Joe chuckled and whispered in my ear, "He wants a strawberry belly washer and moon pie." He could tell by the look on my face that I was still confused so he proceeded to show me the 16-oz. bottles of Town Hall soda which came in several flavors including strawberry. They tasted like colored water with fruit flavoring and were called "belly washers" because they contained enough liquid to wash out a normal stomach. I had heard of moon pies from working at other grocery stores. They were two large cookies, sandwiched together with some kind of sweet spread. Together, the large drink and cookie, for only ten cents, could fill up a hungry ten-year-old. Within a couple of weeks, I could understand almost every thing my young friend said.

I liked working at Maurice's. It was a small neighborhood store where the customers felt very much at home and were very friendly, for the most part. Joe knew the store better than Maurice did and was always there to lend a helping hand, if I couldn't find an item in stock. My biggest problem was selling fresh meat. Orders for pickled pigs' feet didn't pose a problem for me since they were prepackaged in a jar. I could even handle the fresh pig's feet, but I didn't have the constitution for hog maws or pig liver. Beef liver was no problem, it had some body to it, but pig liver was more like Jello. The first and last time I tried to help a customer requesting those two items, I lost my lunch before I could finish wrapping the order. From then on, whenever customers asked for either hog maws or pig liver, I turned them over to Joe.

Ms. Ruth Cockrell was a good history teacher and a strict disciplinarian—which might explain why I never got a good grade in her class even though I loved history. I had a habit of sketching in all of my classes, which was annoying to some of my teachers. Sketching was my form of doodling, my antidote to boredom. I actually found that doodling helped me concentrate on what was being presented in class, or more accurately, kept me from day-dreaming or falling asleep.

Ms. Cockrell noticed me doodling during a class period, and went on with her lesson without any hint that I was annoying her. When the period was over, she asked me stay after class. I wasn't sure why I was about to be reprimanded. She knew that I always sketched in class, but that I knew the class material at test time. Without a word of reprimand, she asked to see what I had been sketching. I reluctantly handed her a drawing of one of the students in the class and she studied it approvingly. She then told me that ever since I had been in her 10th grade history class she had been thinking about a project that would be a great tool for teaching the Civil War and would make good use of my talent. The project consisted of making poster-sized pencil portraits of Confederate generals from photographs she would provide. I would get extra credit for the work as well as her undying gratitude. Anticipating my concerns, she had already checked with Mrs. McKee and Ms. Messer and let them know that this project would not interfere with any artwork that was required by the newspaper or yearbook. This was a challenging project, and sort of like an offer I couldn't refuse. I accepted the assignment although I could not guarantee that the job would be finished by the end of the semester.

I had no idea there were so many Confederate generals. I only finished six or seven by semester's end but I promised that I would work on the rest over the summer. The extra credit probably factored into my history grade, but that wasn't the only A on my report card, an indication that I was taking my schoolwork more seriously. After the summer, with a great deal of pride and relief that I had completed the project, I gave Ms. Cockrel the drawings of the remaining Confederate generals, She said that she never doubted that I would come through as she reached in her desk drawer and pulled out photographs of Union generals for my next assignment. She could sense that I had used up all of my enthusiasm on the first assignment, but she also needed the Union generals to properly teach the subject. I agreed to do as many as I could without committing myself to do them all. I ended finishing five Union generals and left it up to her to find someone else to complete the job.

It was a busy summer. I applied again for a job at Camp Daniel Morgan, and this time the director, Lawrence Posner, hired me as a counselor. Although I was still young for a counselor, Mr. Posner said he hired me because of my special interest and ability in art. He also thought that I could help with religious services. Alan Gilman was also hired as counselor; he was already over the minimum age of 17. He was given waterfront duties and other athletic responsibilities. I had known Alan for years, but we had never been close. He was almost a year older than his cousin, Paul Muldawer and me, which put him in a different crowd even though we were all members of D.S.I. At Daniel Morgan, Alan and I became pretty close even though our assignments were totally different. I spent more time with him those few weeks than in the all of the six or so years we had known each other.

Even though I was only a junior counselor, I was responsible for the boys in my bunk, and I felt like we all got along quite well. I found that I was not mature enough to have the patience to deal with whining kids and ended up showing favoritism to the non-whiners. One way of rewarding my campers for good behavior was to take them boating, one at a time. One such time turned out to be ill advised. The weather appeared threatening, but I felt confident enough in my rowing ability and wasn't too concerned about the choppy waters. Actually, I had suggested postponing our outing but the camper, whose turn it happened to be, was afraid of loosing his turn and pleaded with me to go on.

The further away we rowed from our dock, the choppier the lake's water became. Along with the wind that was causing the lake—known as Hard Labor Creek—to be so turbulent, the sky started getting increasingly dark and rain started to come down in sheets. I informed the young camper that we were going to turn around and go back, but as we tried to change direction, we found ourselves unable to fight the strong current, carrying us away from our Camp's pier. The current carried us windward regardless of how hard we rowed. I noticed an alcove by the shore and we rowed with all our might, perpendicular to the current, in an attempt to reach the alcove's calmer waters. It took about fifteen minutes to navigate the fifty or so feet, but we finally made it out of the storm and into the alcove. We were soaking wet and it was still pouring down rain as we stepped ashore and discovered that we had landed at a girls' camp on the other side of the lake.

The counselors of the girls' camp were kind enough to take us inside their main building and offered us towels, a change of clothes and some hot soup. Eventually they were able to make phone contact with our camp to let them know we were safe. Mr. Posner didn't sound too pleased that I had taken a camper rowing in inclement weather but he was at least relieved that we were safe. A van came to pick us up and I made arrangements to bring back the boat the next day. We did not get a hero's welcome when we returned to camp.

Mr. Posner started criticizing my work as an art instructor, saying that while I was helpful to the talented campers, that I was not teaching those less talented to improve their skills. He was also critical of my help in leading the religious services. I thought that having Orthodox services for *Shabbat* would meet everyone's needs and I was unfamiliar with Conservative or Reform prayer services. Apparently that offended the parents of some of the campers and I was told that other arrangements would be made. Some of the campers had written home about my boating incident in the storm. I was not surprised when Posner told me that my services would not be needed after the first four-week session.

The Daniel Morgan girls' camp was adjacent to the boys' camp and certain activities were done together. Occasionally swimming was one of those. Pat, a junior counselor, was from Valdosta, Georgia. She was very popular with both campers and counselors, the latter probably because she looked so good in her one-piece swimsuit. I remembered her from the Young Judea convention in Birmingham. Both Alan and I took a liking to her, but she didn't pay a lot of attention to either one of us. She was one of the lifeguards, so I did get to talk to her a bit at the joint swimming sessions. She was friendly enough, but I could sense an underlying animosity and I had no idea where it was coming from. As I was preparing to leave after my early dismissal from the camp, she asked me to stay and talk to her after the swimming session.

I went to her figuring she wanted to say goodbye and hoping that she would suggest that we stay in contact. When we were alone she let me have it with both barrels. She reminded me that we had met in Birmingham and informed me that the girl I had taken a liking to then was her best friend. She was aware that the girl had written to me and that I had not responded. She did not believe that I had misplaced the letter with the return address and accused me of being a callous Casanova who took pride in breaking girls' hearts. I felt terrible. As it was, I really liked her friend very much. After we both had gone our own way, however, I got caught up in routine activities and apparently was too lazy or not ready, at sixteen, to get involved in a regular correspondence with a girl.

I didn't feel very good about losing my job as junior counselor after only four weeks, even though Mr. Posner told the Bureau that my job was cut only because enrollment was down for the second session of camp. Pat's send off didn't make me feel any better about myself. Nevertheless, I made up my mind to make the best of what was remaining of the summer and find a job in the art field that I might be able to keep on part time basis during my senior year. I made a list of commercial art firms and advertising firms and tried to get appointments. From the two or three that were kind enough to grant me an interview, I discovered that a portfolio of my high school work just didn't make the grade. They were kind in their appraisal of my potential, but said that I needed a lot of experience and training before I could expect to work as a professional.

Mrs. Goncher was on vacation when I returned to Atlanta from Camp Daniel Morgan. The plan had been for me to stay with the Tucks when camp was over until she returned, so I just moved in with them a little earlier. Worried that I might waste the rest of the summer hanging around York's Pool Hall and the like, Mr. Tuck expressed concern that I didn't have a job. While I was making the motions to seek a job in the art field, he made a few inquiries in my behalf regarding summer employment. After none of my leads panned out, he approached me about a possible job that he had found for me.

He told me to report to Mr. Cohen, a friend of his who owned a battery rebuilding shop on Decatur Street. The establishment consisted of a storefront with a desk, a telephone and a couple of chairs up front and work shop in the rear operated by one man who probably knew more about car batteries and how to rebuild them than the manufacturers did. Joe Tuck convinced the owner, who spent eighty percent of his time traveling in and around the outskirts of Atlanta picking up dead batteries, that he needed someone to open and close the shop for him and man the front desk. Mr. Tuck added that, by hiring me, the owner could be more flexible with his time, and thereby expand his radius of travel. Also, since I was only a high school senior, he could get by with paying me a salary that he felt he could afford. I, in turn, would answer the telephones, take orders for rebuilt batteries or for the pick of old batteries and take any other messages.

Sam was a one man battery rebuilding department. He had been with the business since it started and while he required no supervision to get his work done, he never answered the phone or opened and closed the shop. Prior to my arrival, Mr. Cohen had always opened the shop at 7 a.m. and came back to lock up at 6 p.m., limiting the range of his daily trips. These trips were to pick up the dead batteries that he brought back to the shop to be rebuilt and delivery of rebuilt batteries. To cover a larger area, he had two or three more employees who drove to regions throughout the southeast. As much as the business relied on Sam to rebuild the otherwise junked batteries and as diligent as Sam appeared to be, I could not understand why he was not trusted with a key to the shop.

Mr. Cohen introduced me, as the new office manager, to the man with whom I would be spending 11 hours a day. He told Sam that I would be opening and closing, when he wasn't there, and that, in his absence, any questions should be referred to me. That got Sam and me off on the wrong foot. If I wondered what possessed Mr. Cohen to put a seventeen year old in charge of a man who had been his employee for so many years and knew the business inside out, I was sure that it crossed Sam's mind as well. In response to my inquiry, Joe Tuck hinted that Sam might have had a drinking problem in past years, but he wasn't quite sure.

Anyway you slice it, I was not comfortable acting as Sam's superior, and I made a point of letting him know that. Sam was not the talkative type, but I persisted in trying to make conversation with him. My gift of gab finally broke him down enough for me to let him know that I had no intention of interfering with the way he did his work, or of being any kind of a threat to him. I told him that I was interested in what he was doing and wanted to watch him, from time to time, to get a better idea of the work that was done. Mainly, I wanted to let him know that I expected to be relying on him for answers when questions came up, instead of the other way around.

Once Sam and I understood each other, everything ran smoothly. I opened every morning at 7 sharp and Sam was always there, waiting for me. After watching him work on batteries for a while, I went to the front desk pulled out a paperback novel and started reading, waiting for the phone to ring. I quickly came to realize that, aside from the work Sam was doing, this shop was not a beehive of activity. For the first week the phone rang an average of six times a day and hardly anyone came in the front door except to be neighborly and say hello. I read an average of two to three books a week, most of which I borrowed from Susan Franco. She worked two doors down in her family's store. Getting to know her better was the bright side of what turned out to be the most boring job in the world.

Having so much time on my hands was the worst part of this job. My smoking habit, which had been less than a pack of cigarettes a day, became exacerbated to the point that I was smoking more than two packs a day after a few weeks. This was not only expensive, cigarettes were about twenty cents a pack, but it affected my health. I had a constant cold accompanied by a deep cough. It got so bad that I had to ask for time off to see a doctor.

Dr. Weinstein examined me and told me, unequivocally, to stop smoking cigarettes. He knew that I had been smoking for some years and that it would be difficult for me stop "cold turkey." He suggested that I might want to switch to cigars as a means of tapering off. He told me later that his suggestion was predicated on his assumption that most cigar smokers do not inhale. I guess that put me in the minority. I was so used to inhaling nicotine that I wasn't able to break the habit.

Over the weeks, I was getting weaker and my cough became almost constant. I had been smoking nearly three packs of cigarettes a day and, in tapering off, switched to about eight stogies daily. While it satisfied my craving for nicotine, it was killing me. I went to see Dr. Weinstein again and he admitted me to the hospital immediately. I had really wrecked my respiratory system. By the time the fever subsided, Dr. Weinstein listed the combination of respiratory ailments that I was recovering from and asked if I was ready to quit all smoking. I nodded affirmatively, and went back to sleep. I backed up that nod with a promise when the doctor released me from the hospital. He told me I was lucky. The only permanent effect from my years of smoking, aside from a strong aversion to cigarette smoke, turned out to be chronic bronchitis.

I went back to the shop after being out less than a week. Sam was genuinely happy to see me, but Mr. Cohen was visibly put out by my absence. He asked me not to lock that evening until he came back from a meeting. I still wasn't feeling a 100 percent, but I waited around for him to show up. Thirty minutes past closing time, I was getting very tired and hungry and I needed to get home and take medication. By 7 in the evening, I started worrying when Mr. Cohen had not shown up. I knew that he was somewhere in the neighborhood, so I locked the door and went looking for him. I found him three doors down playing poker in the back of a pawnshop. He was livid at me for disturbing his privacy and not waiting for him. He fired me on the spot, asked for his keys and paid what he owed me out of his pocket. Even though I felt I was treated shabbily, I was relieved to be out of that job.

My next task was to find a job for the remainder of the summer. One that would become an after school job once the school year started. At Jack's suggestion, I went door to door in the garment district on Pryor Street. I wasn't having much luck, as most firms that hired summer help had done so earlier. That is, until I went into Mr. K's establishment. Mr. K had been looking for reliable part-time help and was impressed that I had so much work experience at such a young age. It reminded him of how he had started working when he was very young. He seemed very interested in my background, that I came from Europe during the war, and that I aspired to be self-sufficient. He asked me if I knew his son, Howard, who was about my age. I knew Howard, but not that well. He was in A.Z.A. 518, which was based at the Alliance just as D.S.I. was, but he wasn't involved in sports because of his handicap, which I believe was cerebral palsy. To my surprise, Mr. K said that I could report for work the next day and that I could continue working on a part-time basis after school commenced. I really felt good about myself as I left Pryor Street. I had gone on my own and attained a job which, according to Mr. K's estimation, might have future career possibilities for me.
 The next morning, I showed up bright and early and was greeted by an embarrassed and sad proprietor. He told me that he had gone home excitedly, the evening before, to tell his son that he had hired a friend of his to help out in the business. When Howard found out who the "friend" was, he reportedly had a tantrum and forbade his father from hiring me for any kind of job. He apparently told his father some very unkind things about me and said that I was a hoodlum from the south side of town, and an orphaned refugee to boot. I was told that Howard also exhorted his father to not trust anyone from D.S.I., all of whom his friend Mickey had called "south side serfs." What amazed me was that my brother, Jack, was an active member of A.Z.A.-518 and though he lived with a wealthy family on the north side of town, he too was an orphaned refugee. Mr. K was apologetic and offered to pay me for the day. I politely

refused the pay, not wanting any part of Howard's inheritance, even though I could have used the money.

I reverted to selling shoes at Burt's on weekends and swimming and playing cards at the Progressive Club several days a week. The Progressive Club played a formative role in my teenage years even though I was not a member. It was one of the three Jewish clubs in Atlanta and the only one where I felt welcome. The Mayfair Club was more exclusive, but had not been as much fun when I went there with the Ungers. The Standard Club's membership was mainly from the Temple and, for the most part, it was of old-line Jewish families of German descent. I was told that it was very exclusive and that one could only get in with a pre-approved guest pass from a member. Some of my friends who tried sneaking into both, said the Standard Club was harder to get into than the Venetian Club in Decatur, which had a policy of not allowing Jews. In later years, I met Jewish people of my age group who grew up as part of the Standard Club crowd. I didn't know them and they had never heard of me. That might have been understandable in a city with a large Jewish community, but Atlanta had fewer than ten thousand Jews at the time.

The Progressive Club had a square diving pool, a long swimming pool and a wading pool for the kiddies. I learned to swim in the diving pool when I was ten years old. Dave Eisenberg had been the lifeguard and he decided that the best way for me to learn to swim was to throw me into the diving pool, stand by and make sure I wouldn't drown. I didn't think too kindly of him as he stood, arms crossed, watching me as I struggled to the side, spitting out chlorinated water. When I realized he taught me to swim I thanked him.

I was very grateful to have a place to swim in the summer, particularly since very few places I frequented had air conditioning in the 1940s. On one side of the pools was the main building with its slot machines, until the city confiscated them. On the other side was a grassy area with tables, chairs and benches dispersed throughout for sunbathing and card playing. There was a softball field on a lower level where I learned that softball was my least favorite sport.

To teenage boys, swimming was the major activity at the Progressive Club pool. With a few exceptions, the teenage girls appeared to be more interested in modeling bathing suits. The on-going "parade" was fun to watch. A group of girl's ranging from fourteen to eighteen years old would parade up and down the pool area all day long, never going into the water lest their hair would get wet. Many of them changed their bathing suits two or three times a day. It was a combination fashion show and beauty contest, except that some of the participants were far from beauty queens. There were some that made it worthwhile, but even they were comical at times, just from the shear predictability of their routine.

I kept busy playing gin rummy, a card game at which I was getting quite a reputation. It was not unusual for six or more spectators to stand around as two card players were matching wits and luck. I became the guy to beat in my age bracket and I was even offered financial backing if I would participate in higher stakes games, against the likes of Wally Cowan or Ben "Dead Eye" Edelstein, both of whom later became professional gamblers.

I was more interested in earning spending money and hanging around with the girls who were not participants in the "parade". I think that was the summer I met Jeannie, who was a member of D.O.Z. (Daughters of Zion). She was one of the few D.O,Z. girls who didn't bother with the "parade." There was something very special about her. She wasn't just pretty; she was very down to earth and fun to be with. I often gave up a lucrative gin game to hang around and play Hearts or Casino with Jeannie and her friends. I had a major crush on her, but as teenagers do, I tried not to show it. Finally, I got up the nerve to ask her to be my date for a D.S.I. hayride and was beside myself when she accepted.

I was going to have a date with the girl of my dreams and it seemed too good to be true. Having a girl of my dreams appeared to be an on-going pattern with me, going back to when I was about seven. There almost always seemed to be a girl that I would dream about and would long to have feel about me as I did about her. In virtually every case, the girl would be unattainable, for one reason or another. Those rare times that I did make some headway, or it seemed that my feelings were returned, I would find a way to mess things up. I wanted to constantly be in love and to be loved in return, but I did not know how to hold up my end of a loving relationship. I was afraid of loving someone, only to have her be separated from me just like my mother had been. I resolved to be on my best behavior, to be aware of my every move, lest I ruin this special date.

When we arrived at the park, Sidney Rich asked me to help out with cooking the hot dogs and Jeannie encouraged me to do so. She had friends that she could talk to while I was busy with my chores. As I was working at the grill, an attractive young girl named Brenda started up a conversation. I had never seen her before and I'm not sure whose date she was or where her date was while she was keeping me company. Without being asked, she told me she was seventeen years old. Had I thought about it, she actually looked older than that, but I had no reason to care.

It took more than half an hour, but I finished grilling the hot dogs and went back to my date. Jeannie had noticed Brenda being very attentive while I was grilling and wanted to know how I knew her. Apparently, she knew Brenda better than I because, when I replied that I had never met her before, she was not surprised. Everywhere Jeannie and I went the rest of the evening, Brenda was right there, anxious to start up a conversation. Jeannie got fed up and asked me if I wanted to take the little girl, whom she thought had a crush on me, home. I assured Jeannie that not only was she my date but that I very much wanted to be with her.

No matter what I said, it appeared that the evening was already ruined. On the way home, she asked me if I knew how young Brenda was. She laughed when I told her that Brenda said she was seventeen, indicating that she may have been a good deal younger, but she would not reveal what she knew. Maybe I had been too responsive to the young girl's advances. I had been nervous about this long anticipated date, and made up my mind to avoid doing anything that would spoil it. Unfortunately, as I was wont to do, somehow I managed to screw up what turned out to be my only date with Jeannie. After numerous refusals, I went on with my life and never asked her out again.

As summer vacation of 1949 was coming to a close in Atlanta, my brother Asher was getting married in Basel, Switzerland. Two years before, he had met Henriette Meyer when he was stationed in Germany, while serving in the armed forces of the United States. He was visiting her father, Max Meyer, our father's first cousin, who had ransomed Dad out of the Buchenwald concentration camp after his arrest on *Kristallnacht* (November 9-10, 1938). Asher and Hennie had corresponded for two years and were married on August 21, with our uncle Philipp Auerbach, our mother's brother, standing up for Asher at the *Chuppah* (wedding canopy). There had been no talk; at least that I was aware of, about any or all of us, Asher's four siblings, attending the wedding. In retrospect, I would have liked to have been there, but except for Jack's Bar Mitzvah and Sarah's wedding, I had not participated in or attended any of the other life cycle events of my family. Asher had been unable to attend my Bar Mitzvah and I had accepted that, and I had not been able to attend his in France, in fact I was not even aware when it was happening. At least Jack had been at Asher's Bar Mitzvah. Even if the Justice Department would have allowed us to leave the country, we could not have afforded such a trip. I'm sure Asher never expected us to be there. Asher was able to come to all of our weddings, and even officiated in Flora's and Sarah's weddings.

There have been many weddings and other live cycle events among the families of the five Hirsch children and we all have made every effort to share these events with each other. Some of us are even having *simchas* (joyous events) of grandchildren and I see the importance of having families sharing in these occasions. In retrospect, I am saddened that we were not able to share Asher's wedding, even though we have since shared many *simchas* with Asher and his family.

ATLANTA CONSTITUTION — OCTOBER 24, 1948

NOW I HAVE A MOTHER

'But I Was One of the Lucky Ones,' Says 'Displaced' Youth at Home Here

"I must have been a bad boy—nobody wanted me."

Sixteen-year-old Benjamin Hirsch gets a whimsical twinkle in his brown eyes when he says that, harking back to "that old bad time" when he was only nine, but already a wanderer on the European Continent.

That brave twinkle had a hard time staying put while Benjamin, with other displaced children of Europe, was shifted from his native Frankfurt, Germany, to Paris, to Vichy, to Madrid, to Lisbon, to some place he doesn't remember in Switzerland . . .

"But I was one of the lucky ones; I finally got to the States, and now I have a mother," he smiled, turning that persistent twinkle on Mrs. Samuel Goncher.

Mrs. Goncher has been mother—and her cozy house at 72 Ormond St., S. W., home—to more orphaned children than she can remember in the years since 1930.

"She's wonderful—and our oldest foster mother in point of service," declares Mrs. Ethel Copelan, Executive Director of the Jewish Children's Service, a Red Feather agency affiliated with the Atlanta Community Chest.

Mrs. Goncher already had four children of her own when she answered a Service appeal 18 years ago, but her home and heart were big enough for all the foster children who have found a haven there, sometimes for months, often for years.

Formerly the Hebrew Orphans' Home, the Service places in foster homes Jewish children who for any reason need care outside their own homes; subsidizes children and widowed mothers in their own homes; helps unmarried women prior to and after birth of children, and places such children for adoption.

Because of the Service's Student Aid Loan Program, Benjamin can take advantage of his artistic ability. The adopted Atlantan is cartoonist for his high school newspaper.

The Service last year had 83 different children under care provided 10,317 days' care in foster homes. The Chest will provide this Red Feather agency with $15,386 in 1949.

"I HAVE A HOME NOW"—Benjamin Hirsch, once a displaced European shifted from place to place, makes that proud boast now. He chats here with his foster mother, Mrs. Samuel Goncher, of 72 Ormond St., S. W., who 18 years ago answered an appeal from the Jewish Children's Service and has been foster mother to more than 15 orphans since then. She holds a photograph of "my first boy." The Service is a Red Feather agency aided by the Atlanta Community Chest.

Eleventh grade class at Hoke Smith High School, 1949. Ben, above on the back row, Frances Tiller and Betty Meadows, front row, 3rd and 4th from left.

Photos of Doyle "Whitey" Kugler from the 1948 Hoke Smith annual, *The Smithsonian*. Photos courtesy Asher Banator.

168 Home Is Where You Find It

Some of Ben's cartoons from *The Senator*, 1948-'49 school year.

X

LIGHT ON THE HORIZON— SENIOR YEAR, September 1949 –June 1950

A cease-fire ended the Arab-Israeli conflict on January 7, 1949, nearly nine months after the nascent state of Israel was attacked by its Egyptian and Jordanian neighbors. This may have been the time for me to think in terms of eventually making my way to the newly-formed Jewish State that came into being, in no small measure, as a result of the Holocaust. I heard about young Jews who went to Palestine to fight for the new state and others who now were going to Israel to participate in building up the new nation. For some reason, I never felt that, as a ward of the U.S. State Department, I had the option to make such a choice. Over the years, there have been times that I regretted not taking any action toward that end.

Whether I had a choice or not, the road I took was to focus on my future in the country that had offered me and my siblings refuge, the United States of America. By the time the summer was over, I was, with great anticipation, looking forward to my senior year at Hoke Smith High School, even though it would include the angst of making decisions regarding higher education and career choices. Foregoing higher education, as many of my classmates were contemplating, was not an option for me. I just needed to find the field that would best utilize my talents while enabling me to become a self-sufficient and productive member of American society.

Starting a new school year had always been exciting for me. There was a special feeling this senior year; being in the upper echelon of the student body and knowing that this could be my sixth and last year at Hoke Smith. Thinking of the future was a mixed bag, with both the excitement and apprehension of all the challenges that lie ahead. But things were beginning to look good for the physical plant of the junior high school turned high school. After only two years of existence, Hoke Smith High had a stadium, although the new facility on Georgia Avenue was shared as a home stadium with Roosevelt High. The formal dedication of W. O. Cheney Stadium appropriately took place at the Smith High versus Roosevelt High game on September 30, which Smith won

18 to 13, on a late rally, before a bipartisan crowd of five thousand fans. For their first two years, both schools had been playing their home games at whatever facility had been available. This new stadium, together with the excitement of the game itself, accounted for the euphoric mood of the crowd.

The staff of *The Senator* finally decided to add the title of Staff Cartoonist on the masthead and, thus, my contribution to the school newspaper was officially recognized. I had been contributing cartoons for *The Senator* for the two years since its inception, but had not continued the "Hoke and Smitty" comic strip that appeared regularly in the junior high school paper, *The Vanguard*. Mrs. McKee asked me to resurrect the strip. We decided to change the name to "Smitty," even though his girl friend, Hoke, would still be an integral part of the strip. I had to assure our staff advisor that Hoke would be drawn as an attractive high school senior, not as buxom femme fatale. In the meantime, Ms. Messer had me start working on the artwork for *The Smithsonian* so it could go to press early enough to come out in the spring.

I had turned seventeen and was ready for new adventures. I was at that awkward age when facial hair began to appear, but not enough of it to justify shaving, so I thought. "Pig" Crane, a guard on the football team and a friend, pulled me aside and told me that my not shaving annoyed several of the football players, including him, and that if I didn't shave the fuzz off, one or all of them would do it for me. I wondered out loud why anyone would care if I shaved or not. He responded that I should trust him, that he was forewarning me as a friend. I still didn't understand, but I trusted "Pig," and shaved that night.

My interest in girls had not diminished, but I couldn't get over my obsession with Jeannie. Maybe it was because she was not available after that one botched date. I found myself drawing intricate doodling around her name and even carved up the top of my desk in Mr. Byrd's English class. It was the most elaborate doodle/etching I had ever done and it took up over eighty percent of the desk top. It became a conversation piece among the girls in the senior class. No one knew who Jeannie was, but that didn't stop them from teasing me incessantly about her, a fate that I had brought upon myself. Charlie Byrd looked the other way. As long as I did well on his assignments and tests and I let him keep the sketches I made of him, he was not interested in having me report to the principal. I saw Mr. Byrd twenty years later after he had retired from the school system and was working for the Biltmore Hotel. Among other things, he remembered the desk top and said that, to his knowledge, it was still in the same classroom and had become the subject of several legends.

The time had come to pick senior superlatives for posterity. I don't remember whether the senior class, or the entire student body, voted on the most likable, most representative, most athletic, most likely to succeed, most intellectual, and most attractive senior. To select the most talented senior, a talent contest was staged in the auditorium. I was told that I was in contention and encouraged to find a way to display my talent on stage. Fred Azar was a drummer in the band and he had no problem performing to an audience of the student body. Jimmy Woods sang a couple of popular tunes.

For my talent, I entered the stage in a smock with a beret, carrying an easel with a large sketch pad. I asked for a volunteer from the audience to come on the stage and pose for me. An eighth grader volunteered and sat on the stage and, as the audience watched, I sketched his likeness in the ten minutes that I was allotted. I actually thought that act, which had been dreamed up by one of the faculty, was about as interesting as watching ice melt or honey dripping from a bee hive. By the time I finished the sketch, I had lost the attention of most of the audience. I could have painted the Mona Lisa and they would not have been impressed. Deservedly, Fred Azar won. I was pleased at coming in second, but I was embarrassed at the spectacle I made of myself I would have preferred to try my luck at singing, but I wasn't offered that choice.

The biggest event of the winter vacation was the regional A.Z.A. convention in Savannah, Georgia. D.S.I. had become affiliated with A.Z.A. since our fallout with Young Judea more than a year before. Virtually everyone from Atlanta who was going to the convention went by train. Several cars were booked to accommodate all of the A.Z.A. and B.B.G. (Bnai Brith Girls) chapters from Atlanta on the *Nancy Hanks*, the latest in train design, leaving from Terminal Station. Unofficially, interaction and rivalries between chapters started on the train. Predictably, card games sprang up throughout the cars. I was playing gin rummy with Bobby Chaitte, who insisted on raising the stakes with every game he lost. Within a short time, he ran out of money and decided to quit rather than go into debt. Burton had been watching me play and left for a few minutes. He came back just as Bobby and I were finishing our game and told me that five other 518 guys had a poker game going and that they wanted me for a sixth. He mentioned, in passing, that he had been touting my poker skills to them and taunting them with the fact that I had taken one of their members to the cleaners in a game of gin rummy.

Burton introduced me to the other players, although I knew most of them, and I sat down to play. I had never played poker with so many spectators before. It made me feel as if we were playing the world series of poker. Fortunately for those watching, it was a good game. The 518 boys were not novices, and seemed to have played extensively with each other. I had the advantage of being the new guy in the game with no predictable habits. With the build up that Burton had given me, the other players watched me like a hawk to see if they could determine when and if I were bluffing and to make sure that I didn't cheat. They insisted on limiting the dealers' choices to five card draw or five card stud with no wild cards. This made it more of game of skill and suited me to a tee.

I was getting my share of good cards, but I made it a point to stay in with some bad hands and even to bluff a couple of times with obvious losers just to throw them off. Then came the hand of which legends are made. Billy was sitting across from me and he opted to deal five card stud. Unbeknownst to him, he flashed my hole card to me as he was dealing. It took my best poker face to keep from revealing my joy when I saw that it was an ace. Before he dealt the first face card, I declared that I was going to play this one blind, that is, not to look at my hole card until all four face cards have been dealt. That caught everyone's attention, particularly after my first face card also had been an ace.

Being high man, I opened the bidding and only got one raise from someone who either paired up or was feeling me out to see if I would look at my hole card. I raised him back on "general principles." The game went on with more raises after each card and nobody going out. By the third up card, it was obvious that this was going to be the largest pot of the day. Finally, the last round of face cards had been dealt and fortunately not a pair was showing on the board. The bidding was getting furious and since nobody was going out, I had to assume that everybody had paired up their hole card somewhere along the way or at least could beat the ace high that I had showing. After the bidding was over, I let everyone declare and show their hand before I touched my hole card. As it turned out, everyone had paired up their hole card with the best of their hands being a pair of kings. Then one of the players grabbed my hole card and turned it over.

There was an initial moment of shock as at least the five other players gaped at the pair of aces, then cheers from the D.S.I. partisans. The game broke up with all kinds of rumors and allegations. No one could figure out how I had known that I had aces wired, but most of them were convinced that somehow I did know. It was not my deck of cards, so I couldn't have marked the cards. I was not the dealer, so I could not have cheated on the deal. And, more than a dozen people were watching and saw that I never touched my hole card. It made for great conversation and lots of speculation, but I offered no comment. Later, I confided in Burton, only because he wouldn't leave me alone until I did, that it was as simple as the dealer flashing my hole card. I was actually quite surprised that no one else noticed the sloppy way the dealer had dealt out the cards. Probably every player had his hole card flashed to him. The question was, did any of them pay that much attention?

The *Nancy Hanks* pulled into Savannah and everyone was ready to start having a good time. Some of us had already been having a good time and word got around to the staff leaders that there had been a card-sharp on board. I was pulled aside and reprimanded for gambling. The staff person was aware that one person alone could not gamble at poker or gin rummy, but he was especially disturbed because he had gotten a telephone call from Dr. Chaitte, who complained that his son had called home for more money. I was forced to promise that I would not play cards for money for the remainder of the convention, at least not with anyone from the Atlanta chapters.

Everyone was having fun at the convention. The basketball tournament was exciting, but compared to Birmingham, uneventful. Burton was still trying to set up poker games for me, even though he knew that I was grounded from gambling at the convention. There were many pretty girls there, but boys outnumbered them by a wide margin and my buddies and I chose not to get involved in the chase. Most of my friends did not have dates for the final banquet. They stood on the sidelines critiquing everyone else's choice of dates and enjoyed having fun at everyone else's expense. Each A.Z.A. chapter had its own little pack of groupies without dates. They all, my friends included, were acting like a pack of disgusting teenage hoodlams, thankfully not violent. I tried to distance myself from that scene and mingled on the dance floor trying to socialize and meet people.

There had been a lot of drinking going on. Apparently the liquor stores in Savannah were not big on checking identification. Throughout the evening, booze was flowing freely. Everywhere I turned, I was offered a shot of bourbon or Canadian Club. I wondered where the chaperones, who had grounded me from gambling, were. Burton kept asking me to come with him for some kind of mischief, but I was more interested in socializing and people watching. After the last dance, as the band was putting away their instruments, he pulled me aside and told me that a bunch of guys from other chapters had been waiting to meet me. As I followed him to one of the side rooms of the main hall, I wondered why they would want to meet me. There must have been twenty boys waiting anxiously for my arrival. I had absolutely no idea what Burton had organized or what was going to happen next.

Everyone was standing and one guy in the middle was holding a pint bottle of booze. Burton pulled me into what felt like the middle of the ring in a boxing match. He put his arm around my shoulder and proclaimed that I was D.S.I.'s champion drinker, that I could drink anyone there under the table. In astonishment and amazement at that ridiculous assertion, I protested that I already had consumed several drinks of hard liquor and that I had no desire for any more. At this point several boys started teasing Burton, saying things like, "so is this the guy who's going drink us all under the table? Hah!" I can't believe that I actually felt bad for Burton at that point. Someone handed me an almost full pint bottle of Canadian Club and the chants started egging me on to chugalug it. Attribute it to peer pressure and sheer stupidity, but the next thing I knew, accompanied by raucous cheers, I was downing the bottle.

The last thing I remembered was hearing Burton say, "See, what did I tell you?!" I had no idea how much time elapsed when I was awakened by slaps to my face. I was lying on a sofa in one of the hotel rooms. I could not remember how I got there, but there was quite a crowd intent on sobering me up. I was finally awake, but I was nowhere near sober. I heard Paul suggest that they put me under a cold shower. I resisted, saying that all I needed was to sleep it off. Paul and his followers were persistent. I would not let them take my clothes off so they held me under the cold shower, fully clothed. I was angrily fighting back and, in the process, I grabbed at Paul, clutching his cashmere sweater which was torn in the tussle. Finally, some of the more sensible people in the group got me out of the shower, dried me off as best they could and took me outside to walk off my condition so that I could at least appear sober when we caught the train back to Atlanta. My well intentioned friends would have done me a service if they had prevailed before I was thrown in shower with my clothes on. It was New Years Eve and very cold outside. As they were walking with me, I started shivering and my teeth were chattering. Yet, I felt as if I were burning up. I was thankful when they finally took me back upstairs and allowed me to try to sleep it off.

When I woke up, we were on the *Nancy Hanks* on our way back to Atlanta. I was told that I had not been carried to the train, but had walked to the station with some help, and gotten onto the train without raising the chaperones' suspicion. I had been asleep on the train for more than an hour and had no recollection of getting on. When I woke up, several girls passed by and shook their head at the spectacle. Jeannie was among them.

I sat up and started thinking about what an absolute fool I had made of myself. Burton was glad to see that I was alright, but expressed no remorse about egging me on to get drunk. Several people came up to see how I was doing. I told them all that I would be fine, even though I felt feverish and achy all over. Paul came up and handed me a bill for sixteen dollars for tearing his cashmere sweater.

I was relieved to be back home so I could jump in bed and sleep until I felt better. Mrs. Goncher greeted me at the door and before I could say a word, I passed out right in front of her. When I came to, I told her that I wasn't feeling well and asked to go to bed. My fever was 103 degrees and I had a slight case of pneumonia. Thankfully, Mrs. Goncher never knew the whole story. She heard something about the shower incident, but not about what had precipitated it. She just took care of me and nursed me back to health. She told people that I was run down from lack of sleep. Alice had heard the details from Sidney but was kind enough to not report my self-destructive behavior.

Sarah and Harry moved into a larger apartment 305 Atlanta Avenue and she renewed her efforts to have me come live with them. She suggested to the Bureau that I should make the move in June, after my graduation from high school. Mrs. Goncher suggested, as long as this was what I wanted, that the move could take place when she was going out of town. She was leaving for Nebraska on March 1 and thought this would be the appropriate time to make the move. Sarah began broaching the subject with me. I was not unhappy at the Goncher house, but I knew that Sarah wanted me to come live with her. She probed me for any complaints I had with Mrs. Goncher and the only one I could come up with was that she disapproved of my smoking. Sarah was quick to point out that Harry smoked and that therefore it would be okay for me to smoke. That tilted the scale. The next time my case worker, Ed Zabell, broached the subject with me, I told him that I would be agreeable to moving in with Sarah, although I had no complaints with Mrs. Goncher. He said he would start the process and, if all went well, I would be able to move in with Sarah and Harry in March.

Mr. Zabell had done a lot of investigating about Sarah and Harry's ability to take on the responsibility of caring for my needs, even though I was almost a high school graduate. It was expected, regardless of where I was living, that I would start to become self sufficient after high school, even if I were attending college. At my request, expenses for medical treatment were still to be covered by the Bureau. The last item we discussed was whether I should apply for a scholarship in art from either the University of Georgia or the High Museum of Art.

I was in the process of putting a portfolio together for my scholarship application to the High. I had started a couple of oil paintings in school. One of them was from a photographic portrait of my mother and father at their engagement. Neither painting was finished, but I had many pencil drawings and some ink drawings, including some of Ms. Cockrell's generals and some of the art work and cartoons I had been making for *The Senator* and the *Smithsonian*. I was told, however, that my application could not be submitted until the oil paintings were completed.

In the meantime, my algebra teacher, Miss Ruth Rogers, who was the first woman graduate of Georgia Tech's night school, wanted to submit my name for a four-year U.S. Navy scholarship to Georgia Tech. She felt that with my math aptitude, I would be a shoo-in for the one Georgia Tech scholarship that was being offered to a senior at Hoke Smith. Under this scholarship, the Navy would pay all of my expenses, including a living allowance, for four years. I would have to keep a 2.5 or better grade point average and after graduation, I would have to serve four years as an officer in the Navy. I was very proud that she wanted to recommend me, since I was not one of top students in the senior class.

I did have the best average in her algebra and geometry classes and I attributed that to her ability to motivate me. We got to know each other when I did a profile on her for *The Vanguard* in junior high school. In every issue, I included a drawing of one of the teachers along with an interview, without naming the teacher. The reader would have to guess the teacher's identity from the drawing and interview. I learned about her pioneering graduation from Georgia Tech's night school and about her deep religious convictions from that interview. I had great respect for her and when she told me she would not tolerate anything but my best in her class, she got it. Since it was up to her to make the recommendation from our senior class, I gratefully gave her permission to submit my name.

I had been having nosebleeds off and on for years, but lately they were coming much more frequently. I was sent to see Dr. Nathan Gershon who had cauterized my nose years before as a treatment for nosebleeds. He took a quick look, told me that I had a broken blood vessel in one of my nasal passages and proceeded to give me a shot of Novocain to deaden the area in preparation for cauterization. He took a phone call while waiting for the Novocain to do its job. The phone conversation seemed to last forever as I sat in the doctor's chair waiting to be worked on. He apologized for the delay and proceeded with the cauterization. A minute or so into the procedure, I started to feel pain. I suggested that the Novocain may have worn off, to which he shook his head and responded that he gave me enough Novocain to put a bull elephant to sleep. The doctor was a pretty big guy and was built like a football player. In fact, I was told he had played college football. More importantly, he was the doctor and I was supposed to have faith in what he said. I sat back and relaxed, reassured that this would be over in a few minutes. He started with the cauterization again and within seconds it felt as if he hit a nerve. The pain was so sharp that both of my arms automatically swung out and one of my fists hit his nose. The doctor calmly wiped the blood from his nose and decided to give me another shot of Novocain. That seemed to do the trick and I was out of there in about thirty minutes. I apologized to Dr. Gershon, but he felt that no apology was needed, even though his nose was broken.

Harry came over to help me move on February 1. He and Sarah had a one-bedroom apartment and I was going to sleep in the living room on a sofa that opened up into a bed. The move was good for the agency. As far as they were concerned, this was a free home with no expense to the agency. They agreed, however, to continue to pay some of my medical and dental expenses, until I could become totally self reliant. Although she had been fighting to have me move in with her for a long time, Sarah soon found out that I came with my own baggage and the need to deal with all kinds of issues. I still had four months left in high school. I was very concerned about making good grades to enhance my chance for a scholarship. Even though I had just been inducted into the Hoke Smith chapter of the Quill & Scroll journalistic honor society, I could not convince Sarah that good grades and a scholarship for higher education were priorities of mine. Particularly since I had seldom brought books home for homework and, as had been my custom, I was keeping late hours. She eventually laid down the law and I started letting her know where I would be and when I would be home.

Miss Rogers gave me the sad news that I was ineligible for the Navy scholarship because I was not yet a citizen of the United States. She pleaded with the powers that be assuring them that I was the most qualified and the only reason I was not yet a citizen was that the law did not contain provisions for a refugee to apply until his eighteenth birthday. She felt that because I had come from an alien country might have affected the decision to disqualify me. I was heartbroken. Deep down inside, I was depending on this scholarship and had slacked off work on my portfolio for art scholarships. The scholarship went to Grady Waters, vice president of the school, an all A student, halfback on the football team and an all around nice guy. He flunked out of Georgia Tech before the end of the first year.

The plan became to enter the High Museum of Art competition in hopes of getting a scholarship there. Ms. Beacom was very confident that I would win, and encouraged me to work hard. Many of my friends in the senior class said they envied me because the course for my future had been set, while they did not know what careers they wanted to pursue after high school. Victor Copeland and I had many conversations on the subject. He thought I should become a commercial artist or a cartoonist and bemoaned that he still had no direction after graduation. Art was an enjoyable pastime for me, but I wasn't sure I was good enough at it to make a living and I wasn't certain that I wanted to try. Victor convinced me that I should make the best of the gift God gave me and pursue some form of art as a vocation.

Sarah kept me informed about our claims under the German indemnification laws. Asher had found that our house on Grünestrasse was still been standing and occupied by tenants, six families, who paid rent to an administrator appointed by the government of Frankfurt am Main. The house was in our father's name although the title was encumbered by a small mortgage. To get the title in our name, Asher paid the mortgage from his savings while he was serving in Germany in the army of occupation. She also told me that Asher had filed claims for all of us for Dad's loss of practice. All of this was interesting, but I had too many other things on my mind. I was glad that Asher was handling these matters. I was busy trying to make the best grades I could, and getting a scholarship to a college. I still had commitments to the school paper and was almost finished with the artwork for the yearbook, and I also had a part time job at Beck's Shoe Store.

Ms. Beacom offered an advanced art class in which she allowed me to work on my own creating more work for my portfolio. In March, she was called to be an expert witness for the G.B.I. in a case that would require at least two or three days of her time. She found a substitute for her regular classes, but she felt, as she instructed our class, that an advance art class should be able to get its work done without constant supervision. She referred the class to me, in the event that anyone needed some help or a problem came up. She reminded them that I had my own work to do and interruptions should be kept to a minimum. Finally, she said that she trusted a group that was interested enough in taking an advance art course to behave. With that, she went on to her assignment and left me in charge.

The first day, the class did well. Interruptions were few and far between and everyone worked on his or her own project. The next day, I was in my own little corner, working on a pencil drawing of Venus de Milo. Ronnie Watkins, a football player who had a flair for art, finished his project and came over to get some advice on what to work on next. He looked at my drawing as I was completing the shades and shadows, and waited patiently for me to finish it. He expressed great admiration for the drawing and asked if he could hold it up to the light to study my technique further. I should have known better. I knew Ronnie to be a mischievous trouble maker and I should not have fallen for his ruse.

As I started to put my materials away, Ronnie put Ann Lovell's name on my drawing and pinned it in the display case facing the hall. Ann, a pretty and very statuesque girl, had been in the class, although she was not a senior. She was very upset and embarrassed and demanded that Ronnie take the drawing out of the display case, which happened to be facing the principal's office. I pleaded with him as he put the key in his pocket and dared me to try and get it from him. He was much bigger and stronger than I, but for more reasons than one, I had to try to get the key from him. I didn't know whether to be more afraid of Ronnie or of Ann's brother, an all-city tackle on the football team bigger than Ronnie and me put together, or of Ms. Beacom, who had put her trust in me by leaving me in charge of this advanced art class.

I tried to get some of the other boys in the class to help me get the key from Ronnie while Ann ran into the principal's office crying hysterically. The drawing was in the display case for more than an hour before Mr. Keith was able to get Ronnie to open the case by threatening to expel him from school. The damage had been done. More than a hundred students and teachers had seen my drawing. This was only problematic because it was identified as being the drawing of a student, Ann, instead of the enchanting, armless statue of Venus de Milo. As soon as the case was opened, I took out the drawing and erased her name. Ann, still sniffling as she thanked me, said she was satisfied and didn't hold me responsible for the incident. She was really annoyed with Ronnie and she let him know it. I had to promise Mr. Keith that I would do no more drawings of nudes or bare breasted females, even if they were world famous statues. I thought the issue was taken care of, with the exception of my having to come face to face with Ms. Beacom, and I had gone on to my next class. A student assistant interrupted the class to tell me that I was to report to the principal's office immediately.

Mr. Keith looked a little uncomfortable, as he too thought the incident was over, but two teachers had come to his office because felt that they wanted to pursue it further. To my surprise, they were Mrs. McKee and Miss Messer, both teachers for whom I had done a lot of artwork. They were both known to be somewhat prudish, but I felt comfortable in justifying the bare breasts on Venus de Milo and pointed out that Ms. Beacom had approved the project. Before my arrival, the two of them had suggested that I be expelled from school and not allowed to participate in the graduation. After hearing my explanation of the events and that I had approval for the subject matter of my drawing, Mrs. McKee relented and no longer demanded my expulsion. I wondered if the fact that I had not yet completed all of the cartoons for *The Senator* played a part in her decision.

Miss Messer, whose yearbook had already gone to press, would not let up. She said that it was totally unacceptable to display a drawing of a woman with bare breasts and that I was responsible for the drawing, which she considered to be pornography. Mr. Keith tried to reiterate all of the explanations and rationalizations given and added that expelling an otherwise fine student a few weeks before graduation was not warranted. We were at an impasse. Mrs. McKee left the meeting and Mr. Keith had work to do. He suggested that Miss Messer and I discuss the issue further and come back to him with an agreed upon reprimand.

Without conversation, Miss Messer and I walked back to her room. School had already been dismissed, but Mr. Keith was going to wait for our resolution. I always considered Frances Messer a friend. I never had her for a class, but had worked extensively with her on the yearbook. To my mind, we related more like colleagues. She started off by telling me that I let her down, that she never knew I was a sex pervert who got thrills from bare breasts. I protested that the human body is a thing of beauty and that Venus de Milo is a recognized masterpiece of ancient Greek art. The more we talked, the angrier she appeared. I stayed calm, trying to make my points. She insisted that my "behavior" called for expulsion. I reminded her that Ronnie's punishment was a week of detention, to which she screamed, "But he did not draw that filth!" I just looked at her. She was shaking and visibly very agitated. I actually felt compassion for her. Something was bothering her and I couldn't figure out what it was. After a long silence, I said something that I was afraid I might regret, but as a friend, I had thought should be said.

"I think you're frustrated, you need a man," just came out of my mouth. I couldn't believe I had the *chutzpah* to actually mouth what I was thinking, but it was my untrained analysis of what was going on. She was so shocked she could hardly speak or catch her breath. Her eyes were wide as if she had seen a ghost. She caught her breath and ran to the principal's office, with me right behind her. Mr. Keith looked up at her from his desk and couldn't help but notice her agitated state. She pointed at me and screamed, "Do you know what he said to me?!"

"No. What did he say?" was all the principal could respond.

She stammered, "He said—he said—never mind, I wash my hands off this mess. He can graduate magna cum laude for all I care." She then stormed out of the office, slamming the door behind her.

Mr. Keith looked at me quizzically. "What did you say to her, anyway?"

I told him that it had been just a personal observation and that it had been said with the best of intentions and left it at that.

Ms. Beacom came back to an advanced art class that was industriously working on projects without the usual banter and horsing around. Even if she had not heard reports of the "unfortunate event," she would have suspected the class was covering something up. I stayed after class to face the music, but she didn't seem too disturbed. We agreed that had I been more careful, I could have kept Ronnie from abducting my drawing, but she was glad that it had been resolved. She did not ask me about Miss Messer and I did not offer anything.

I won a prize at the High Museum of Art Competition, but I did not win the scholarship award. With no scholarship in hand, I made the decision to attend the Atlanta Division of the University of Georgia after graduation and major in art. I would be able to live at home, get a job and try to be self-supporting.

The idea of being self-supporting was scary. The agency had been preparing me for some time to think in those terms after graduation from high school, and for the last six months, Sarah along with Harry had been stressing the importance of my becoming self-sufficient. I had been looking forward to winning a scholarship to help me with higher education. I had put so much stock in getting the Navy scholarship, that I let my other applications slide until it was too late. Now I would have to work my way through school or take out student loans. I did not cherish the thought of being in debt, so the plan for Atlanta Division became my best option.

Graduation was scheduled for May 24 at the Municipal Auditorium in the heart of downtown Atlanta. Our class of eighty-four graduates was going to be the largest in Smith High's three year history. Mrs. Lankford, the music teacher, had the whole graduation class rehearse the songs we would sing at graduation. I still remember the words to "*The Lost Chord*" by Sir Arthur Sullivan, her favorite song which we seemed to rehearse over and over. All of the songs were spiritual and those like Haydn's "*Praise the Lord! Ye Heavens Adore Him*," would have been more appropriate in a church. The only song I liked well enough to memorize was "*The Lost Chord.*" Though it probably was written as a church hymn, it could be appreciated regardless of the listener's religion. It was also the only song that every graduate felt comfortable enough to sing.

To some of the seniors, the graduation couldn't come soon enough. That is, they were celebrating long before the ceremony. For the ceremony, the graduates were seated on portable bleachers and I was afraid that some of the boys who had been drinking before the ceremony would fall off. The boys all wore white dinner jackets and the girls were arrayed in traditional white. D.S.I. was well represented in the program. Leon Tuck gave the welcoming address, Stanford Firestone spoke on "Education, The Basis of Democracy" and Jack Rosenberg was the class orator.

Finally, it was time to receive our diplomas. Mr. Keith read out the names of graduates and we came up to get the piece of paper that was twelve years in the making. Fred Azar was among those who started celebrating early and he barely made it back to his seat. I was glad for him that he was not sitting at the end of the bleachers. Mr. Keith continued on and graduates kept coming: "Dorothy Baxter," (a pause) "Dorothy Huiet," (a pause) "Dorothy Lee," (a pause) "Mary Grammas," (a pause). All of a sudden, Fred Azar who was still sober enough to recognize three girls named Dorothy in a row, blurted out "Where the Hell did she come from!," a split second after Mary's name was called out. The audience and graduating class broke out in laughter and Mr. Keith was visibly agitated. Had Fred not already received his diploma, it might have been held back. The laughter quieted down, Mr. Keith continued and no more was heard from Fred.

After the ceremony there was a dance in the Sky Room. I had a date with Rachel, whom I considered to be a friend. I had wanted to ask Jeannie, but she had turned me down too many times before and I did not want to be turned down for my own graduation. After the dance, at one in the morning, there was a breakfast at Leb's. I started to feel nostalgic at the dance and felt even more so at the breakfast. I knew that I may never see some of my classmates again after that evening. It reminded me of how I felt when I left the children's home at Château du Masgelier in France nine years earlier, knowing that I probably would never see any of the friends I left behind again. I didn't have that feeling when my mother put us on the *Kindertransport* train in Frankfurt because I had been convinced that the separation was meant to be short lived. By the time I had left Masgelier, I had become accustomed to separations that abruptly changed lives. Separations invariably left me with a feeling of loss, along with anxiety about the unknown and the feeling physically translated into my inability to catch my breath.

We took our dates home after the breakfast and about ten of the boys rendezvoused in front of the public library at Georgia Avenue and Capitol Avenue. We stayed there, singing songs, arm in arm, until daybreak. Then it was over. There would be no more Hoke Smith High School for any of us. Some would get jobs, some had plans to get married, some went on to college or university and some joined the armed services. I was going to look for a summer job, hopefully in an art-related field, one that I could, hopefully, continue on part time basis when I planned to start Atlanta Division in the fall. I had not been allowed to take ROTC in high school because I was not able to become a citizen. So it followed that I did not ever consider joining the armed services after graduation, as quite a few of my classmates did. I was told by the head of ROTC that I would not be eligible for army service until I became a citizen and that the age requirement for aliens to apply for citizenship was being raised to twenty-one.

In June, 1950, the American Displaced Persons Act of 1948 was modified by Congress to allow equitable Jewish emigration to the United States. The original act favored Jews whose homelands were under Soviet rule after World War II. This gave new hope to Sarah and me that Werner and Roselene might still be found and allowed to emigrate to the U.S. Sarah had been even more convinced than I that our younger siblings were still alive. The news reignited my desire to join the army and try to get to Europe to find them, but the ROTC instructor's pronouncement of my temporary ineligibility curbed my enthusiasm and made me realize that my quest would have to be put on hold. It became clear that my best course of action was to obtain as much higher education as possible, until I reached the age of eligibility to volunteer for the armed services of the United States.

Ben, c.1950.

Samples of Smitty comic strip, published in *The Senator*, 1949.

XI

A YEAR IN TRANSITION, June 1950–December 1951

Finding a job in an art-related field was easier said than done. Commercial art firms were not really interested in high school graduates, but some of them did indicate that they would take the time to look at my portfolio. The problem was that I did not have a portfolio and didn't know enough about how to put one together. I must have given Ms. Beacom the impression that I had it all together and that I did not require any help. Truth be known, her faith in me was unwarranted. I knew I had talent, but I was very unsure of myself in spite of the confidence that I projected. That lack of confidence in knowing what works to include, coupled with my innate tendency to procrastinate, resulted in no portfolio.

I really wanted to find a job cartooning. I heard about a relatively new company that was doing cartoon animation for the film industry and excitedly called for an appointment. The company consisted of two men in a small office in the Flatiron Building opposite the Loew's Grand Theater. I spoke with them and felt that I made a good enough impression to gain an interview. They seemed interested in hiring someone right out of high school, as long as that person had talent and was trainable. It was an opportunity to get in on the ground floor of a budding industry. After the interview, they asked that I put together a portfolio of the work I had done and come back to see them. I felt very confident while I was in their office. As soon as I started to work on putting my portfolio together, I began to fear that they would not like my work and I started finding reasons to not pursue this job. I never went back to see them and I never even called them to thank them for meeting with me. To this day, I regret not following up on this incredibly unusual opportunity, which in retrospect might have been a heaven sent chance for me to help myself.

I mentioned to my case worker, Ed Zabell, that I needed a job for the summer, one that I would be able to keep on a part-time basis, when I planned to go to the Atlanta Division of the University of Georgia in the fall. He contacted Mr. Max Borenstein, the manager of the basement shoe department at Davison's. Mr. Borenstein had a reputation for helping refugee boys get employment and, I was told, he had himself come to America from Germany in the early 1930s. As expected, Max Borenstein was very gracious as well as helpful. I had a good meeting with him, after which he tried to get me a job with Davison's art department. Unfortunately, they had no openings for young apprentices. He offered me a job as a salesman in his department, which he probably would have done even if I had no experience selling shoes.

Working for Mr. Borenstein was good training. He was attentive to his sales staff and a good mentor. More than once, he suggested that I get an education in fashion design and become a shoe designer. He was a buyer for the department as well as the manager and, as a result, was not always on the sales floor. He, therefore, relied heavily on his assistant manager. The assistant manager was very short, an impeccable dresser, and a slight person with a Caesar complex that manifested itself only when Mr. Borenstein was away from the floor.

My friend, Burton Clein, was hired about two weeks after I started and we worked very well together. We were consistently among the top salespeople in the department, but we were not favorites of the assistant manager, or "Little Caesar" as Burton liked to call him, who took great issue with our friendly approach to the customers, who were, mostly females. I can't deny that several young ladies gave Burton their phone numbers—not a breach of sales ethics—and neither of us rebuffed customers who were flirtatious, but that was part of dealing with the public. "Little Caesar" was open in his disapproval. At first, he reported us to Mr. Borenstein who pulled us aside individually to find out what was going on. Realizing that there had been no customer complaints and that his assistant was a small-minded prude, Mr. Borenstein told us to be careful to not step on his assistant's toes.

A few weeks later, Burton was called to the personnel department to address complaints by anonymous customers about his "aggressively suggestive behavior toward female customers." Personnel would not disclose who had made the complaint, but Burton was sure that it was "Little Caesar." He was given a warning and sent back to the sales floor. As Burton was telling me what transpired, "Little Caesar" came up, with a smug look on his face, and ordered him to go in the stock room and to help straighten out the stock. Burton got into an argument with him, and accused him of making up complaints to the personnel department.

Burton was only about 5'-6" tall, but he was a couple inches taller than "Little Caesar" and a lot stockier, not to mention athletic. He threatened to punch the assistant manager out if he didn't get off his back. That threat played into "Little Caesar's" hand. He ran straight to Mr. Borenstein and reported the altercation. Before he could be fired, Burton quit and left me there to deal with the little tyrant by myself. School had already started and Burton did not particularly want to work during the school quarter anyway.

Not much time elapsed before I was called up to the personnel department with similar complaints. I insisted on knowing who made the complaint against me, but I was told that it would be a violation of store policy to name the accuser. Vociferously, I denied the allegations. Still, I was put on probation and sent back to the sales floor. When Mr. Borenstein came back from an out-of-town buying trip, I asked to see him and recounted what I felt was harassment by his assistant. "Little Caesar" had preempted me and had already delivered a bevy of accusations about me.

Mr. Borenstein wanted to believe me, but I was accused of so many indiscretions that he found it difficult to believe they were all trumped up. I still had a job, but I did not have the trust of my employer. "Little Caesar" waited for the manager to go on another buying trip before he started harassing me in front of the sales staff and customers. I told him to get off my back or I would forget how small he was. He fired me on the spot for threatening him, making me half-way sorry that I didn't follow through on my threat. When Mr. Borenstein came back he called and asked me to come back if I could get along with his assistant. I thanked him but declined, saying that I did not wish to be seduced into committing homicide. I heard through the grapevine that "Little Caesar" was fired a few months later. By that time I already had another job. About twelve years later, I ran into Max Borenstein at a bridge tournament, at the Mayfair Club. We ended up being bridge partners for about a year, never once mentioning "Little Caeser."

I signed up for the fall quarter at the Atlanta Division of the University of Georgia, which was in a single building on Ivey Street in downtown Atlanta, and in walking distance from Five Points and the Hurt Building. A few years later the school became Georgia State University and has since grown tremendously, both in student body and facilities. The courses started in September and I was taking a full load, including algebra, English, history, and art. I declared my intention to major in art even though the range of art classes available was quite limited. With the exception of the history course which required a considerable amount of reading, the course work was not much of a challenge. Algebra was a breeze, but I enjoyed it anyway. Art was the biggest disappointment. I wanted to learn the techniques and technicalities of working with various media, instead students were virtually left on their own.

The class comprised of students ranging from freshmen to seniors and even some post graduates. I was the sole freshman and was totally unprepared for such an unstructured set up. The instructor told me to spend time with the upperclassmen and learn from them as they tackled their projects. The little exposure that I had to abstract impressionism did not prepare me for the direction that work in this class was taking. I was most impressed with the grad student I was assigned to whose project was being painted on a piece of glass about eight feet by three feet. With a cigarette hanging from his lips, he poured house paint directly from a gallon can onto the glass from a distance of about three feet. He created his design as he poured different colors, mostly primary, and occasionally would tip ashes from his cigarette at strategic spots.

I asked him if he was doing this because he didn't have the talent to draw or paint in the manner of Michelangelo or DaVinci. With a wry laid back, smile he took me aside and showed me drawings and paintings that he created that were masterful. In my naivete, I asked him why he was throwing house paint from cans onto a large piece of glass when he was capable of doing such exquisite work. He didn't bother giving me the explanation that artists should not compete with photography for realism, but should be creative and continually explore new media. He just told me that I was young and in a few years I would understand. I was in awe of his talent, but I still could not understand the merits of his project. When I told him that I was going to have to work my way through college and that I needed to feel I was learning a profession to support myself, he agreed that majoring in art at Atlanta Division was not the place for me. That advice came toward the end of the quarter.

One nice thing about going to Atlanta Division was that I was one of six students from D.S.I. and there were quite a few other Jewish boys and girls there along with us. This was a plus until the issue of fraternities came up. There were two Jewish fraternities at the school, AEPi and TEP, and the competition between them was stiff. From the beginning of the school year, both fraternities made the assumption that the six D.S.I. boys would stick together in their choice of fraternity. When rush week came along, the pressure got heavy. Everywhere I turned, I was being hot-boxed by a member of one fraternity or the other. Basically, these were all people who had grown up together with us at the Alliance. I found it hard to figure out how they had such horrible things to say about each other in the name of fraternity, which I had always thought was defined as brotherly love.

The final night of rush week both frats had a party. The six of us went as a group from one party to the other. Free beer and booze was flowing. Every frat member at each party treated us as if each on of us was the most important person in the school. The problem was that I liked everybody and I wanted to keep it that way. I could never remember how many times we went back and forth that evening. I do remember being quite inebriated when I fell asleep that night. I woke up in the morning noticing that I had been pinned by both fraternities the evening before, and I did not remember committing myself to either group.

I decided to let the situation work its way out. I attended all of my classes, wearing both pins just as they had been pinned to my sweater. Between classes, I started getting funny looks and comments. Finally at lunch time, I was approached by both groups and told that I couldn't pledge both fraternities and that I would have to make up my mind which one I wanted. With representatives from both fraternities standing there, I told them that I did not knowingly pledge either fraternity, and protested that getting me drunk was not the way to get a commitment from me.

The TEP guys pulled me aside and extolled the virtues of Tau Epsilon Phi while denigrating Alpha Epsilon Pi and its members. I asked them if it was possible to pledge TEP and still to have friends in AEPi. The answer was a resounding "No." When the AEPi guys pulled me over, I asked them the same question in reverse and received another resounding "No." I gave each group its pin back and told each of them that I had no desire to be part of any group that dictated with whom I could and could not associate. In retrospect, I had no regrets about my decision not to pledge any fraternity, especially when I became aware of how many extra hours I would have to work just to pay my dues.

It was during the first two weeks of the quarter that I was fired from Davison's shoe department. Within days, I found a job that did not interfere with school hours, though it did put a dent in my social life. I don't remember how I found out about Dittler Brothers Printing Company, but I got a job there for the night shift. The hours were 2:30 in the afternoon to 11:30 at night and, being on Hunter Street, it was accessible by bus. As I recall, my job was running a small printing press, printing mostly calendars. Gil Bachman was the foreman and my boss. For optimum production, it took two men run the press. Gil put me together with an experienced journeyman who trained me to do both jobs so that we could rotate as desired. I liked the job and I liked my co-worker. It was a good thing that most of my course work did not require a lot of after school work, because I had precious little time to get homework done if I were going to get any sleep at all. My history grade suffered as a result. I knew I could pass the history exams without rereading the text but, in doing so I had to settle for a mediocre grade.

Eventually, my experienced co-worker switched to the day shift. At first he stayed with me until about 5:00 in the evening and then I would be on my own for the rest of my shift. After a few days of trying it alone, someone was hired to work with me on the night shift. Even though he had some printing experience, he was hired to help me. That, along with the fact that he was at least ten years older than I, made him resent working as my assistant. He was a real greasy-looking guy, almost my height with a wiry, thin but muscular build. He had black slicked-down hair and tattoos all over his arms. Every night at the end of our shift, we would have to leave through an overhead door and the last one out would pull it down by the handles to close and secure the shop.

My new co-worker was not very friendly. He liked to brag a lot about his exploits and as long as I listened without questioning the veracity of any of the exaggerated accounts of his macho activities, we got along fine. We took turns closing up. By the time 11:30 p,m. came around, I could hardly stay awake long enough to reach up for the handles on the overhead door, pull the door down, shut it, and catch a bus for home. One Monday night when it was my turn to close up, I instinctively reached up for the handles and I was too tired to realize that they weren't there. Apparently, they had been broken off during the weekend or earlier that day, and no one warned me about it. My fingers lodged in the open groove between two panels of the open overhead door and I pulled down to close the door. The open groove disappeared as the door came down and smashed the three middle fingers on both of my hands. I let out a blood-curdling scream as pain went writhing through my body. Luckily, others in the building heard me and came running. They opened the door, freeing my hands, and called Gil Bachman to come and take me to the hospital. By the time Gil arrived, my fingers were twice their normal size but the pain had subsided a bit. Not bothering to pump me for details of the accident, he rushed me to the emergency room at Grady Hospital.

Once there, we waited patiently for someone to take care of me, while my fingers kept swelling. Finally, a lady in a nurse's uniform came up and, oblivious to my pain, gave me a very long form to fill out. At that point Gil lost his cool. "Look at his hands!" he yelled at her. "How is he supposed to be able to fill out a form?" The lady was not rattled. She merely told Gil that he could fill it out for me. Gil asked if a doctor could see me while he was filling out the form. That, of course, was against hospital policy. By the time a medic came, I couldn't feel the ends of my fingers. The medic spent all of three minutes looking at my fingers. He suggested that I go home take two aspirins, and soak my fingers in Epsom salts. Gil was shaking his head, and I wasn't too impressed either, as he watched the medic zip in, give his medical advice and zip out of the examination room. Gil took me home and said that he would pick me up first thing in the morning to take me to the company doctor's office. He did not trust the diagnosis of the medic at "The Gradies," and I was just as anxious to get a second opinion.

I hated the idea of cutting classes, but I had confidence in Gil and went with him to the doctor's office. The doctor examined my fingers. The swelling of those on my right hand had gone down somewhat, but my entire left hand was starting to swell along with the fingers. He told us that we came to him just in time as he had to remove the nail of my middle finger and puncture small holes in the other two fingernails, in order to drain blood that had accumulated under them. Before removing the nail, he mentioned to Gil that if he had waited another day to bring me in, I probably would have lost my finger. He bandaged up the fingers on my left hand, told me to soak the right hand, gave me medication for the pain and told me to come back in a week. I quickly became a believer in second opinions.

Even though it was Tuesday morning, Gil realized that I would not be able to run the printing machine with my arm in a sling, so he told me to take the rest of the week off and come back to work on Monday. This meant that my erstwhile coworker would be the lead man on the press and I would be his assistant, which didn't really bother me. He, however, became emboldened by the change. The stories of his exploits started taking a racist and anti-Semitic turn. Every confrontation he recounted was with a black man and every conquest was with a rich Jewish woman. As he probably anticipated, I quickly grew angry with his racist stories and suggested that we just work and not talk. He asked to step outside so he could beat me to a pulp, as my "Jew ass deserved." I congratulated him on his bravery for waiting until my hand was bandaged up to challenge me to a fight. I told him that if he could be patient and wait for my hand to heal, I'd be happy to go toe-to-toe with him. About a week later, he failed to show up for work. I thought he had quit, but somehow without any action on my part, word of the confrontation made its way to the front office and my coworker wasn't around when my fingers finally healed and my nail grew back. As it turned out, without him there, I was able to do more work all by myself.

Half way through the quarter, I had about decided that I needed to rethink my pursuit of higher learning. The art program didn't impress me and it was too easy to get by without studying in the other courses. I thoroughly enjoyed Dr. Sutton's English class although I had the terrible habit of always turning in my assignments late. I was having a good time in Mr. Cope's algebra class, though I didn't feel as if the material was at a much higher level than what we covered in high school. As a result, a few of us had free time in his class which we spent on mathematical puzzles. I became fascinated with one of that started with a penny and doubled it every day for a month and, at the conclusion, two to the 29th power plus two to the 29th power equaled two to the 30th power. I found that by asking people, even one of my high school algebra teachers, what two to the 29th plus two to the 29th was, none of them came up with the right answer. In my free time, I decided to develop a formula postulating that any number to any power plus that number to the same power times that number minus one equals that number to the next power. I put it in the form of an algebraic equation, $X^n + X^n(X-1) = X^{n+1}$, proudly showed it to Mr. Cope and explained to him what I had in mind. He studied the equation for a moment and suddenly got very excited. He told me that I had developed what mathematicians call an Identity, and added that he thought it was ingenious.

Toward the end of the quarter, I made the decision not to continue with Atlanta Division's day program for the next quarter, but to take a full time job and decide what to do with the rest of my life. I went to see Mr. Cope to tell him that I wouldn't be coming back next quarter. He was distraught with my decision, and pleaded with me to sign up for Trigonometry, which he would be teaching in night school. I was flattered that he wanted me to be in his class and agreed to sign up for it. When the quarter was over, I left the job at Dittler Brothers, took a full-time job with Alterman Brothers wholesale grocers warehouse for $.75 per hour, and signed up for Mr. Cope's trigonometry class in night school.

I wanted to work in the warehouse loading trucks to build up my upper body strength, but Sam Alterman thought I should be in charge of the special room that had small, higher priced items not necessarily sold by the case, such as chewing gum and cigarettes. In that room, there was a machine to stamp the cigarettes for state taxes. My primary responsibility was keeping on hand a sufficient amount of stamped cigarette cartons of the various brands. That alone took a better part of my day that started when I punched the time card at 7:30 in the morning. While I was proud of my first full-time job, I knew that I would have to use this year to decide on a course of study to pursue and where to do it. Jack was working as a bookkeeper in the office so I saw him every day. He was still living at the home of Rosalie and George Alterman and he was like one of their family. Though I hid it well, I really envied his sense of belonging.

Late in February 1951, I received my naturalization papers but was told that, because of a change in the law, I would not become a U.S. citizen until after my twenty-first birthday, instead of my eighteenth birthday as the law had been until recent months. I met with Mrs. Fink at the Children's Service Bureau and we established that I was to be self-supporting with the exception of expenses for medical emergencies. Without school, I had more time for a social life, but getting up before six in the morning every morning didn't make for staying out late many nights a week.

For three or four weeks, I tried going to Mr. Cope's trig class in night school and finally dropped out for lack of motivation. The pace was excruciatingly slow and though I was interested in the subject matter, I was not getting enough from the class to justify the effort it took to attend. I felt bad for Mr. Cope, he had talked about trying to get my "identity" published in a magazine, which I appreciated. He was aware that the level of the class was very basic and uninteresting and explained that this was due to the fact that most of the students had failed the course at least once before and needed that pace to keep from failing again. I fully understood the situation and hated to let Mr. Cope down, but I asked him to understand how difficult it was for me to stay awake in his class, if the material was not going to be challenging, after a long day of working in a warehouse. Reluctantly, he said that he understood and suggested that I get back into the day program. As a token of my appreciation of him, I gave him the sketch I made of him, complete with the hair on his nose, in the last class, and went my way.

What I enjoyed most about working at Alterman's was the workers in the warehouse. With the exception of myself and a couple of warehouse superintendents, everyone was African-American. They were such colorful fellows, no pun intended. Charlie Bell was my favorite. Like all the others, he was strong as an ox, but while many of the guys were friendly, he was the most personable. Several of the guys were good athletes. Charlie was a natural. He had played baseball, football, and basketball in high school, but baseball was his love. From what I had heard and seen of his talent, I felt that he could have played professional ball if he had not been black. After I went back to school, I often thought about many of the guys in the warehouse crew. Working and spending most of every day with them reinforced my advocacy for civil rights. Charlie Bell was the one I could never get out of my mind. He was not just another good athlete. He was charismatic, had a way with people, and had leadership ability. If he had been born ten years later, the chances for him to reach his potential would have been so much greater.

There was one man in the warehouse we lovingly called the "Phantom." At first, I didn't know how that appellation came to be. He was mostly very quiet and to himself, but very personable when you took the time to talk to him. It wasn't long before his nick-name became apparent. Every Monday morning was his time to get in character. Many of the warehouse workers came in still hung over from the weekend and, because of the large turnover in warehouse "pickers," there was always someone who had never heard his *shtick*. He would come in about nine in the morning, still a bit inebriated himself, and walk over to the "bitch box," as we called the intercom speaker system. By this time, the hung-over workers had all found cozy spots among cases of canned groceries throughout the warehouse and were fast asleep. As if on cue, he would walk up to the "bitch box," turn it on, and start his ritual.

"Who knows what evil lurks in hearts of men," he would say with his mouth on the speaker, sounding like Lamar Cranston. Then after a slight pause, he continued, in a louder voice, "The Shadow do!" Invariably this would wake up and startle the men napping, even if they had heard it before. Those who had never heard him do his thing were usually scared out of their wits and would come running out, wide-eyed as-if they had seen a ghost, ready for their next assignment. He was never reprimanded for this unconventional behavior. Not only was it hilarious entertainment, it was a very effective way of getting improved production from the warehouse pickers on Mondays.

My sister, Flo, announced early in the year, that she was engaged to marry Herbert Spiegel. Herb was an electrical engineer working for the U.S. Government in Kodiak, Alaska. The Spiegel family had emigrated to the U.S. from Cologne, Germany just before the start of World War II and settled in Albany, N.Y. where his father established a medical practice. Flo had been living in New York for a couple of years and met Herb on one of his trips to the Big Apple. The wedding was set for May 23 in New York City and Reverend A. Asher Hirsch, my brother the rabbi, would be performing the wedding.

Jack and I decided to take a train to New York. That may have been my only trip on a pullman train and it was like being on a vacation. We watched the passing scenery and played gin rummy. Of course we played for money, keeping a written record as to who owed what to whom. When we reached New York, I asked Jack to pay up which didn't set well with him. He told me that if he had won, he would not have asked me for the money. I had no idea if he was conning me or not and responded that I had no intention of losing so his point was moot. That type of wise ass remark was no way to resolve an issue between brothers. After more heated words I told Jack to forget it. At that point, he reached in his pocket and paid me the five dollars and change and refused to allow me to give it back making me feel guilty as hell—for at least five minutes.

I have no idea who made the housing arrangements for Jack and me. We stayed at a hotel in the 42nd Street area, which was an eye opener for me as I had never seen so much hustle and bustle. This was a place that never slept. Lights were flashing and places were open all hours of the day or night. Everywhere we turned, someone was trying to hustle us. Everything was available for a price. There was a certain excitement in being there, but along with it came a sense of danger and a small measure of disgust at the depth of depravity to which some human beings can go to make a buck. My favorite hangout was a record store that continuously played Nat King Cole's latest hits. I remember learning the words to *"Mona Lisa," "They tried to tell us we're too young,"* and *"Nature Boy,"* which I had not heard before. That we did not get sucked into a poker game, buying a hot watch or enjoying the pleasures of one of the many ladies of the streets says something for our refusal to give in to temptation. Another important factor, at least in my case, was that I didn't have nearly the amount of money needed for what was being offered.

The wedding took place in Congregation Mishkan Israel of Astoria, where Asher was the spiritual leader. Flo looked beautiful. I had not been to a New York wedding before and didn't know what to expect. Jack and I got there early and there was already a decent crowd. Asher started introducing me to relatives and friends of our parents, none of which I had ever met before or, for that matter, knew about. People came in droves and the introductions had to be postponed as Asher was busy greeting them. I was especially taken with my cousin Helen who was Uncle Philipp's daughter. I asked Asher why I had never been told of these relatives and friends of our parents. He responded that, had I moved to New York when he asked me to, I would have met them all before. I was less than satisfied with that answer.

After the wedding and reception, where I was able to spend a little time with my new found cousin, Herb asked Jack and me to ride with him to Albany. He wanted us to help bring some of the necessities for the *Sheva Brochos* (seven blessings) dinner the next evening at the Spiegel residence, and to keep him company for the long ride. Jack declined, but I didn't have the heart to turn Herb down. So, I spent the evening and a good part of the night, doing exactly what Jack said he would not do on his vacation, riding in a pickup truck from New York City to Albany and back. Jack told me that I was a sap for allowing myself to be used and I didn't argue with him, but I did make some points with Herb. At the dinner, Helen sat between Jack and me and we got to know and appreciate each other and developed a lasting relationship.

The train ride home was not as much fun as the ride to New York. Jack refused to play gin rummy with me. The most he would consider was occasional game of hearts, and he wasn't interested in rehashing our trip. I caught up on my sleep, read a paperback novel and tried to get my mind back to the issues facing me at home.

In June, I got a raise to 85 cents per hour, averaging $42.00 a week, and I felt rich. I still had not decided where to go to school in the fall, or what to study for that matter. My choices were Emory (which I couldn't begin to afford), Georgia Tech (which I would have attended on a full Navy scholarship, had I been a citizen of the United States upon graduation from high school), and, of course, the Atlanta Division, with a different major. The longer I worked at

Alterman Brothers' warehouse, the more I realized that I had to pursue higher education that would lead to a professional career.

I had been complaining about a pain in my side, off and on, for over a year. I told my sister, Sarah the summer before that I thought it was appendicitis, but the doctor couldn't find anything. In June, the pains got worse and this time, Dr. Weinstein's diagnosis was an immediate appendectomy. I was admitted in Crawford Long Hospital to have the operation that the doctors in Marseilles mistakenly diagnosed ten years earlier.

Not wanting to be bored, I brought my sketch pad along with me. I had no time to draw anything before they took me to anesthesia in preparation for the emergency operation. When I woke up, I was in a ward with two elderly patients and in more pain than I had bargained for. The first time I complained to the nurse, she gave me a shot of morphine for the pain. That was my first experience with pain-killing drugs. I could have easily become hooked on morphine had the nurses given me the opportunity. The next morning, I was feeling much more chipper but I still had some pain. In spite of my pleas, no one would give me another shot of morphine. To keep my mind off the pain, I picked up my sketch pad and made pencil drawings of the two patients in my room. One of the nurses was very cute and a little flirtatious. She saw the drawings of the two patients and asked me to sketch her. When the sketch was done, she asked to see it and proceeded to put her phone number on it. I can't remember if I ever called her, but I still have the sketch to remember her.

I spent about a week recuperating at home before going back to work and used the time to think about my future. The only thing I was sure of was that I did not want to spend the rest of my working life as a career warehouse worker. That I needed higher education was a foregone conclusion. I just needed to determine what and where. Of all my D.S.I. contemporaries, Abe Esral was the only one studying at Georgia Tech (the Georgia Institute of Technology) and he was determined to talk me into joining him. He and I had discussed my search for direction he was well aware of my financial limitations. One evening, as we were sipping coffee at our favorite hangout, The Crossroads restaurant at Pershing Point, he offered his studied opinion. He said he had given a lot of thought to my dilemma and concluded that, since my two strongest areas were art and mathematics, I should major in architecture at Georgia Tech. I admitted to being totally unfamiliar with the profession of architecture, but that did not deter Abe. He said that architecture was a blend of art and math and the end product was beautiful buildings that were structurally sound.

While I was convinced that Abe was trying to con me into joining him at Tech, his argument peaked my interest enough to get me to discuss it with

Gertrude Fink, who had taken over as my case worker again. Mrs. Fink agreed that further vocational testing was in order before I made such a momentous decision. She mentioned that Georgia State Employment Service offered a battery of tests for just that purpose and referred me to Mr. Scarborough, the person in charge. The tests bore out Abe's conclusion, even if his reasoning that led to it was specious at best. It sealed my decision to enroll at Georgia Tech for the fall quarter and to seek work at Rich's Department Store for as many hours as my schedule would allow, since they had earlier expressed a willingness to be flexible with my hours, as long as I remained a student. Mrs. Fink reminded me that the Bureau's Student Aid Loan was available to me, but I expressed my fear of, and wish to avoid, getting into debt for my college education, at least as long as I would be able to work while in school.

I formally applied at Georgia Tech only to learn that I did not have all of the prerequisite courses for acceptance. I was lacking a course in either physics or biology, neither of which had been offered to me at Hoke Smith High. To move things along, I signed up for a night school course in physics at Georgia Tech and took a job at Rich's Department Store's warehouse for the basement clothing departments. To not be on the sales floor would allow me to be more flexible with my hours when I started the day program at Georgia Tech the next quarter. For the most part, the job was very boring. I filled orders from department managers and worked at keeping the huge volume of stock in some semblance of order. It needed to be organized enough to allow any stock clerk to fill orders in a timely fashion. The warehouse was across Forsyth Street, so I was transporting rolling tables full of goods down a service elevator, through a tunnel below the street, and onto the sales floor in the basement of the store. The boring part was being alone about half of the time, on the third floor of the warehouse. The job kept me busy, but I was used to being around people and missed that interaction. At least I was able to work full time, earning eighty-five cents per hour, thus allowing me the opportunity to save a little money while giving me another few months of vacation from school.

Raymond Maloof taught me the ropes when it came to the third floor of Rich's warehouse and the various departments it served. We developed a close friendship that lasted way beyond our months of working together in Rich's warehouse. Between Ray and the department managers, I learned a few things about merchandising. Sales always kept us busy, changing the price tags on merchandise going on sale. The most unique sale that comes to mind was Dollar Day. Everything item on the floor or in the warehouse was marked up or down to the nearest dollar. An item selling for $2.01 up to $2.49, for instance, was marked down to $2.00, while an item selling for $2.51 up to

$2.99 was marked up to $3.00. The amazing phenomenon was that the marked up items invariably sold faster than the marked down items. Go figure!

Since we did the pricing, Ray and I always found out which items were going on sale days before anyone except the department manager. Therefore, we were able to pick up the best buys before the general public had a chance at them. No one, including department managers and buyers, saw anything wrong with that practice. It was one of the perks of the job. We were even allowed to pick up sale items for members of our families before the items hit the floor. It's a good thing that neither of us ever tried to run for public office. By twenty-first century standards, Ray and I could have been prosecuted for insider purchasing.

As the quarter progressed, I realized how much I loved going to school even though, or maybe because, it was just one course in night school. Most of my classmates were taking the course over because they had flunked freshman physics. They found it hard to believe that anyone could actually enjoy physics. My enthusiasm for the material was infectious to at least the two students who needed to pass to get back into architectural school. They opted to study with me and gave me the opportunity to better understand the material we were supposed to be learning by explaining it to them. The exercise helped me gain confidence in my understanding of the material and proved to me that I had the ability to impart information, or tutor students who were unable to learn in the classroom environment. My material reward was free beer after every session; my real reward was seeing them both pass and join me as freshmen in the department of architecture.

Flo's wedding, May 23, 1951, New York City. From left: Ben, Jack, Flora Hirsch Spiegel, Herb Spiegel, Sarah, and Rev. A. Asher Hirsch, who performed the wedding.

Ben's sketch of nurse at Crawford Long Hospital when he was there for his appendectomy.

XII

GEORGIA TECH, A NEW OUTLOOK, January 1952 –October 1953

At the beginning of the winter quarter in January 1952, I finally started my freshman year in the architectural school at Georgia Tech. It was the beginning of my quest to make a career for myself, the first step toward making a new life with, someday, a family of my own. While I would never forget who I was or where I came from, I was spending less of my time thinking about the past. My new focus was energized by the goal of becoming a productive member of American society, and trying to live the American dream. I had a new outlook on life. Up to this point, school had been a mixture of drudgery and fun challenges, but never too taxing and with no specific direction. The material I had learned in night school exhilarated me. I expected that my time at Georgia Tech was going to be an all consuming adventure of learning and I was excited with the prospect of learning new things.

Starting the school year in January was a little disorienting. All of the other freshmen had started in the fall quarter. I was a year older than most of the other freshman and, to the horror of some—I did not belong to a fraternity. On the brighter side, I was past the quarter of freshman hazing. I had not been issued a "rat cap," those yellow-gold little baseball caps with a navy blue "T" on the front. I didn't have to worry about getting forced to get a "T cut," the infamous hair cut that left nothing but a T-shaped crop of hair, and was the penalty for being caught not wearing the rat cap. The T-cut was also a punishment for freshmen who did not "properly respond" to spurious questions and/or demands from upperclassmen, and was generally limited to the first quarter of the freshman year. I felt extremely fortunate to have by-passed that demeaning ritual.

My two new friends, who were allowed to resume their freshman year after passing physics in night school, were convinced that in my infinite wisdom I planned it that way. Both of them had lived through freshman hazing rituals the previous year, but were still freshmen because of their grades. I pleaded with them to quit spreading the word around that I had beaten the system. These guys held me responsible for helping them pass the night school courses they had been taking which included remedial algebra. Until I let them know that I did not appreciate being put on a pedestal, they felt compelled to toot my horn at every opportunity. The last thing I wanted was to advertise that I was the only member of the freshman class that did not wear a "rat cap," so we agreed to keep that little tidbit of information to ourselves.

I was chafing at the bit to start learning about architecture and to learn how to design buildings and draw with instruments. The only architectural labs for freshmen were two hour credit drawing courses. Freshmen had to take a number of required core courses that did not relate to architecture. Architecture 101 was engineering drawing and in it, I learned much of what I should have been learned in Mr. Martin's class at Hoke Smith had I not been playing chess with him.

I was allowed to take twenty hours of course credits the first quarter because of the A average I maintained in night school. My class load consisted of seven courses: College Algebra a five hour credit course; Chemistry a four hour credit course; English Composition and Western Civilization three credit hours each; while ROTC and Engineering Drawing were two credit hours each. Swimming, a course that left a major impact on me, was only a one credit hour course. As long as I maintained a 3.0 average or above, I would be allowed to take between nineteen to twenty-one credits per quarter, which I ended up doing the first two quarters to catch up with the rest of my class.

I felt like an outsider. I was taking more hours than most students and to make ends meet financially, I had to rush to work every day as soon as my last class was over. All of this, and the fact that I did not have a fraternity to socialize with, was of my own doing. I was learning new things and I felt as if I were on my way to a career. It didn't matter that much that I was not one of the pack.

Freddy Lanoux's swimming course was an unforgettable experience. Mr. Lanoux had been a Seabee in World War II and taught his "survival course" to the U.S. Navy. His reputation preceded him, so most of the students in his class had an inkling of what to expect. Dan Santocroce and I did not. I knew how to swim, which was more than one could say for Dan. I had expected a PT course in swimming to be about recreational and competitive swimming skills. I soon learned that this course focused on survival skills and, if we passed, we would be prepared in the event that any of us was on a ship sinking in the ocean.

We first learned to swim with our hands tied behind our backs, and to pass we had to swim four lengths of the pool that way. Next we learned to swim with our feet bound and tied behind our backs and, eventually, had to swim four lengths that way as well. The *coup de grace* was when we had to learn to swim with both our hands and feet tied behind our backs and, of course, swim four lengths of the pool under those circumstances. In all of these exercises, our grades depended on the speed with which we completed the four laps. Dan became a legend for his intestinal fortitude. He never learned to swim and he was a sinker instead of a floater. He completed each of the four lap exercises, with appropriate limbs tied behind his back, by crawling on the bottom of the pool until he completed his required four lengths.

Lanoux rode us all mercilessly and egged us on by yelling, "Come on sucker!" Dan got a lot of his attention and cajoling, but when he finished his fourth lap with both hands and feet tied behind his back, you could see tears of admiration and pride running down Freddy Lanoux's cheek. Dan may have been the only non-swimmer to ever pass Mr. Lanoux's swimming class.

I was guaranteed to get an A in the class until we were required to jump off the high dive platform. We were not allowed to wear anything in the swimming class. This was at least two years before the school became co-ed. I had no problem jumping in from the side of the pool or from the low dive platform. I asked for permission to put on a jock strap or at least swim trunks before jumping from the high platform and, as expected, my request was denied. I kept hoping that he would turn his back so I could dive in the water, but he watched me like a hawk, yelling "Come on sucker, jump!" Each time I would stand at the edge of the platform with the intention of jumping and end up either diving or holding on to my family jewels, before I hit the water. After many tries, it became apparent that my fearless nature did not include endangering my reproductive organs. I settled for a B in the course.

Fraternities served the function of making students feel like they belonged and, in the case of an out of town student, provided a place to live. Most fraternities were also the repositories of files of previously given tests, by various professors, which members used as study tools. There were three Jewish fraternities at Tech. AEPi and TEP were the largest with Phi Epsilon Pi not far behind. All three were fiercely competitive. Even though I had missed rush week while attending night school, I was approached by members of all three fraternities with offers to join. In declining each of them, I described the debacle of rush week at Atlanta Division and explained that, in the little time I had to socialize, I did not want to be restricted in choosing with whom I could keep company. I wanted to have friends in each fraternity and to feel free to accept invitations to visit each fraternity house.

Unlike Atlanta Division, the engineering and industrial management students in the fraternities at Tech had no problem with my remaining independent. The fact that I probably could not have afforded joining any fraternity never came up. I saw the advantages of living on campus and having time for a social life in the midst of studying, but that was beyond my reach. Fortunately, I was able to maintain a few friendships in each fraternity and often found study partners for major exams in the different frat houses.

I remembered the Hillel group at Georgia Tech having a team in the basketball league at the Alliance when I was in high school. Hillel is a college-level national Jewish student organization, open to all Jewish students in the school. I had hoped to join the organization with the idea of playing with their team. To my disappointment, I found out that Hillel had been inactive at Tech for about a year. I tried to create some interest in reviving the group and fielding a team in Tech's intramural league as well as in the Alliance league.

Another aspect of Hillel—providing religious services on Friday nights and on holidays—didn't seem to be of interest to the Jewish student body and there were just not enough Jewish students who didn't belong to one of the three fraternities to field a team. There was no paid Hillel director and there were no students, including myself, who had time or were willing to put in the work needed to resuscitate the organization.

Among the mandatory courses I was taking the first quarter was Air Force ROTC. I mentioned to the sergeant in charge that I was not allowed to participate in ROTC in high school because I was not yet a citizen of the United States. I was happy to have the opportunity to take Air Force ROTC, as it could lead to becoming an Air Force officer upon graduation, but I wanted to make him aware that I was not yet twenty-one years old and, therefore, I was still not an American citizen. The instructor told me that I would have no problem because I had lived in the U.S. for so many years and my application for citizenship was already in the works, I had received my Naturalization papers when I turned eighteen. A couple of weeks into the quarter, we were measured for uniforms. Every cadet had to pay for his own uniform but would receive monthly compensation, which more than covered that cost. I was advised that I could not receive the compensation since I was not a citizen, but that I could be reimbursed for the cost of the uniform—$69.56—once I became a citizen. I had to make a decision that day. Unable to reach Harry or Sarah, I called and discussed the dilemma with Mrs. Fink, who listened as I presented the options. I finally decided, even though citizenship was over a year away, that I would join ROTC without compensation and bite the bullet for the cost of the uniform, which was slightly more than one quarter's tuition.

Dr. Wahab, my algebra professor, took a special interest in me and almost convinced me to change my major to math. When I was first assigned to his class in College Algebra, I argued that I had taken the course at Atlanta Division and had made an A+. He promised me that by the end of the quarter I would understand why I was required to repeat the course. It didn't take that long.

Our first exam was very basic. I completed it in twenty minutes, took another five minutes to check my answers and turned it in. Dr. Wahab took less than a minute to review my test, wrote ninety-nine at the top of the paper and handed it back to me. I was curious about what I had missed to keep me from getting a 100 and asked him about it. He took the paper back, looked me in the eye, said "Nobody's perfect." He then crumpled up the paper and threw it in the wastebasket. That left a lasting impression on me.

I had a special passion for math. I had read an article by a mathematician stating that while most people know that Pi (3.1417....) is an irrational number, very few people are aware that Pi^2 is a rational number. I wondered how in the world anyone could prove that so I asked Dr. Wahab, who was also the head of the math department at Tech. He responded that if I were interested enough to stay after class for at least fifteen minutes he would prove it to me. It meant skipping lunch, but I stayed and was treated to an explanation that filled up the entire wall of blackboards and took about twenty-five minutes. I was amazed at his ability to attack the problem and explain it as he chalked it on the board. I barely understood the complex proof as he was explaining to me and gasped when it concluded with a long, but rational, number. I thanked him for taking the time to go over the proof with me and he in turn thanked me for being interested enough to ask. I wished that I had a wide-angle camera to record the work he had done on the chalkboard, because there was no way I could remember that amazing proof.

From that point on, Dr. Wahab took an interest in lessening my non-academic diversions and responsibilities. He encouraged me to apply for an U.S. Navy scholarship, which would pay for four years of college and living expenses. He felt strongly that if I could avoid working while attending Georgia Tech, my opportunity to achieve academic heights he expected of me would be greatly improved. The fact that I had applied for that scholarship at the behest of Ms. Rogers, when I was still in high school, and that I had been turned down then, for lack of U.S. citizenship did not thwart him. He knew that the Navy was looking for people with high math aptitudes and felt that with his recommendation, and the fact that I was enrolled in Air Force ROTC, things would be different. He had not taken into account the inflexibility of government bureaucracy. I was not even allowed to take the examination.

I was enjoying all of my courses, even Chemistry 101, which scared me in the beginning since I had never had it in high school. It was hard work, but the professor was very good at teaching the basics and making it enjoyable to anyone willing to learn. Not everybody was willing to make the effort. We had a celebrated football player in our class. His name was Peavy and he had been a High School All-American end. The word was out that this jock had to pass chemistry in order to maintain his scholarship. He was given a special tutor who was allowed to use questions from upcoming exams in preparation for the exam. Some students complained about the advantage this gave Peavy, thinking that he might bust the curve. It was all moot. Peavy still failed chemistry and most of his other courses, claiming that he had already decided to play football for another school where the course work would not be as taxing. As for me, all in all, it was a good first quarter. I made the honor roll and was able to keep working, while trying to maintain a normal social life, though the pace was taking its toll. My chronic bronchitis made my sister very concerned and she called Dr. Weinstein to express her worry about for my health. He assured her that I was just run down from burning the candle at both ends and that playing basketball was not too strenuous for me but, in fact, good for my overall health.

Spring quarter was going to be interesting. I was looking forward to trigonometry, which had not been available to me in high school. I was told that I could not sign up for the second quarter of Air Force ROTC. The citizenship thing had become an issue for the officer in charge, but he didn't know how to resolve the fact that I was allowed to sign up in the first place. After an extensive physical, I was declared 4-F citing my flat feet and chronic bronchitis as the reason. I strongly suspected this was the officer's way out of the question of my citizenship. This was borne out less than a year later, when I was drafted in the U.S. Army, in spite of my flat feet and chronic bronchitis. I was allowed to return the uniform and was reimbursed for the cost.

I was excited to finally have a class on architectural drawing. Architecture 102 was still only a course with two hours of credit, but it was my introduction to architecture. Our initial assignment was to copy the working drawing floor plan of a small house that had been designed by our teacher George Heery, who was in private practice with his father. Next came the elevation, then cross sections. Before the quarter was over, we each had copied a simple set of working drawings for a small house and learned what working drawings, or construction documents, were meant to achieve as well as the importance of accuracy and clarity. I was not able to fully appreciate the lessons being taught even though I was one of the more focused students. After I graduated, I wished that I had taken that course in my fourth year, when I could have appreciated the importance of what was being taught and applied myself more.

There was a classroom discussion component of the lab in which all sorts of basic first year architectural questions were aired. Early in the quarter, one full session was devoted to having every student tell how he decided to go into architecture. It seemed that everyone but I had known in advance that this question would be asked, and had prepared accordingly. As I listened to one after another presentation of flowery testimony, I began to wonder where my aesthetic sensibilities had been all these years. Only later did I find out that most of the stories were variations on what had been penned by the likes of Louis Sullivan and Frank Lloyd Wright in writings that were readily available in the architectural school library.

When it came my turn, I related that prior to Abe Esral's suggestion that I consider studying architecture at Georgia Tech, I had not known what an architect was or did. Without embellishment, I went into full detail of the events that lead to my enrolling in the school of architecture. Even though I heard some snickers and quite a few chuckles, I felt no embarrassment at telling it as it was. At least no one had a reason to think that I made the story up. Many of those in the class appreciated my candor, but there was a definite group from "prestigious fraternities" whose opinion that I was of the proletariat was only reinforced. It took most of them at least another quarter to warm up to me. Some of them never did.

To stay on the honor roll, I was going to have to ace trigonometry, which was the only course I was taking with five hours of credit. I became overconfident after completing homework assignments in a matter of minutes. Our first test was my Waterloo. I finished it in twenty minutes and turned it in without checking the work. I don't remember where I was rushing off to, but it must have been important for me to pull such a bonehead stunt. I was aghast when the professor handed out the graded exams, and I had flunked because of a few sloppy mistakes. The teacher acknowledged that it was obvious that I knew the work, but he had no mercy. "Just be more careful on exams from now on and hand in all of your assignments, and you will do well," was the best advice he could give me.

I worked extra hard to make sure that I double-checked every assignment before it was handed in and did the same for all exams. After getting an A on the semi-final exam, I approached the professor and asked him if it was mathematically possible for me to get an A in the course, considering how I blew the first exam. He was quick to mention that many professors drop the worst test grade in calculating a student's grade for the course, but that he was not of that ilk. However, he continued, if I made a 100 on the final exam, he would assure me an A in the course. With that incentive in mind, I studied extra hard and even tutored some of the slower students in the class to sharpen my own skills. As he was handing out the test papers, he wished me luck and, as an aside, mentioned that no one ever made a 100 on his final exam.

At least he remembered his promise, I thought to myself. I was very confident, but I was not going to allow myself to make any sloppy overconfident mistakes. I checked all of my answers twice before turning in my paper, hoping that he would grade it then, since no on else had finished yet. He grinned at me and said that he would prefer to keep me in suspense. He returned our papers on the last day of the quarter and I did get 100 as well as hearty congratulations from the professor. By the time my grades for the quarter were delivered by mail, the professor had gone for his summer vacation. I tried to see him when he returned, so he could explain to me why he only gave me a B in the course. He said that it was only a grade, that even if he wanted to, it was too late to change it now, and that I should learn to live with it. For my own curiosity, I double-checked the numbers, and found that, because of my abysmal grade on the first exam, my average for the quarter was 89.6. Be that as it may, I trusted this professor to live up to his word and he didn't.

On the lighter side of the schedule, Social Science 106, besides being an 8:00 a.m. class every Tuesday, Thursday, and Saturday, was taught by a professor who provided the comic relief needed to stay awake that early in the morning. This professor had a propensity for discussing with the entire class, very private matters relating to his relationship with his wife. This made it difficult to focus on the subject matter we were supposed to be learning. I doubt if any of the students in that class could remember the course material, but I'm confident that many of them remember some of the more raunchy anecdotes. Rumors were rampant that Georgia Tech was going to become co-ed in the near future. Many of us wondered how this professor, who jokingly called himself a pervert on occasion, was going to function in a classroom with female students.

I found it difficult to take this class seriously, which unfortunately, made it too easy for me to rationalize staying in bed (rather than getting up to make the 8 a.m. class, which was the only Saturday class on my schedule.) As a result, because of my poor attendance record, my grade was lowered from B to C. Without any A's to balance it, my grade point average went down to 2.85 for the quarter. That was still enough for the honor society at the school of architecture, but below the goal of 3.0 or better that I had set for myself. I became despondent and decided to limit my summer schedule to seventeen hours.

My social life for the first two quarters at Georgia Tech had been limited by my school and work schedules, but I still found time to hang around with my friends once or twice a week, play a little basketball and even host or join an occasional poker game. I was spending as much time with Ray Maloof, whom I had met a Rich's, as with my old D.S.I. buddies. Ray and I found that we had a great deal in common. He was going to night school at Atlanta Division, so both of us had limiting schedules, but we did find time to go for an occasional beer.

I started using Crossroads restaurant as a place to study in the evenings. Crossroads was the favorite hangout of Jewish teenagers and college age kids. It was located in the triangle formed by the intersection of Spring and Peachtree Streets. I found it very difficult to concentrate on my studies at home. It was so quiet that the occasional sounds coming from a radio, television, or telephone would disrupt my concentration. I needed either total quiet, which often would put me to sleep, or a constant din of noise.

Crossroads was the perfect answer for the constant din of noise. I could sit there nursing a few cups of coffee, catch up on all of my reading assignments and even do some of my math homework. I welcomed the occasional interruptions, if I felt I could use the break, and other times I ignored them. I realized that I was considered eccentric by many of my friends, but it worked for me. I found it to be an effective way for me to concentrate on reading texts, and I was able to keep in social contact with many people whom I otherwise would not have seen for a long time.

I really wanted to attend the D.S.I. banquet because it was the occasion for members attending universities outside of the Atlanta area to get together with those of us who were still in the city. I had a date with Sandy Marcus, whom I thought of as a Kim Novak look alike with personality. I had known Sandy's brother, Sidney, for years. He used to bet me that I couldn't do more than ten push-ups in the Progressive Club's steam room with the steam on high. Even though he kept losing money, he seemed to enjoy the ritual of our little bet, until I built up to twenty-five push-ups and he decided to call it quits. Sandy, who had always been the cute little sister, had grown into a very attractive young lady, and I was more than pleased, when I saw her at Crossroads, that she agreed to go with me to the banquet. It was the ninth annual D.S.I. banquet and may have been our last before most of us went our own ways, many of us into the armed services of the United States.

As the quarter moved along, I began to see the wisdom of taking the summer off from school. Chemistry 103 was all it was cracked up to be and more, and I didn't have enough interest in the material or the drive to work for a good grade, to give the course the effort it required. I allowed my disappointment with the past quarter's trig grade to affect my attitude toward studying. I was enjoying Analytic Geometry, but I didn't approach it with the same enthusiasm as I had Trig and Algebra.

After acing my first of two compositions in English 103, I decided to test the rumor that our professor was a racist bigot. Our first two papers had been on assigned subjects but we were free to select the topic for the next one. For the third paper, I wrote a critique lambasting two recently printed magazine articles claiming to prove that Caucasians were genetically superior to Negroes. I had researched this topic before and still had the material I had used in high school. I made sure that everything was in my words, composed as we had been instructed and neatly typed. I even had a senior student teacher in the English department check my paper out to make sure that my point was clearly made and that I made no grammatical or sentence structure errors. Then I submitted the paper, fully confident of getting an A, even if the professor disagreed with my premise. We received our papers back within a week and I was disappointed, but not shocked, at the C marked at the top of my paper. Although the lowest grade in the class, my paper was the only one that had no red marks on it, save for the note below the grade which read, "Faulty premise!" It was worth the gamble. I still had a B in the course and I had made my point, for what it was worth. About ten years later, Georgia Tech opened up to Black students. I suspect that professor retired before that happened.

I continued working part-time at Rich's, but was switched from the basement warehouse to the sporting goods stock room. A lighter school schedule left me time to spend some time at the Progressive Club pool two or three days a week and even to shoot a little pool at York's. Every week, Jack Taffel had a standing game of poker, which included Marshal Cohen, Walter Huebner, Paul Klein, and myself. Between the poker, occasional pool games and especially the gin rummy at the Progressive Club, I made enough money to pay for another year's tuition, but it didn't always come easily.

The few times that I went to York's Pool Hall, Alan Levitt was hanging out there. He was a year or two older but he had no problem shooting pool with younger guys. We used to play eight ball or rotation for fun. Then he suggested, even though I almost always beat him, that we play nine ball, a faster game usually played by gamblers, for money. I was not averse to gambling, but I was wary of playing with someone I thought I could beat anytime I wanted to. Reluctantly, I agreed to play as long as we paid up after each game. We played for an hour or two, once or twice a week, and it provided me with pocket change. After we had played several times, he came in one day wanting raise the stakes. After losing the first game, he sheepishly told me he left his wallet at home but promised if I continued to play he would find me and pay me the next day. We agreed to quit when he owed me forty dollars, and after checking my schedule with me, he assured me he would pay me the next day.

He didn't find me, as he said he would, and every time I spoke with him he apologized and set a time to get the money to me. When I didn't see him for several weeks, I figured that he had set up the raised stakes game to get even but never really intended to pay me when he lost. I finally ran into him at the Varsity on North Avenue. I had gone there after a disastrous night at our standing poker game, at which I lost an unheard of forty-one dollars in a game that had some disturbing and suspicious undertones. As I walked out of the Varsity, there was Alan standing on the sidewalk. When he saw me, he tried to turn and run, but the sidewalk was too crowded.

I squared off in front of him and demanded my money. He was several inches taller than I and wore heavy-rimmed glasses. He claimed to not have his wallet with him and I told him that was just not good enough. I thought to myself that of all the fistfights I had been in, I had never started one but there was always a first time. I asked him to take off his glasses if he didn't want to get them broken. He refused, and tried to convince me that it was against the law to hit a man with glasses. I replied that I would count to ten and if his glasses were not off by then, I was coming at him anyway. By that time, a fairly large crowd had gathered around us, cheering us on. I reached ten and his glasses were still on his face until I knocked them off. We got in less than a dozen swings before a policeman came and broke up the fight. The cop first threatened to take us to jail, but then agreed to let us go if we separated and went our own ways. The crowd cheered. I never got my forty-one bucks and Alan had to get new glasses. I found out later that the poker game had been rigged with a marked deck and all of the players were reimbursed for their losses. The offender claimed to have done it as joke and an experiment of sorts.

Jack Taffel asked if I would take out his cousin who had just moved into town. I hated blind dates, but he said she was pretty, that I could double with him and he would drive. I figured that I had nothing to lose. We would go to a movie, then to Crossroads and I would be doing Jack a favor. And, if I got lucky, she may be very nice to be with. I was one of the few guys who didn't have a car available to him or, for that matter, knew how to drive. That Sunday night, I must have gotten a ride to Jack's house which was on the other side of town. I was still living with my sister, Sarah, on Atlanta Avenue on the south side. Once there, Jack picked up his date first and drove to his cousin's house. I was expecting the worst when I went to the door and was pleasantly surprised when I saw Gail. Jack's description of her was an understatement. She was very pretty and wholesome looking.

Gail Haskell was an army brat. Her father was a Colonel in the U.S. Army, and her family traveled with him from base to base. There seemed to be an instant connection between the two of us. We had a delightful evening and she even asked me if I would bring her to the Progressive Club to swim the next day when I told her that I had commitments to play gin rummy near the pool. I agreed, without hesitation, thinking that my neighbor, Jerry Zimmerman, with whom I was going, wouldn't mind taking a little detour to pick up Gail. Ziggy was very gracious, but I didn't know he had ulterior motives. He had heard about Gail moving to town and wanted to ask her for a date. He was hoping that once she saw his convertible, she would be dying to go out with him.

We picked up Gail and brought her to the Club. I spent some time with her in the swimming pool and introduced her around before my appointed gin rummy matches. The card games were serious challenges to my reputation as a player, and were also my source for tuition for the coming school year. Gail was very understanding and just lazed around the pool until I finished my games. She was not much at small talk or gossip, so she didn't fit in that well with the cliques of girls around the pool, but that didn't seem to bother her. While I was busy, Ziggy asked her for a date. She not only turned him down, but she made it clear that she had no interest in making a date with him while she was out with me. I wasn't aware of that exchange when he came up to me while I was playing cards and told me I needed to find another ride home because he was leaving.

I finished playing about 3:30 in the afternoon and sat on the edge of the pool with Gail as she told me of Ziggy's unwelcome advances. She said several guys had approached her, but none quite as brazenly as Ziggy. She knew that Jerry had left because he had threatened to leave her with me, with no means of transportation. I looked around to see if anyone would be able to give me a ride to take Gail home. I figured that my chances of getting a ride to the south side were slim to none.

Jules Cavalier was the only one around with a car who said he had the time to give us a ride. I told him to just take me to Gail's house and I would find my way home from there. Feigning magnanimity, he insisted that if I hurried back to the car after dropping Gail off, he would drive me home to the south side.

I really wanted to spend more time with Gail, but it was getting late and my sister was waiting for me. I took Gail to her front door and she invited me in, saying that her father would be home soon and I could meet him. Jules started tooting the car horn and I tried to wave him off. He would not leave. He came running up to the door telling me that if I wanted a ride home I had better come now and that the next bus wasn't scheduled for another hour. Gail gave me a kiss and told me to go.

Jules was not a person that I had a lot of trust in, and he remained true to form. He drove me about two miles to a bus stop, and said he forgot about an appointment. The next day Gail told me that he drove back to her house after dropping me off, and tried to hit on her. She wouldn't let him in the house, but he spread the word around that she did and that they had sex. Mostly everyone knew to discount any such bragging on Jule's part, but Gail's reputation suffered nonetheless.

I signed up for driving lessons with a private instructor. I didn't have access to a car, but wanted to be ready whenever a car would become available to me. The incident with Gail was the catalyst for me to learn to drive. I could always rent a car rather than be dependent on someone like Jules. I finished with the lessons about the time that Harry and Sarah bought a house on Spring Valley Lane on the north side of town, but I never bothered going for my license. There was no car for me to drive in the foreseeable future and I didn't want to take the test in the instructor's car.

I helped Harry and Sarah move into the new house by taking care of Thyle and Neal, their almost two-year-old daughter and infant son. Sarah was beyond excited. She had dreamed of having a house in the suburbs and this was it, a small ranch house at the end of a cul-de-sac. She was pleased to point out that most of our neighbors were Jewish. The builder of many of the houses, Mickey Kuniansky was our next door neighbor on the right side of the cul-de-sac and next to him was the family whose daughter Brenda I had dated shortly before the move, thinking she was seventeen when she told me she was nineteen. I was more embarrassed than she or her parents when I found out that she was just thirteen years old. They saw nothing wrong with her dating older boys and I had to agree that she had the maturity of a twenty-one-year-old, if lying about her age didn't count.

I had to figure out how I would get from the new house to Georgia Tech. Public transportation was problematic, to say the least. My only choice was to catch a bus on Highland Avenue, going south toward to Five Points and transfer to a bus going back north toward to Georgia Tech. To make an 8:00 a.m. class using that system, I would have to leave the house no later than 6:30 in the morning, and that would be cutting it close. Desperate, I sought out students and faculty who lived in the vicinity and discovered ways to meet them along the way and catch a ride for the rest of the journey. For my 8:00 a.m. classes, I left with Harry and he took me to school on his way to work. It only took fifteen to twenty minutes by car and I arrived an hour early for class, but that was better than depending on the bus system when I would have to start out at the same time and still possibly be late for class. Within a month, I had a whole system of ride sharing worked out, although all I could contribute, except for my company, was a share of the cost of gasoline.

Shearith Israel Congregation bought the old Lanier College building on University Avenue by Spring Valley Lane and was using the old building, which had a quaint Greek revival façade, as a temporary home until the synagogue was ready to build a new building on the remainder of the site. I had not lived so close to a synagogue since *Kristallnacht* when I witnessed the destruction of the *Friedberger-Anlage* Synagogue, close to our house in Frankfurt am Main, Germany. Although I had removed myself from religious observance for a few years, I began going to services on occasion, especially on Saturday mornings if I didn't have a class. The more I attended prayer services, the more interested I became in the content of the prayers.

I was at the age at which I began to question everything I was expected to do, including long established rituals such as daily prayer. I had been used to reciting the proscribed Hebrew passages in the *sidur,* prayer book, without giving a great deal of thought to the meaning of the words. More out of curiosity than skepticism, I began paying attention to the English translation of the passages during prayer services.

The prayers for *Rosh Hashonah,* the New Year, are sufficiently different that a *Machzor,* a special prayer book for the High Holy Days is used. Aside from the extended length of the services, synagogue attendance on *Rosh Hashonah* and *Yom Kippur,* the Day of Atonement, which falls ten days later, is greater than any other time of the year. The focus on socializing on those special days bothered me even more than in previous years. In years past, I too participated in socializing during the service, but this year I was in quest for meaning of the solemn High Holy Day services. On the second day of *Rosh Hashonah,* not wanting to appear as if I were snubbing well wishers whom I hadn't seen for months, I announced to my friends that I was taking my *Machzor* home to study it and try to understand why these passages were chosen by our sages of old, for us to recite on these auspicious days.

What started out as a private search for meaning in ritual was touted by my friends as a radical rebellion on my part. Luckily, I didn't have far to walk. I went home and told Sarah's kids I would not be able to play with them until I completed an assignment, and spent the rest of the day in the living room poring over the *Machzor.* That evening I received a few calls from my peers asking me what revelations I came up with. I cynically responded the *Machzor* is a compilation of praises of God, written by various sages throughout the ages, with a little bit of historical data, all to the end of praising God, and individual supplications to God to grant the supplicant life, with health and enough food to eat. I questioned why I had to read prayers written by others. Why, I wondered, would I not be encouraged to make up my own prayers? Maybe then I could put my heart and soul into to praying to God. I was so twenty, but to my friends, who had never given a second thought to what the contents of prescribed prayer books were all about, I was as radical a Jewish thinker as Spinoza.

I had planned to take twenty or twenty-one hours during the fall quarter, but registration day was on *Yom Kippur* and by the time I tried to sign up for classes on the following day, many of those classes I had planned to take were full. As a result, I was able to only schedule sixteen hours of courses; still it promised to be an interesting quarter. Luckily, Architecture 103-Graphics was still available so I could finish that required freshman course. It was perspective drawing, which was initially difficult for me because I had been so accustomed to making free hand three-dimensional drawings, without a graphics system. It took a while for our professor, Rufus Reyhard Green, to convince me to forget my instincts for free hand sketching and learn the system. He was a soft-spoken, gentle and patient man and a very good teacher. It amazed me how someone with so much artistic talent could be so humble and unassuming. I learned a great deal in that class and it was due, for the most part, to his perseverance and gentle approach.

Math-201 was Differential Calculus and I was very excited at the prospect of tackling new horizons in math. Through my friends in the fraternities, I had the names of the more lenient, or rather, preferred professors teaching this course, but their classes were all filled up by the time I registered. I was prepared for the worst with a visiting professor from Illinois Tech who had built up quite a reputation the previous quarter for his teaching methods. He was a strict disciplinarian with a German accent that made me uncomfortable at first. He believed in teaching by stressing basic concepts and had a strong aversion to memorization without comprehension.

For the first half of the quarter, I was among the majority who disliked this professor who lectured us daily in suit and bow tie with total lack of warmth. He knew how to present and teach the subject matter, however, and he did get my attention when he kept stressing differentiation by definition. We spent many hours in class and were assigned homework problems in differentiation by definition. This was the longer way to arrive at an answer, but it gave assurance that the answer was correct. To most of my classmates, this lengthy proof method was a waste of time since, early in the quarter; we all could get the answers to these simple differentiation problems by memorizing the tables. He cautioned us in his heavy accent to not approach the homework problems in that manner, but to understand the fundamental principals and be able to delineate how we arrived at the answers.

Apparently, I was the only one who wasn't surprised at the first problem on his 150 point, two-hour long, mid-quarter exam. The problem was to differentiate 2X by definition and it carried a value of 35 points on the exam. Everyone in the class could give the answer in a matter of seconds, however, to arrive at the answer by definition took twenty to thirty minutes, and I was the only one in the class who took the time to respond correctly to that problem. The end result was a grading disaster. I had made a grade of 137 while the next highest grade was in the seventies. The professor posed the problem of assigning letter grades to the class for the exam. Even if he curved the grades, he could not justify giving anyone else higher that a C. Had I not been in the class, he could have accepted that the first problem of his test was unfair. He ended up curving the grades and generously gave those with 75 or higher (out of 150) a B-minus and flunked only the very lowest grades. He endeared himself to the class with this generosity and I became a pariah to the rest of the class for the remainder of the quarter.

Physics-207 was a course in mechanics specifically designed for architects. It was more of an overview of mechanics than a preparation for more detailed physics courses that other engineering students had to take. Professor Mendelker had a heavy European accent and a way of endearing himself to all of his students. He had been my roommate at Mrs. Goncher's house, when he first came to this country from Shanghai in 1946, after World War II. I remembered being in awe of him when I first met him and he shared that, before coming to America, he had authored a paper challenging one of Einstein's theories and his challenge had been under consideration by the academic community. Before I came to Georgia Tech, I heard that his challenging theory had been accepted as being on par with Einstein's. As pleased as I was to have him as my professor, I could not understand how a man of his stature and knowledge could be teaching a course that had to be simplified for the non-mathematical students who were taking this course.

Professor Mendelker had the perfect disposition for this course. Any other serious physicist would have lost patience quickly with the students whose only goal in taking the course was to pass it and forget it. He seemed to understand the mindset of most architectural students. He had a practice of walking around the class looking over students' shoulders as they were taking his exams. He would shake his head if he saw a student making a mistake and continue to do so in an attempt to get him to correct it. He had a famous saying that he was known to repeat as he picked up test papers after one of his exams. "Ooltimaatly," he would say in his heavy European accent, "architects are very religious people. They come to the test knowing nossing and expect the good Lord to give them the answers." That always brought the house down. Even though all of the other courses he taught were at a very high level, he was known in the student body for this course, and many non-architectural students—particularly football players—tried to sign up for it. He was a much loved-professor, who may have responded to the adoration of his students as a substitute for the family he lost in the Holocaust.

My only other course, English-201, was uneventful and enjoyable. We read and analyzed plays such as *Juno and the Paycock* and *Playboy of the Western World*. We also were given the assignment of making a model of a set design for the play of our choice. The course gave me an appreciation of theater, which later spurred me on to get involved with Drama Tech and other theater groups.

My brother Jack decided to get married. He had met Gladys Denaburg while he was attending the wedding of Henry Birnbrey in Birmingham, Alabama. Jack had worked with Henry who was a certified public accountant and was also one of the Jewish children who had come to the United States without parents. Henry had arrived from Germany in 1938. Jack had been going back and forth from Birmingham since Henry's wedding and he finally convinced Gladys to marry him.

The wedding was in Birmingham on November 30, 1952. It did not dawn on me, when I met Gladys' father, that he was the famous Sy Denaburg who had controlled the sale of colors at the Alabama football games, especially the ones in Birmingham. In my days of selling colors, all of my colleagues had painted such a fearful picture of him that I found it hard to believe that this kind gentle man was the Sy Denaburg.

Gladys was the third of four siblings and she had cousins galore. Her younger brother, Bobby, was closer to my age than anyone else at the wedding and we soon found out that we shared a penchant for mischief. Bobby was quite the athlete, having made the Alabama All-State High School football team as a full back. The wedding was a lot of fun. Bobby pulled me aside, to tell me about the tradition of decorating the groom's car—an absolute must in America.

Together, we did Jack's car justice. Of course, we had to sneak out of the reception to decorate it before the newlywed couple left for their honeymoon. came up with some ideas that I thought were bizarre enough, but Bobby's s lifted the car's décor to a new plane. I never would have thought of condoms on the gearshift as a finishing touch. As Jack and Gladys were leaving, he grinned at both of us and said that he could not wait for our weddings to get his payback. As they sped off, I stopped to think for a moment. All my siblings were now married. Somehow that realization didn't have that much of an impact on me. I was focused on what I had to do. I would not consider getting married and starting a family until I graduated from college and had a job in my chosen profession. Even though Jack was only a year-and-a-half older than I, he was much more mature and settled and I looked up to him as a mentor.

When Jack and Gladys returned from their honeymoon, Jack suggested that I should apply for a driver's license so, from time to time, I could help Sarah with errands and car-pooling the kids. Feeling that I needed a refresher course, I contacted the driving instructor that gave me lessons in the summer and asked him to help me get ready for the licensing tests. He was nice enough to pick me up three days a week after classes and drop me off at work after the lesson. At first, I was afraid that I had forgotten everything he had taught me, but after a while it all started to come back faster than I would have imagined. After three weeks, I was ready to take both the written and the driving test and my instructor was kind enough to take me, stay there for moral support and afterwards, take me to work. The written test was a piece of cake and though I needed more practice with parallel parking, I was granted a driver's license. He let me drive his car to Rich's, but cautioned me that I should not solo at night driving until I gained some experience with someone else in the car.

It was dusk when I arrived home from work and proudly announced that I had a driver's license. Jack and Gladys had come over after supper on their way to a card game in the neighborhood. Sarah told Jack about my license and he immediately threw me his car keys and suggested that I take his car for a spin. I didn't want to tell him that I was nervous about driving at night, especially alone. I thought I would take the car to Ray Maloof's house, just off the By Way, chat with him for fifteen minutes and come back so Jack and Gladys could go to their card game. Ray lived less than a mile away and I was being extra cautious, remembering my driving instructor's admonition.

I made sure that I knew where the lights and windshield wipers were before starting the car. After cranking it up, I held my breath and drove off down Spring Valley Lane holding it to twenty miles per hour. I took the hairpin left onto University and felt that I was home free, until shortly thereafter a car appeared behind me with its bright lights on. I waived for the driver to turn off the brights, which he did, but he kept on tailing me. I thought to lose him when I turned right on Briarcliff Road., but that didn't happen. I slowed down for him to pass and he slowed down, refusing to pass. I sped up and he sped up. It was obvious that the driver was playing games with me. If he or she had been trying to unnerve me, it was working. I kept the speed at twenty mph and kept looking back every few seconds to see if I was still being followed.

I knew I was getting close to the By Way and took a quick last look in my rearview mirror. The car was still there, tailing me. I saw what appeared to be the By Way, but was, in fact, a driveway that had recently been widened, fifty to a hundred feet before it. I signaled and started to make a left hand turn into what I thought was the By Way, before my final glance back. When I looked forward to see where I was going, the By Way was no longer in front of me. Frantically, I started to turn the steering wheel to the right and passed out in sheer panic.

By the time that I came to, I had hit two trees and a telephone pole along the By Way, less than 100 feet from Briarcliff. I was out of the car, lying on the ground, and Arnold Gross, a friend from D.S.I., was tending to me. I was told that an ambulance and the police were on the way. Arnold offered me a cigarette and, when I took one, told me to keep the pack. I hadn't smoked in two years, but by the time Jack arrived, I had smoked the whole pack. I expected Jack to be enraged at me for wrecking his car, but he was far more concerned about me. The policemen told me it was not my fault and that I would not get a ticket. I didn't want to look a gift horse in the mouth, but I had to wonder whether the fault lie with one of the trees or the telephone pole. I was taken to the Emergency Room at Emory Hospital for stitches. Arnold wanted to come along but I thanked him and told him I was all right. Deep down inside, I suspected that it was Arnold who was tailing me. He had no way of knowing that I had never driven at night before. He never owned up it and maybe it wasn't he, but it sure was strange that he happened to be there when I regained consciousness.

I needed seven stitches next to my left eye where my head had landed on the key in the dashboard after I passed out. The doctor said I was very lucky not to have lost an eye. I needed three more stitches on my chin and I was as good as new, physically that is. The car, on the other hand, had been totaled. Emotionally, I too was a total wreck. I didn't want to ever drive again. To Jack's credit, he took me out to an empty parking lot every Sunday morning with a friend of his, and forced me to drive his new yellow Plymouth convertible. It took quite a few weeks but he finally got me to shake the fear of driving and never mentioned the accident again. Well, almost never.

I was looking forward to registering for the winter quarter. I had a 9:00 a.m. time slot, which promised to allow me my choice of subjects and instructors. I ˙s finally able to schedule twenty-one credit hours of courses, which was ˙ up of eight courses including PT 201 & 202, since I had been unable to schedule 201 the previous quarter. One was supposed to be indoor games and the other, outdoor games. The instructor was the basketball coach, Whack Hyder, and he allowed those who wanted to, to play basketball for the outdoor games as well. Math 202 was Integral Calculus, which was challenging but enjoyable. I missed the priggish German professor from Illinois Tech, even though we had one of the best profs in the department.

Along with another graphics course, I was able to sign up for Architecture 207, my first real design lab. I was looking forward to trying my hand at designing a building, but this was not to be the quarter for that. The design lab was called "Abstract Design" and was taught by Professor Jim Grady, a very fastidious man who was often accused of being prejudiced against Hispanics and Jews, and in later years, women. I got along very well with Dr. Grady, and made an effort to glean as much knowledge from him as possible.

For our main project of the quarter, each student was assigned a painting of one of the modern masters to use in the project. The assignment was to dissect the painting by color, calculate the quantities of each color in relation to the other colors and design an abstract painting using the same colors in the same proportion. It was a tedious and grueling project, which demanded analytical skills and ultimately design skills. As Dr. Grady predicted, about six students dropped out of architecture, more than twenty percent of the class, before the quarter was over. My assigned painting was by Paul Gaughin of a native girl in Tahiti. The analytic part of the project was very time-consuming yet rewarding, but I found myself ill equipped to start the abstract design. I remembered the grad student at Atlanta Division and wished that I had taken the time to learn the concepts of abstract design from him. I ended up with a stilted cubistic design of which I was not very proud, and felt fortunate to walk away with a C in the course.

I loved History of Architecture, but I couldn't afford the book. I wound up sharing a loaner with one of the other students who was in similar financial straits. We ended up studying for exams together, but neither of us cared much for memorizing dates and places. The test scores were not indicative of the knowledge and respect that Fred and I had for the subject matter. Years later, after I graduated, I used my first paycheck to buy a brand new copy of *A History of Architecture* by Sir Banister Fletcher.

I had needed to take the twenty-one credit hours to catch up with the courses that kept me behind the rest of my class in the department, but the strain was beginning to take its toll. I started to wonder how much longer I was going to be able to work while going to school. The course work was becoming more demanding and my grade average had gradually slipped to 2.8, the minimum requirement for Tau Sigma Delta, the honor society of the architectural school. That coupled with the amount of time required for design lab, left me with precious little time for any social life. My adviser strongly suggested that I limit my hours to eighteen for the spring quarter or give up my job at Rich's. I opted for limiting the hours.

The biggest challenge of spring quarter was also the one most anticipated by me. I was finally going to take a design lab that had to do with architecture. I heard about the two major five week design projects and the occasional "sketch projects," to be issued, completed and turned in during the same four-hour lab. The first five-week design project was issued on the first day of lab and, within an hour, the lab was virtually empty. I found out later that most of my classmates went straight to the library to look up solutions to similar projects in periodicals. After reading and studying the design program, I took out my pencils, sketch paper, and drawing instruments and started sketching. There were three design critics/professors assigned to the lab, but I was the only design student left for them to critique. D. J. Edwards was the professor for the class/lab while Jim Grady and Rufus Green were the other critics. Professor Green stayed to answer any of my questions while the other two went about their business.

The project was to design a five-house subdivision on a cul-de-sac that was part of a larger subdivision. We were given the site boundaries, topography, and point of entry of the road into the property. Our assignment was to design the overall site, including the cul-de-sac and the site plan of each house, a design task that should take an experienced designer less than an hour to do. When our designs were gelled, we each had to build a model of our site design in order to present our design solution. I had several questions for Rufus Green. What materials would I need to build a model and where would I get them? How much time should I allot for building and completing the model? And where, in hell, did all the other students go? He answered the first two and laughed at the last. It was refreshing to him, he noted, to see a student who had not been indoctrinated by fraternity brothers who had taken the course. He opined that I was much better off not rushing to the library to find other peoples' design solutions to copy since the purpose of the class was to learn how to design, not vie for a good grade by cribbing old designs. I took that as good advice, and never used the library in that way.

The five weeks were a learning experience for me. Since most of the other students spent an average of less than two hours per lab in the building, I had an inordinate amount of time to chat with the critics and glean from them. At the same time, I couldn't help but take notice of how unmotivated many students seemed to me. I knew several engineering students working their way gh school, but they did it by alternating quarters of work and school. I found it interesting that all other engineering disciplines had a co-op program, but that only the school of architecture did not allow for one. This did not make sense to me, so I became interested in trying to help other interested students in trying to establish a co-op program at the school of architecture. Predictably, our efforts were for naught. While no one could give us an adequate reason for not having such a program, we were never able to make any progress.

The lab started filling up about three weeks into the project. A lot of people had been working on designs in their dorm room or frat house and only bringing the work in for an occasional critique. I was told that this was done to avoid having other students copy their work. The last two weeks, however, we spent building our individual models and that necessitated doing the work in the lab. It wasn't until the last week that I started noticing what others were doing. I had never seen an airbrush used to spray paint before, and was duly impressed with the handful of students who not only had one but knew how to use it. All of the models were to be composed of layers of gray chipboard, cut to the contour lines, and either rubber cemented or Elmer's glued together. Several models were being painted with water-based paint using a standard brush. That resulted in curling layers of chipboard and that was where the airbrush came in handy. Not only was it quicker, but it applied the paint with less moisture and gave the designer tremendous flexibility with colors and shading.

When I was able to view the array of models submitted for the jury at the deadline, I was in awe of the technological capability of the airbrush. After I had a chance to look carefully at all of the models, I was amused at the Disney-like character of many of the submissions. Not only had they sprayed the base of the model in colors ranging from chartreuse to fuchsia but, many of them also sprayed the lichen tree foliage. Some otherwise good designs were, in my opinion, ruined by a surrealistic paint job. While I felt embarrassed at having submitted the only model that didn't have a painted chipboard base, I really hadn't felt the need to change the earthy gray color of the chipboard. I also relied on the natural colors of the lichen to provide an autumn scene of foliage, instead of experimenting with airbrushed psychedelic colors.

We were not allowed to sit in on the design jury, but word came to me that there was disagreement among the jurors with regard to my submittal. Two of the jurors wanted to give me a twenty-one, which was an A+, but Mr. Edwards was reported to have said I should have been more daring and experimented with color. To compromise, the jury gave me a nineteen, which was an A-, the highest grade in the class. I was overwhelmed. I truly had not expected to do that well and was feeling bad for some of others who worked so hard and did not get rewarded for their hard work. Rufus Green was so happy for me that he offered to give me a ride home so I could show the model to my family. He saw how hard I had worked, staying in the lab for the full session every day, and he was delighted that my diligence was rewarded. Jim Grady was also very congratulatory. Jim Edwards, on the other hand, said he was waiting to see how I did on the next project to make sure that this one had not been a fluke.

He succeeded in taking the joy out of what had been a very special day for me. As Rufus Green was driving me home, he tried to explain Mr. Edwards' insistence on putting me down as standard behavior for him. "In his own way," Mr. Green said, "Jim loves his students, he just doesn't want them to become overconfident and complacent about what they need to learn." That sounded plausible and I was willing to accept it and go on with the next project. I introduced Rufus Green to Sarah as he helped me bring the model in the house. I had to bring it back the next day to use on the next project. Also, as was the practice with projects that received high grades, my model was going to be retained for the archives.

Our second project was to design one of the houses in the subdivision. It was to be a simple two-bedroom house on a limited budget and I took that directive literally. I spent the first two weeks exploring different floor plan possibilities and looking for ways to be innovative within the program constrictions. Ultimately, I came up with a very simple rectangular house and almost everyone in the class did also. I was not prepared for our submissions to be judged primarily on presentation. As in the first project, I chose not to be flowery in presenting my simple, but well thought out, design. The guy with the fuchsia model turned out to be an excellent renderer and his presentation was a knockout. There were quite a few very well-rendered elevations that focused more on the foliage and the sky than the building, but they looked good. As D. J. put it, "You can have the best design in the world, but if you can't sell it to the client, it won't get built." That thought inspired me to work harder on presentation techniques in the future. It was too late for this project, and I ended up with a disappointing fourteen, which was the equivalent of a C.

I figured that this project had been a good learning experience and was pleased that I still had a B in the main course of my major. When the final course grades were posted at the end of the quarter, I was aghast when I saw a C next to my name. First I went to Rufus Green to see if he could give me an explanation. We jotted down the two project grades and factored the sketch projects, all of which I had received a B or higher on, and came up with a high B average. He was sure that D. J. Edwards, who was responsible for the grades, had made an error and convinced me to go see him. Professor Edwards looked up and asked me what I wanted, prefaced by his famous, "My Gawd!" When I suggested that there might be an error in the grading, he opened up his grade book. He pointed to the two five week projects, for both of which he had inserted a grade of fourteen. I pointed out that the first fourteen was in error, that in fact I had received a nineteen. He vociferously denied having entered the wrong grade and challenged me to prove it. I started to call in Professor Green and he stopped me. He changed the entry for the first project to nineteen then looked up at me and said, "This doesn't change your course grade. You are a C student and that's all you're going to get in my class."

I was angry and hurt beyond belief. I scrapped my plans to register for summer quarter and decided to re-evaluate my pursuit of architecture as a career. I also had flunked my first course ever that quarter. It was a two-hour credit course on building materials. I had not known that Professor Grif Edwards (no relation to D.J. Edwards) had, several years before, prepared three different versions of each test he scheduled and that these versions were readily available in the frat houses. I found out later that the professor knew his students would study all three versions. Therefore, he figured that they would be learning what he wanted them to know. The only problem with that system was that, occasionally, someone would come along (like me) who was totally unaware of the availability of these tests. That student would not be able to compete. Unfortunately, I proved that point.

There are setbacks and then there are setbacks. I had been working hard for two years, taking a full load of courses and earning my keep at Rich's. I wondered if I was doing the right thing in pursuing a degree in architecture. Were professors D. J. Edwards, Grif Edwards and my trigonometry professor trying to prepare me for a profession that has no level playing field? I needed time to sort things out in my mind and I needed to find a way to continue my college education without having to work full time to support myself.

I was going to turn twenty-one in September and finally be eligible for U.S. citizenship, which I had been led to believe was a criterion for joining any of the branches of the military of this country. The armed services of the United States was deeply involved in the Korean Conflict. I heard that the G.I. Bill, which provided assistance in college tuition and was available to all war veterans including vets of the Korean Conflict, would no longer be offered to veterans that joined the armed services after the end of the Korean Conflict.

I had never given up on someday going to Europe to find Werner and Roselene. Even though Uncle Philipp testified that he had seen them walking into the "showers" (gas chambers) with my mother, I could never accept the report that they were dead. Several of my friends had already enlisted or been drafted into the U. S. armed services. With each letter that I received from them, I felt more envious that they and not I were serving the country that had opened its doors to me and four of my siblings when we otherwise might have been killed.

Even though the Korean Conflict was in full gear in the summer of 1953, there was an outside chance that, if I enlisted, the Army might send me to serve in Germany. After all, they had done that with my brother Asher in 1946. From Germany, I fantasized I might be able start my search for Werner and Roselene and bring them to America to live with us.

I called the local draft board and explained that I wished to volunteer for the draft even though I held a student exemption. They were more than happy to oblige. We agreed on the date of Ocober 22, 1953 for me to report to Chamblee, Georgia for induction into the United States Army. Another phase of my life was about to begin.

EPILOGUE

In 1991 in New York City, along with 1,500 child survivors of the Holocaust, I attended the first International Conference of Child Survivors, also billed as the Hidden Child. This was the first large scale gathering of Holocaust survivors who had been children during the years of the Holocaust. Being among and sharing with so many Jews who had undergone similar experiences was such a catharsis for me that I started attending some of the annual gatherings, and in recent years, I have made it a point to attend every annual conference of child survivors, as well as the occasional reunions of survivors of the OSE homes in France.

At the various sessions of these conferences we share our memories, our thoughts on how our survivorship has shaped our lives and how some of our experiences have affected the lives of our loved ones and others around us. Most importantly, we meet others with similar and sometimes shared experiences. We make friends in the few days together and depart hoping that we see each other again. The last day is always bitter sweet for me. I return to my family and my community with new stories of new friends, but the anxiety of separation from the fellow survivors usually stays with me for a few days. It reminds me of the many times I had to leave friends and family behind as I was taken from one place to another.

I have had the good fortune to meet child survivors from OSE that settled all over the world, from Europe, Israel and South and Central America. At the OSE reunion in Paris and in recent conferences in Denver and Amsterdam, I was surprised to meet child survivors who live in Australia. Where they were sent in the aftermath of the Holocaust is where they found and made their home. Truly their home is where they found it

It is at these gatherings that I have come to grips with some of the aspects of my early life and realized how some of these experiences affected my decision making processes in later years. We tend to keep our inner emotions close to the vest, but many of us find the sessions at these gatherings to be an opportunity to open up as we never have before. Many things have come out for me that I did not know were hidden inside.

I never came to grips with the sudden separation from my older siblings upon our arrival in Paris, France in December 1938. I had been prepared by my mother for our departure from Frankfurt, even though I had been made to believe that it would be a short separation, but I was totally caught off guard when my siblings and I were separated upon our arrival in Paris. I saw them on rare occasions during our almost three years sojourn in France. After coming to Atlanta until I turned twelve, at least one of my siblings was living in the same home with me. I thought I had accepted the separation as "just the way it was."

I never viewed the sudden separation from my siblings as a traumatic experience, though it did affect me at the time, that is, until recently. Our daughter, Adina, has been living in our house with her two daughters and two sons since her divorce some eight years ago. In accordance with the divorce agreement, the children, Ashira, Naftali, Rina Leah and Aharon, have been living with Adina who had full custody.

On May 21, 2005, Naftali celebrated his *Bar Mitzvah*. Somewhere along the way, I became aware that during his *Bar Mitzvah* preparations, Naftali was being pressured by this father to leave his mother and siblings to come live with him after his fourteenth birthday, when, according to Georgia law, children can decide where and with whom they wish to live.

It was this whole process that brought back the scene of the train station in Paris, the splitting up of the Hirsch children that would leave me alone without a sibling. I had never given it all that much thought before now. It hit me like a ton of bricks. I knew that I had missed out on the closeness that siblings often have when growing up under the same roof, but I never realized how much I had missed it. I would cry when Asher and Jack would leave after a visit when I was six years old, but thought I had accepted my situation by the time I arrived in the United States. What happened to me was foisted on me by the circumstances of Hitler's war against the Jews. I was saddened and found it hard to comprehend how my very intelligent grandson could voluntarily make such a choice.

After losing sleep one night, I felt compelled to share my thoughts with my daughter and she, in turn, knowing that Naftali cared about the feelings of his *zadi* (grandfather), shared them with her son. She explained that even though he would be living in the same city and would see his brother and sisters, his decision was tantamount to leaving them. The two younger children tearfully pleaded with him not to leave.

After a few days of sadness and sorrow, the three remaining siblings seemed to accept the change. It was sad for me to observe that even after a few short months of not living under the same roof, there seems to be a palpable difference in the relationship between Naftali and his brother and sisters. They are no longer used to him being there and their once natural interaction appears to have become stilted.

I love my grandson no matter with whom he chooses to live. It took his actions to awaken hidden feelings about my own youth. Still I find it ironic that he would voluntarily choose to separate from his siblings.

When I saw the pain and anguish that this limited separation of one child from his mother and siblings caused my daughter, I began to realize that I could never begin to fathom the enormity of the pain my dear mother must have felt, or how she garnered the courage to send the five of us away to live another day.

Recently I, along with three other local Holocaust survivors who had each written a book on their experiences, was asked to appear before an assembly of students of Temima High School for girls in Atlanta. The students read excerpts from each of the four books, which included my first book, *HEARING A DIFFERENT DRUMMER, A Holocaust Survivor's Search for Identity*, and prepared questions for our response. Among the poignant questions addressed to me, there was one that I had never been confronted with before and it sticks with me as the defining question of all my years of speaking to school groups.

She asked, "If you had a chance to change your life and not have gone through all you did, would you?" Without hesitation, I answered "No—then I wouldn't be who I am." I surprised myself with that answer. Obviously, I would have preferred that my family not be killed and that we not be separated, but that would have required a total change of history with the Holocaust never happening. I firmly believe that God, in His infinite wisdom, controls all of history while we as individuals have the freedom to choose our paths within God's framework. I am who I am because of my experiences and though the losses have been many, the gains of the next generations begin to shed some light on God's incomprehensible plan.

Ben and Jacquie at Raphael's wedding, January 31, 1995.

(above) The Hirsch siblings at Raphi's bar mitzvah (1980). From left: Jack, Flo, Claire Heyman (who stayed with our parents from 1939-1941), Ben and Asher.

(below) Ben, with his children (L-r) Raphael, Shoshanah, Michal, and Adina Chaya, c.1982.

(above) L-r: Herb, Mark, Bobby, Sam and Flo Spiegel, c.1980.

(below) Asher, with his family, 1974.
Seated, L-r: Ruthi, Henny, Asher and Samson; standing: Naftali, Miriam, Eli and Mayer Hirsch.

(above) Front row, L-r: Harry, Sarah and Edward; rear: Neil and Thyle Shartar, c.1974.

(below) L-r: Stuart, Jack, Gladys and Bryan Hirsch, c.1982.

Ben Hirsch speaking to a group of school students about the Holocaust and his experiences at The Breman Jewish Heritage Museum, c.2000.

(above) Ben giving a tour of the Holocaust gallery he designed, to the Counsel General to the United States from the Federal Republic of Germany, c.2000.

(below) With Nechama Tec in the Holocaust gallery of The Breman Museum, c.2002.

The Hirsch family gathers to celebrate the bar mitzvah of Ben's and Jacquie's grandson, Nachliel, in Jerusalem, 1987.

ACKNOWLEDGMENTS

Writing a memoir fifty years after the fact requires a respect for and memory of the past and willingness, or better yet a passion, to track down sources to corroborate and enhance those memories. I mentioned in the Introduction, eventually obtaining access to my and my siblings' case records from the Children's Service Bureau in Atlanta. In the case of my records these files went beyond corroborating memory, they shed light on my behavior as a foster child and how that behavior affected the various foster parents who cared for me then. I owe a great debt of gratitude to Fritzi Lainoff and Sandy Berman for making these files available to me

I am very grateful to Mary Helmer for making me aware of *Transplanted Children,* a historical review of The United States Committee for the Care of European Children, Inc., which opened my eyes to activities in the U.S. on behalf of Jewish European Children victimized by Hitler's Nazi regime. This book answered a lot of long standing questions for me. I dearly hope that Mary finds her real identity soon.

Thanks to Leon Tuck for sharing articles from *The Senator* that corroborated a story I remembered but could not verify and for providing photographs for use in this memoir. Thanks also to my scout master, Josiah Benator, for the photograph of our scout troop and to his cousin, Asher Benator, for finding photos of Doyle "Whitey" Kugler after I had exhausted all archival leads. Thanks to Malcolm Minsk for providing what appears to be the only photo of Alex Zomper in captivity, and a special thanks to Dr. Perry Brickman for photographing some of my photos in the *Absence of Humanity* exhibit of The Breman Museum for use in this memoir. The originals along with their negatives had been lost.

I am indebted to Genya Markon and Maren Read of the United States Holocaust Memorial Museum for the photos from the museum's collection that they made available for this memoir and to Nathalie Mook of *Oeuvre de Secours aux Enfants,* (OSE) in Paris for bringing me in contact with *Centre de Documentation Juive Contemporaine* who made photos of the OSE homes available to me.

A special thanks is due to the many friends who helped in various stages of editing of the manuscript, among them to Hazel Karp, Sue Ann Pliner, Maureen MacLaughlin, various members of my immediate family and Lynn & James Taylor for their encouragement.

Kudos to Ruth Einstein for her technical expertise and support, for copying all of the photos into the computer and placing them in their assigned place in the manuscript and finalizing the complete document in the computer format proscribed by the publisher. This was a yeoman's job and greatly appreciated.

To Jane Leavey, who took a manuscript that I had been made to believe was almost ready to print and proceeded to rip through it with a "tough love" edit. After many hours of sweat and toil, I can only say, "Thanks, I needed that!"

The *Holocaust Chronicles*, published by Publications International, Ltd was invaluable in refreshing my memory on Holocaust era events that were occurring in Europe while I was growing up in the United States and putting the various events in the proper chronological context.

Last but not least, I thank my family for putting up with me as I stole time from them and my architectural clients in order to create the time required to write and publish this memoir. My wife, Jacqueline Robkin Hirsch, who deserves special credit for putting up with me and all of my projects for forty-seven years, our children Shoshanah and Barnea Selavan, Adina Chaya Hirsch, Michal and Sholom Apelbaum, Raphael and Sherri Hirsch and our twenty-one grandchildren were encouraging, each in his or her own way.

Once again I thank God Almighty for allowing me to live long enough to complete this second memoir. May it be his will that I have the time to continue to chronicle some of my experiences as an adult.

Benjamin Hirsch
Atlanta, Georgia

978-0-595-39002-1
0-595-39002-1